Jumbo

Jumbo

SCOTT BATEMAN
WITH LYNNE BARRETT-LEE

PENGUIN MICHAEL JOSEPH

UK | USA | Canada | Ireland | Australia
India | New Zealand | South Africa

Penguin Michael Joseph is part of the Penguin Random House group of companies whose addresses can be found at global.penguinrandomhouse.com

Penguin Random House UK,
One Embassy Gardens, 8 Viaduct Gardens, London SW11 7BW

penguin.co.uk

First published 2026
001

Copyright © Scott Bateman & Lynne Barrett-Lee, 2026

The moral right of the author has been asserted

Penguin Random House values and supports copyright.
Copyright fuels creativity, encourages diverse voices, promotes freedom of expression and supports a vibrant culture. Thank you for purchasing an authorized edition of this book and for respecting intellectual property laws by not reproducing, scanning or distributing any part of it by any means without permission. You are supporting authors and enabling Penguin Random House to continue to publish books for everyone.
No part of this book may be used or reproduced in any manner for the purpose of training artificial intelligence technologies or systems. In accordance with Article 4(3) of the DSM Directive 2019/790, Penguin Random House expressly reserves this work from the text and data mining exception

Set in 13.5/16pt Garamond MT Std
Typeset by Six Red Marbles UK, Thetford, Norfolk
Printed and bound in Great Britain by Clays Ltd, Elcograf S.p.A.

The authorized representative in the EEA is Penguin Random House Ireland, Morrison Chambers, 32 Nassau Street, Dublin D02 YH68

A CIP catalogue record for this book is available from the British Library

HARDBACK ISBN: 978–0–241–67328–7
TRADE PAPERBACK ISBN: 978–0–241–67329–4

Penguin Random House is committed to a sustainable future for our business, our readers and our planet. This book is made from Forest Stewardship Council® certified paper.

To the aviation visionary, Joe Sutter, and all the
'Incredibles' who made this possible

Contents

	Foreword by Ray Conner	1
1	Cleared for Take-off	5
2	The Aircraft That Was Supposed to Change the World	17
3	The Incredibles	29
4	If You Build It, They Will Come	49
5	The Jumbos Are Coming	65
6	Carrying the World	75
7	Delivering the World	85
8	Tragedy on Tenerife	93
9	The Galunggung Glider	113
10	Air Force One	129
11	Getting Lost	155
12	Learning through Failure	181
13	Lockerbie	207
14	The Human Factor	221
15	The 40-Year-Old Virgin	233
16	A Force for Good	249
17	SOFIA	267

18	Those Bits I Just Couldn't Leave Out	281
19	Hopes and Dreamlifters	303
20	Forever Incredible	317
	Epilogue	331
	Afterword by Michael Lombardi, former Senior Historian, Boeing	335
	Acknowledgements	340
	Index	345
	Picture Credits	357

Foreword

By Ray Conner, former Boeing Commercial Aeroplanes CEO & President

Every day, millions of people get on and off aeroplanes around the globe and the convenience of flying is largely taken for granted, but there was an earlier time when this was not the case. In the 1950s, a trans-Atlantic roundtrip ticket could cost the equivalent of an annual income, putting air travel beyond the reach of most people. Aeroplane performance was limited and to get between distant destinations required multiple stops, with flying times measured in days!

In February 1969, an altogether different shape took to the wintery skies over Seattle and marked the start of a new era that changed the face of commercial air transportation forever. The plane, christened the *City of Everett*, was the prototype 747 and the first of 1,574 Super Jets to be built by 2023. For many of the 7.5 billion people that have flown on the plane over the last half century, she became the 'Queen of the Skies'.

The Queen was created by the men and women of Boeing, from brilliant engineers to highly skilled machinists using imagination, courage, hard work, dedication and, above all, passion. They numbered some 50,000 people in total and sacrificed much over long hours to create something that the world said could not be done. They were called the 'The Incredibles' and their dedication, pioneering spirit and amazing accomplishment are an inspiration for Boeing employees to this day.

The 747 was the product of great leadership, in particular from Joe Sutter, who headed the design team and who in time became known as the 'Father of the 747'. It started with the brilliant direction of Boeing CEO William Allen and his decision to take great financial and technical risk on a plane that many said had no future and were instead placing their bet on supersonic transportation.

It was Allen's friendship with Juan Trippe, the legendary leader of Pan American Airways, that brought the 747 to life. Together they had ushered in the jet age in 1958, when Pan Am took delivery of its first Boeing 707-120 and inaugurated daily transatlantic jet services. Air travel quickly ballooned, and Trippe was soon in search of an aeroplane that would carry more people and fly further.

Following an agreement with Trippe, Boeing in April 1966 embarked on developing an aeroplane more than twice the size of the 707. Less than twemty-eight months later, the first giant jet rolled out Boeing's equally new and gargantuan plant at Everett in Washington. Constructed as the first 747 was assembled within, the building remains, to this day, the world's largest by volume.

The 747 heralded many technological and aviation firsts, the most significant being the wide body design able to accommodate 350 passengers across two aisles. With an eye to a future freighter and ease of loading through the nose, it featured an upper deck giving the plane its distinctive hump. It marked the first commercial use of high-bypass turbofans, delivering a huge leap in power and fuel efficiency. Most importantly, the design was anchored around safety, introducing quadruple hydraulic systems, redundant structures and quadruple main landing gear, as well as revamped pilot training.

It did not take long for the 747 to make its mark, carrying over a million passengers in the first six months of

1970 – twice the total traffic for all types flown for the same period in 1958. With the failure of supersonic transport as a commercial proposition, the 747 became the flagship for more than 100 airlines around the world. The appeal was not simply its size, but world-shrinking range and operational efficiency, making it affordable for everyday people to fly anywhere on the globe.

Over more than fifty years, the 747 family evolved into many different versions: the SP, −100, −200, −300, −400 and finally the −8. The body length was both shortened and increasingly lengthened, more powerful engines added, weights increased, flight deck avionics modernized and the wing refined, enabling greater numbers of passengers and freight to be carried over longer distances.

Specially modified variants have carried heads of states, the Space Shuttle, airborne command posts, lasers and even a giant telescope to gaze into the heavens. The 747 remains the finest cargo plane in the air today and along with the new VC-25B Air Force One now in development, the Queen will be with us for decades to come. This is testament to a design built to last and serves as a reminder of the power of the human spirit and what can be accomplished with vision and the collective application of ingenuity and labour.

1. Cleared for Take-off

It is a warm summer's evening in August 2008 and before I kiss my wife goodbye and put my suitcase in the car I double-check my smaller bag for the tenth time that afternoon. Do I have all I need for the trip? After so many years as a member of the military, it seems strange to swap essentials such as flying suits and body armour for a packing list that includes shorts and flip-flops.

I am simultaneously excited and petrified. This is such a big moment, in both my life, and my professional career. I am on my way to Heathrow Airport, which for the last three months has been my place of work, and I am about to achieve what has become one of my greatest ambitions: to pilot a Boeing 747 Jumbo Jet.

This evening will see a few firsts for me. It will be my first time flying a real 747 as opposed to a simulator, my first time flying a jet aircraft, and my first flight for my new employer. And all this with an accompaniment of 299 paying passengers who are expecting to wake up in Hong Kong tomorrow morning.

I drive down the motorway without my usual company of Radio One, choosing to spend the entire time engaged in rehearsals in my head of all the procedures and briefings I will be expected to carry out this evening if I'm to get the 747 safely airborne. By the time I've surfaced from those thoughts I am already coming off the M4, and as I turn on to the M25, bound for the staff parking area at the western end of the airport, I see what I hope is a personal good-luck message: a 747 gliding gracefully into the air from the northern runway at Heathrow. Its lights, shape and size are all so easily recognizable. Good lord, I think. In a couple of hours that'll be me. Despite years piloting Hercules transporters for the RAF, it's like I'm seventeen again, and I'm feeling slightly sick.

I pull up in the car park adjacent to the runway and just sit for a few moments, gathering my thoughts. I accept that I am feeling nervous, and not without reason. I've been in the air force the entirety of my adult life. It's all I've ever known. I was comfortable in that environment. I felt at home in that environment. I also knew my aircraft inside out, almost as if it was a part of my own body. This is very different, and I feel like I'm the new boy at school – where everyone knows the drill apart from me.

Leaving the car, finally, I follow the crowd of chattering crew on to a bus which will take us to the recently opened Terminal 5. The terminal is quite a sight and as we drive along the perimeter road it looks vast and resplendent against the dark sky. A newly built edifice, a sea of glass and light and LEDs, its sensuous shape now entirely dominates the Heathrow skyline.

I have already agreed to meet the training captain who is going to take me through my paces in the cafe on the departures level shortly, to guide me through navigating the terminal and check-in procedures. When I arrive, it is packed, with both travellers and crew.

'You must be Scott,' the captain says as he approaches. My heart sinks just a little. I clearly stick out as a newbie, like the veritable sore thumb, so it seems the confident demeanour I'm trying to channel isn't quite as effective as I'd imagined.

A coffee and the reassuring words of the training captain calm me down; just what I need to make me feel I can do this, even if a part of me still can't quite believe I am. I am now ready to start my first day as a commercial airline pilot, flying the largest and most iconic of all airliners, the famous 'Queen of the Skies'. The Jumbo Jet.

I'm travelling to an equally iconic location. For all the travelling I've done in the military, which amounts to many thousands of miles, I've never flown into Hong Kong in my life, either as a pilot or a passenger – unlike the crew, who I meet in a small glass cube off the main briefing area. They all look very experienced, and I am introduced as the new guy, although that must be already obvious, as there aren't many pilots on the Jumbo with only two silver stripes on their arm. Most go through several years on short-haul aircraft before moving to the big jets and long haul, because they need to have four years of flying under their belts before graduating to the three stripes of senior first officer, like the other co-pilot on this trip.

My RAF experience, however, means that although I am the most junior pilot in the aircraft today I already have sufficient experience flying large transport aircraft to have gone straight to long haul, and the coveted Jumbo Jet. I am also doubly blessed. Assuming everything goes okay today, my mandatory four years flying with the airline, to earn my third stripe, will be completed on the 747.

The briefing for the flight is given by the training captain and is very different to those I have been used to in the RAF. The operation is of a different kind, and so is the approach, and I am beginning to realize how much I have to learn, and how little my RAF training counts here. The fuel required for the trip, for example, at over 110T, is a whopping forty tons heavier than the maximum total weight of the Hercules. This is when I begin to grasp the sheer scale of this aircraft – everything is enormous and therefore difficult to comprehend.

This evening our departure is from Terminal 4, so we get on another bus and the chatter on the way is all about what's likely to be happening post-flight; from favoured restaurants for our layover to the best place to buy cheap electronics. It's a very different world to the one I'm used to. My thoughts, however, are very much in the here and now. Can I actually *do* this? I will very soon find out.

As the bus pulls up alongside our ride for tonight – a Boeing 747-436, registration G-BNLG – I marvel anew at the size of the aircraft. Like the C-5 transporter – the biggest aircraft I've ever been this close to – this thing needs a whole new definition of the word 'big'. It is over 250 feet long and 244 feet wide, and to the top of the fin it stands at 63 feet, as high as a six-storey building. Tonight, we will be close to the maximum take-off weight of almost 400 tons, and I am in awe of the engineering miracle I am gazing up at, devised in Seattle *over forty years* previously.

I go up the two flights of steps to the entry door and as I do so take a look back at the wing. For a moment, I am tempted to turn around and wave, in the style of US presidents as they board Air Force One. Happily, the urge passes, so I avoid looking ridiculous, and instead, once inside, climb the further eleven stairs that will take me up on to the upper deck. This part of the aircraft is famously big. Bigger even than the *entire cabin space* of another Boeing icon, the 737. I jump into the right-hand seat for the first time, and what strikes me immediately is just how high up we are. We are a long way off the ground, a very long way indeed.

The next forty minutes are predictably busy, as we get the aircraft ready for departure, doing everything from entering the route into the flight management computer to working out the performance and speeds required for take-off. These vary, depending on destination, volume of cargo and number of passengers. And, of course, the massive amount of fuel we have on board.

Tonight, we are extremely heavy, even for a Jumbo. We will therefore be using almost all the 237,600 pounds of available power, from the four Rolls-Royce RB-211 engines.

The customers are boarding as we go through the final briefing, which is led by the training captain. Though I am essentially going to be the pilot flying tonight, he will guide me through it all from his seat to my left. The briefing now complete, we are finally good to go and, as we finish the checklist and I am putting my straps on I realize it's been an incredibly long time since I've been this nervous flying an aircraft. Right back to my first ever solo flight, in fact – which was in a single-engine piston aircraft, the Slingsby Firefly. The contrast in size could hardly be more different. The species of stomach-dwelling butterflies are just the same.

I try to still them as the instruction comes in from air traffic control: clear to push to face north. I relay this to the ground team who are waiting to push us away from the terminal and, with the parking brake making a reassuring clunk as it disengages, we begin to move back from the gate. We are underway.

When cleared by the ground crew, we start each of the four engines in turn and, having been so used, for so long, to the massive noise made by a Hercules, I'm astonished that we can hardly hear these jets up on the flight deck – almost the only indication that they are working is the dials all being nicely aligned on the instruments. This is a *jet* airliner. Shouldn't it be even noisier than a Herc? It all adds to the sense of disconnected unreality.

The pushback complete, the ground crew detach the tug, then make their way from the aircraft. Another checklist and we are ready to taxi this block of flats around the airport. We call ready for taxi, and the instructions come back: 'Speedbird 25, Taxi Tango, Sierra, hold short of runway two-seven left at Sierra One, call ready.'

The time has at last come; we are off.

As a teenager, I never saw myself flying big aircraft. Like many other wet-behind-the-ears would-be pilots, I initially set my sights on the more obviously macho planes. I wanted to be a fighter pilot – at least for a bit. A day spent on a search and rescue helicopter put paid to all that. Search and rescue seemed the pinnacle of career options for me now; exciting flying, great views and a chance to feel heroic. At the end of that day, it was yellow-painted paraffin-fuelled canaries all the way.

So I was not at all happy when, early in my RAF career, I was selected to become not a pilot but an air loadmaster. And not on a helicopter either (pretty obviously, to be fair), but on the RAF's trusty transport aircraft, the Hercules. I was crushed. A transporter aircraft just seemed so, well, boring. No exciting aerobatics, no heroic rescues, just lumbering about the place delivering troops and equipment. I was going to become a loadie on the aircraft colloquially known in the forces as a flying Pickfords Removals van.

How naïve I was. I not only fell in love with the transporter aircraft widely recognized as one of the finest in the world – first and last out of any conflict, or skirmish, or humanitarian aid mission you could think of – but I was also now on a trajectory that would see me set to become a pilot on one too, which meant I would be well placed, after my years in the forces, to make the leap into the pilot's seat of the incomparable Jumbo Jet. And as we prepare to taxi, something occurs to me. I owe that RAF selection guy a pint.

I'm also here, I know, due to an unfortunate event – one

that happened in Kabul, back in 2004. We were three weeks into a six-week detachment in Afghanistan at the time and, as the only UK-operated fixed-wing asset in theatre, our beloved Hercules was the go-to heavy-lift workhorse for both the SAS and all the regular troops. And since both were engaged in a cycle of constant operations against the Taliban, the workload had been reliably intense.

I started that particular morning by being given a mug of coffee by my room-mate, Barry. We shared a 10-foot-square room in downtown Kabul, which, apart from us, contained nothing but a set of iron bunk beds. Bar the fan, there was nothing as fancy as actual furniture. And were it not for the fact that the window was boarded up rather than barred (in case of an explosion and shards of glass being rained down all over us), it would have felt more like a prison cell. As it was, at least compared to most field accommodation I'd experienced, it was as palatial as one could reasonably expect. It was also a haven from the heat of the fierce Afghan sun, which, at that time of year, was relentless.

The coffee having done its work, I was feeling almost human, a transformation which would only become fully complete once I'd taken a much-needed shower. So I swung my legs out of bed, grabbed my towel and my sunglasses and emerged from the room into the cooler air of the corridor wearing nothing bar my flip-flops and a pair of shorts.

It was then time to open the door and face the meteorological onslaught. Going from the chill of the air con to the intense morning heat was always an assault on the senses. It was already in excess of 30°C out there, and the next breath I took, as I quickly closed the door behind me, filled my lungs with a sickly cocktail of heat and dust. Squinting and grimacing as my eyes tried to adjust to the intense morning light, I donned the shades and set off for the showers.

What with the shorts, sunshine and Aviators, you could almost imagine I was in Ibiza. Except for the fact that I was immediately passed by two guys in full body armour, which, along with their weapons, did make things feel a bit more 'war zone'. Plus, the place I was now approaching – the nearby shipping container which housed the 'facilities' – meant there was absolutely no doubt. But I didn't mind. I was a proud Hercules pilot, from 47 Squadron, RAF, and right there was precisely where I should be.

Not that I'd want to over-romanticize things. RAF banter suggested, and with a fair degree of licence, that with some 300 young soldiers using the same 20x40-foot space, the toxicity of the stench that greeted anyone who entered could rival the worst of Saddam's chemical weapons. And in that kind of heat, it was a reliably potent recipe. Take all those men, all those ablutions, mix in a few dicky tummies, seal tightly, then let everything marinate. What resulted, and intensified with every passing hour, was probably against the Geneva Convention. Still, the water was clean, and I needed to be likewise.

After a quick shave, done mostly blind as the steel 'mirrors' were so scratched, it was off with the shorts and, still in my flip-flops, a careful manoeuvre into the nearest shower cubicle. I say 'careful' because the greatest care needed to be taken to avoid one's shorts or, indeed, any part of one's body making contact with the gloop on the floor, which had long since caked on and was supplemented daily, and too much of a biohazard to risk.

Still, the feeling of tepid water coursing over my dusty, salty skin represented a few moments of pure bliss. Yes, I knew the whole sweaty cycle would repeat once I was dressed and off to work, but for a couple of precious minutes I could wash it all away and enjoy perhaps the most rewarding of life's simple pleasures.

At least in theory, because that morning, as was sometimes the case, the water went off without warning. So that was it. My shower was over. I had no choice but to take it on the chin, though, so I did, reaching for the towel I'd placed so carefully on the nearby hook and taking that first flip-flopped step out of the cubicle.

But my best-laid plans for the day conspired to fall apart. I'm not sure how, I'm not sure why – I'd done this so many times before – but my foot slipped on something treacherous on the floor and I was suddenly, shockingly, frighteningly airborne.

I landed hard, half a second later, on my back and my side, right across the lip of the metal shower tray. *God*, I remember thinking. Jesus, that really, *really* hurt. But there was work to be done, so I took two paracetamol and two ibuprofen, and, like the military man I was then, I soldiered on. After all, what's a little back ache when you're in a war zone?

Over the following four years, a realization slowly dawned. Though an operation down the line went some way to fix the problem, I was now faced with a painful reality. Though I was still fine to fly, I was no longer able to fly combat missions; I could no longer run, I couldn't shoot, and I couldn't wear full body armour, so I would have to see out my military career far away from any front line. It was with the heaviest of hearts, then, that I made the decision to end that career prematurely and, with that, my decades-long affair with the iconic Hercules.

But I was obsessive about aircraft. An avgeek. An addict. If I couldn't fly on the front line, I needed to find a new passion. But what possible new aviation challenge could compare?

There was only one, really.

The one I'm about to taxi across London Heathrow. The Jumbo.

*

The C-130 Hercules is not a small aircraft to taxi around an airport, but the 747 is on a whole different level. Operating it from three storeys up makes it very difficult to judge speed, and with the nose wheel, your steering point, quite a distance behind you, it is not uncommon for the pilot to be over the grass at the edge of the taxiway before turning. No doubt about it – the whole thing feels very alien.

Taxi lights on now, and we are moving, and the first thing that strikes me is the power needed to get the almost-400T aircraft moving in the first place. Nothing is happening fast, which I reflect is probably for the best when, just like a ship manoeuvring in an ocean, we are so vast and have so much momentum. We come to the first turn, which the captain is going to talk me through. In my head, I think 'turn now', because we seem to have gone so far, but the captain says nothing. Then, having noticed my obvious discomfort, he reassures me. 'Stick with it,' he says.

He only says 'turn now' after what feels like a lifetime, so I pull the tiller towards me and the aircraft responds with all the grace of a cruise liner. We go around the corner and straighten on the centre line, and I feel pride that I have done my first turn. I'm anxious too, though, in anticipation of doing the next one, which will be on to the runway and all my own work.

We stop short of the runway to allow the cabin crew to complete their checks and prepare for departure, and while they are doing this I am mentally running through all the possible scenarios in my head – from a high-speed abort to an engine failure at rotate. I know that all these anomalies are extremely rare, but, still, I'm steering this monster, and I need to be prepared. A ding in the flight deck signals that we are ready to go, and the captain lets air traffic control know. The instruction is to line-up runway two-seven left.

The clunk of the parking brake again, and we are moving forward on to the runway. I am judging the turn, and I almost get it right, only a little to the right of the centre line, something I can sort out as we roll down the runway. Then it happens. 'Speedbird 25 cleared for take-off.' We are ready.

I advance the thrust levers a little and allow the engines to stabilize, then press the TOGA button in front of them, which commands the predetermined take-off power. There is a whirring noise as the motor of the auto-throttle advances the levers, and the noise builds, though it's nowhere near as loud as I had expected. I definitely feel a pressure in the base of my back, however, as the four rollers push out everything they have and we begin to accelerate down the runway. I am totally focused on getting safely airborne now, but, in the background my brain is still going through every scenario. We go through V1 (the speed where we can no longer stop safely in the given conditions) and I take my hands off the thrust levers to prevent me reducing power by accident, then the command comes from the training captain: Rotate!

I pull back on the aircraft. It feels a little heavier than in the simulator, but it pivots nicely, and then it happens – I have done it. We are off the ground.

And I am a Boeing 747 pilot!

It's one hell of a feeling. Meanwhile, the gear comes up and the autopilot is engaged, and it's almost as if I can feel the aircraft gently remonstrating with me. *See?* I can hear her say. *Easy!*

As we soar into the night sky I feel a great surge of joy. I've just experienced the most amazing twenty minutes of my professional life and am now part of an elite band of 747 pilots. And I see why they love it. To have lifted this colossus off the tarmac and into the air feels incredible, and I could not be more besotted. Even now, I already know it. This is the start of another love affair. With an oversized aluminium tube with four engines.

With the autopilot engaged, ready to take over flying duties for the next eleven or so hours, I look out and down. I can't help but wonder how those first test pilots must have felt some forty years before today. What must it have been like for that very first pilot, flying that very first Jumbo? As he roared down that runway, back in 1969, wouldn't his overarching feeling be one of profound disbelief that such a behemoth could ever get off the ground?

And then another thought might have edged into his mind. How on *earth* was he going to get it safely back down again?

How am *I*? It's going to be a long flight.

2. The Aircraft That Was Supposed to Change the World

Conventional wisdom might suggest that an aircraft as well loved and successful as the Boeing 747 must have been the natural outcome of an industry-wide push for design excellence. That the idea was mooted, that billions were thrown at it, and that a landmark in aviation history was the result.

That's not how it happened. Far from it.

It's 2023, and I'm standing outside an unassuming building on the edge of Paine Field International Airport in Everett, Washington State. I'm here as the producer of a documentary about the construction of the very last Boeing 747 for the Smithsonian, and though the film is in the can now, I was invited to return here, to watch as the last ever Jumbo rolled off the production line.

For a superfan like me, it's been an obvious pinch-yourself moment, but it's also given me the opportunity to poke around the place a bit, and one of my personal must-sees is sitting inside this building and is, arguably, where the 747 story began.

Dwarfed by the Everett assembly-line buildings which dominate the skyline around these parts, this nondescript building isn't currently used by Boeing. It's on long-term loan to the Museum of Flight, which is based in nearby Seattle, and here, run and staffed mostly by passionate volunteers, is where they work on various restoration projects.

I am met outside by John, one of the docents who is based here. A cheerful man in what I judge to be his sixties, he greets me warmly before guiding me through a modest gift shop and, via a short corridor, into a bustling hangar – for me a very familiar-feeling place.

There are some interesting aircraft in here. A De Havilland Comet 4 that, due to John's loving ministrations, looks almost immaculate, and a Lockheed Jetstar business jet that was apparently used by Kelly Johnson of Skunk Works fame. The centre of the building is dominated, however, by the aircraft I have come to see, its highly polished blue-and-white livery with a single red stripe shimmering under the bright halogen lights. To any avgeek like me, its sleek lines and presence are unmistakeable. This is the last remnant of a project that back in 1967 cost a staggering $1.44 billion (about $35 billion today), produced no flyable aircraft, and famously (or, rather, infamously) 'almost ate Seattle'. It is the Boeing 2707 Supersonic Transport, or SST.

The metal in front of me isn't an actual aircraft, however. And it's not even whole. It's just the remaining forward 80 feet of the final configuration mock-up, and it's had a life story, John tells me, equally as complex as the finished aircraft it was meant to represent.

'Boeing sold the model to a museum in Florida in 1973,' he explains, 'who displayed it until they went bust in 1981. The building then got bought by the Faith World Church, and for the next seven years they held services beneath it.'

Okay, I'm thinking, a church that prays under an aircraft. I'm obviously not against that per se. 'It was then sold on a few times,' John continues, 'eventually ending up back in Seattle in 2013. It's been here ever since.' He pats it fondly. 'Have a look around, and if you have any questions just holler.'

While John gets back to his restoration work on the

Comet I stand and gaze upon this half-century-old lump of metal. I am taken aback by the size of it. This is no 'lawn dart', the narrow aluminium tube otherwise known as Concorde. No, it looks so obviously what it is – the front end of a much bigger aircraft, one designed to carry up to 300 people. And to carry them at Mach 3, three times the speed of sound, easily outstripping what would turn out to be Concorde's 128 passengers, carried at a slightly less impressive Mach 2. It was not to be. This model is all that is left of that endeavour and, with its signature drooping nose removed, what is left of this mocked-up SST looks a little sorry for itself.

When I tap the aluminium a hollow sound echoes through the hangar. And I can't help but wonder if that's how the designers might have felt, seeing all their hopes and dreams reduced to this shell.

Because that's what happened. They had backed the wrong horse.

Though generally seen as an exciting and innovative time, the late 1950s and early '60s were awful in terms of aviation safety. It seemed that not a month would go by without at least one fatal air accident. One of them, a mid-air collision between a TWA Super Constellation and a United Airlines DC-8 over Staten Island, New York, in December 1960, proved particularly notable. It was the first accident where details for the investigation were provided from a flight recorder, or 'black box', as they are colloquially known today. (Actually, they are orange. The term 'black box' derives from the Second World War, when sensitive aircraft components were kept safe in black metal boxes.) And, it was the deadliest US commercial aviation accident to date, with a loss of 134 lives, 128 aboard, and 6 on the ground.

The following month, January 1961, when John F. Kennedy was sworn in as the thirty-fifth President of the United States, that devastating crash was at the forefront of his mind, along with the whole future of aviation safety. This is why, when Najeeb Halaby was appointed as the second ever director of the Federal Aviation Administration (FAA),* Kennedy gave him a mandate to start Project Horizon, an exploration of what advancements could be made in civil aviation over the next decade.

The resulting report came to twenty-four conclusions, one being that to keep the USA at the forefront of aerospace technology the nation would need to develop a supersonic air-transport aircraft. This bold assertion was met with scepticism by many, including JFK's then vice-president, Lyndon Johnson, who had been given the Supersonic Transport (SST) portfolio. Halaby countered that he was aware of a European collaboration on SSTs between the British Aircraft Corporation and Sud Aviation. They were already working on a project, so the race was truly on, and to Halaby's mind, if the USA failed to enter this emerging market it would be what he termed a 'stunning setback' for its entire aviation industry.

And, for the Boeing Company, incidentally, not the first. Boeing had been exploring SST designs since the early 1950s and in 1958 had established a permanent committee to look at the possibilities in further depth. Under the code name 'Model 733', many options were considered internally, and in early 1960 a design for a new Boeing SST was chosen. This was to be a swing-wing airliner, with origins in the Boeing Defense military TFX programme, but

---

* The first was Elwood Richard Quesada, who served from 1 November 1958 to 3 March 1961.

as it turned out the US government purchased the General Dynamics F-111 rather than the Boeing jet. This left Boeing with a design they had invested time and effort into but had no customer for – not unusual for military programmes, but still a blow. However, they could now return to that concept and re-purpose it. This would give them a head start over their competitors, and JFK's big push might actually deliver them a bigger prize.

Halaby duly pressed ahead with Project Horizon, but in November 1962 there was another setback for the US when the European consortium announced the results of its labours. Concorde, as its new SST was christened, was going to lead the way! And in a flurry of publicity, the consortium grandly announced what Halaby had felt to be true all along – that the future of *all* air travel would in time be supersonic. And that Europe (well, Britain and France in this instance) was going to be at the vanguard.

This was bad enough, but things very soon worsened. Through classified intelligence, it became clear that the Soviets were also well advanced with designs for SST. Halaby wrote in earnest to JFK. If they didn't act, he pointed out, and resurrect their own programme, both jobs and income would be lost to foreign suppliers, as US airlines would of course opt for Concorde, or, worse, choose the Soviet aircraft.

Halaby's letter went further, advocating for an audacious design, one that had Mach 3 performance and that suited the domestic market rather than the transatlantic one – in this, he believed, the ship had already sailed. Being so far ahead, the Europeans would surely dominate.

This was a crucial point in aviation development but, like so many political hot potatoes, decisions were driven not by pure economics but also by industry and public perception.

And so it transpired here. It would be industry that gave the US government the push it so plainly needed. And one business in particular.

Pan American Airlines, by this time generally seen as the USA's unofficial flag-carrying airline, all but dominated the skies over America, and from offices high up in the iconic Chrysler Building it was run by one of its founders, the entrepreneur and airline pioneer Juan Trippe.

In May 1963, Trippe, who'd run the airline since the early 1930s and was never one to stand still when he could push his airline forward, was quick to see the new technology's potential. It was leaked that he had secured six options for Concorde, making no bones about the fact that he really had no choice: Pan Am needed to be at the forefront of the supersonic revolution, but if America's failure to join the race meant he needed to buy from Europe, then so be it.

JFK was reported to be furious. 'Did you see what Juan Trippe did?' he said to Halaby during a meeting in the Oval Office. 'He put out an announcement this afternoon that he's going to buy six planes from the British and the French. How could he do that, when he knew we were about to go ahead? We think that this is a deliberate thing, to beat us when we are about to announce a programme. This looks to the President [himself] as a deliberate act and I'm really going to spend our time screwing Pan Am. If he's so indifferent to what the United States government is doing, I think,' he told Halaby, 'that you ought to call up and stick it right up his ass. We'll give him all the trouble he wants. There isn't going to be anything that's going to make me more excited than doing that.'

Trippe obviously wasn't privy to those words at the time, but as his son Ed Trippe later told me, during our interview for the documentary, his father was subsequently threatened with repercussions by the White House; if he went ahead, Trippe knew he couldn't count on any kind of future government support.

Shortly afterwards, during a visit to the USAF Academy on 5 June 1963, the President announced the National Supersonic Transport programme. And, despite the continuing clamour both from naysayers within his own administration and the wider industry, in February 1964 he supported his VP's request for SST development funding, to the tune of $100 million. The USA had finally joined the race.

They were far behind, so they had to get their skates on. With this in mind, the government placed requests for proposals with three airframers and three engine manufacturers, making it abundantly clear how ambitious their aims were: all the documents supplied carried the bold market estimate of 500 SSTs being needed by 1990.

With time of the essence, they were not given long, now having less than six months to deliver. The chosen airframers, Boeing, Lockheed and North American, all duly produced designs to meet the specifications. Boeing went with the one it had developed in 1960, the swing-wing Model 733 that resembled the yet to be built B-1 Lancer Bomber. Lockheed had gone with a scaled version of the Concorde, using the work already underway with European partners to cut down on the development time. North American chose to take its proven design for the B-70 Valkyrie and scale this up for passenger service. Boeing and North American obviously had one eye on the defence market and applications for this platform, hence the militaristic look and feel of their designs.

This first round saw the removal of North American and its NAC-60 aircraft from the competition – a sad end to what was a truly stunning-looking concept. It also saw one of the engine manufacturers dropped. As a result, Boeing and Lockheed were now competing head to head, with General Electric and Pratt and Whitney the preferred engine manufacturers.

Both airframers now had until September 1966 to develop the plan in detail, including full-scale mock-ups of the aircraft they envisioned, and undergo lengthy review before the winner was chosen. The stakes could not have been higher, or the potential rewards greater, so Boeing and Lockheed naturally placed their most experienced engineers and innovators on the projects. And there was little doubt that this was exactly where everyone wanted to be. This was, after all, and as everyone agreed, going to be the future of *all* air travel.

Or was it?

Let me now take you to Hood Canal, Washington State, a scenic waterway on the edge of the Olympic National Forest a little to the west of Seattle. It's the place where, back in August 1965, a 44-year-old Boeing engineer called Joe Sutter had recently purchased a holiday cabin.

Buying the cabin, it should be noted, was not Joe's idea. Being something of a workaholic, he was rarely keen on taking a holiday, but his wife, Nancy, always conscious of the punishing hours he worked at Boeing, had finally put her foot down. And with their two kids away at summer camp, she was adamant about the two of them taking a break.

Joe's job was a busy one. Now in a management role within the company, overseeing the engineering team responsible for the 737 programme, he was doing work he assumed would occupy him for the next two or three years. And though he was aware of the work going on to try to secure that precious

SST contract, he knew, as a relatively junior engineer within Boeing, that even were that not so he was unlikely to be chosen to land a role in the biggest game in town.

That was just fine by Joe. Yes, he had ambitions, but he was settled where he was, and, right now, also happy to disconnect from any stresses and strains. Heck, as he admitted to his wise and tolerant wife, he was even beginning to enjoy himself. He was close to the water, the air was crisp and fragrant, and with no phone line yet installed in the not-quite-finished cabin, he was finding the enforced isolation surprisingly restorative.

Joe's dedication to his job, however, meant that he couldn't properly relax unless he knew he could be contacted in the case of an emergency, so, before leaving work, he had taken the trouble to give his assistant, Ruth Howland, the number of his nearest neighbour.

A couple of days into the couple's week-long vacation, Joe received a call. Nancy was out with friends and he was cutting wood into logs for the cabin fire at the time; despite it being summer, the evenings were often cool, and the fire really did help take the chill off. He was in full flow with his axe when he was interrupted by the sound of his neighbour calling him.

'Hey, Sutter!' the man yelled as he approached. 'They're calling you on my phone!'

By 'them' Joe could only assume his neighbour meant his employer, since he'd already asked him if he could give Ruth the number. It also seemed the neighbour was a little irritated to have his peaceful afternoon interrupted by someone else's problems. So Joe apologized profusely as he followed him up to his cabin, wondering what kind of crisis might have taken place.

Lifting the phone, though, Joe quickly established that

the person on the end of the line wasn't Ruth. It was Dick Rouzie, chief engineer of Boeing Commercial Airplanes, with whom Joe had recently been discussing how Boeing might improve the 707 – an aircraft he'd previously worked on and which was, all agreed, becoming too small to be fit for purpose, and difficult to adapt. Was this call about that? Surely not.

After apologizing to Joe for interrupting his holiday, Dick explained that it was something bigger. Much bigger. He explained that Pan Am was pressing Boeing to design something that would be *way* larger than the 707. So,' Dick finished, while Joe was trying to take everything in, 'do you fancy leading on that project?'

Joe didn't need to think about it. A request from his boss was, after all, effectively an order. Plus, this would be an opportunity to head up a project of his own.

'Of course,' he confirmed immediately. The deal was, it seemed, sealed.

After once more making his apologies to the neighbour for disturbing his peace and quiet, Joe walked slowly back to his own cabin, deep in thought. Despite the tranquillity of his surroundings and the gentle hissing of the water as it lapped against the oystershell-strewn shore, his mind was already racing. He had just been given a project of his own, and not just any project, either. It was a programme involving a dream he'd had since childhood; being at the forefront of the development of a long-range airliner – actually being the one to *head* the project that might bring it into being. By the time he'd returned to the cabin and picked up his abandoned axe, he was already thinking about the details. About size, features, range, powerplant. In short, Joe was doing what Joe was so good at: beginning to design the aircraft in his head.

He had no idea, however, just how enormous the consequences of the decision he had just made would be. And nor would he. At least, not for another five years.

When, I think it's fair to say, he would end up saving Boeing.

3. The Incredibles

By 2008, when I took up my position as a commercial pilot, what had started life as a bundle of design ideas in the head of one relatively junior aircraft engineer had become one of the most well-loved and recognizable aircraft in the skies. It was also an aircraft, at least to my mind, without equal.

I was by now three months into my employment as a commercial 747 pilot, and my line training had been progressing well. Since my first flight to Hong Kong (where, yes, I did land that Jumbo safely) I'd added several ticks to my required training competencies, including operating in a hot and high environment – in my case, Johannesburg – and, during a trip to São Paulo in Brazil, something called 'shuttle operations', where a short flight is tagged on to the end of a long-haul one to allow another destination to be served.

Today, which saw me 38,000 feet over Newfoundland in a 747-400, I was being exposed to 'two crew operation' and the vagaries of operating to the East Coast of the United States, which is notoriously busy airspace.

I looked out of the front window into a cloudless azure sky. The eastern seaboard of Canada was visible as far as the eye could see, and as we drifted past Gander I reflected that I was back in familiar territory. This was a destination I often visited during my Hercules days. That was of necessity, due to the limited range of that aircraft, but no such refuelling problems existed for us today. We cruised past it over 50 per cent higher than a Hercules, and, due to the amazing aerodynamic work of Joe Sutter and his team, at almost twice the speed. Oh, how my work life had changed.

I was now settling into a routine and the work environment was beginning to feel more familiar, but working for an airline was very different to being in my old military family. For one thing, with almost 3,500 pilots, over 900 of whom flew the 747, how would I even get to know them all?

Yet, in some ways, we were a family, because that's what we had to be. Despite the transient nature of crews, due to rosters and rotas, we had to somehow manage to build close bonds and trust, and at a level that is, I think, perhaps unique to airlines. It was taking time for me to adjust to it, but I was steadily getting there, partly due to the ubiquity of clear standard operating procedures. SOPs are what bind us because they allow an expectation of trust: we will all do what is expected of us, and what we are trained to do.

I was flying with Steve that day, a training captain who was taking me on my first East Coast trip, which was also one with only two pilots on board. This had already added an extra layer of pressure, as with the two-crew operation we could not rely on the support of extra pilots to do tasks such as the pre-flight walk around.

While we rigorously applied the SOPs, Steve guided me into areas where we could save a bit of time, such as preparing the charts only for the departure rather than for the entire route. If it wasn't critical to the departure – a 'nice to do', rather than a 'need to do' – it could be dealt with over the next seven hours.

With a bit of coaching, poking and prodding, therefore, we departed on time, and I used the following six hours to fill my head with preparation for the arrival into Boston. While not as complex or challenging as New York's JFK could be (as flown by others on my course), it was unique in other ways that required consideration.

A busy regional and international airport, Boston saw a mix of both commercial and light general aviation aircraft. This was normal for the US, but for all of us UK pilots it felt a bit bizarre. And not unreasonably; in the UK (and in much of Europe too) you'd never see a 747, or any other big commercial aircraft, sharing airport space with a single-engine propeller-driven aircraft such as a Cessna. To manage that mix was incredibly complex. You couldn't, for example, have a Cessna land following a Jumbo, because the wake turbulence from the Jumbo would flip the Cessna upside down. Still, it was what it was, and, having been told about it during the briefing, I was now going to experience it for myself.

Boston Logan sits on a peninsula reaching out from East Boston into Boston Harbor and has six runways ranging from 779 to 3,073 metres long. They are laid out in the sort of pattern you might get if you threw six pencils of varying lengths on the floor – i.e. a series of random intersecting lines. Only four of them are usable for a 747, the shortest of those – also the shortest on the airline's entire 747 network – a mere 2,134 metres long, a figure I urge you to note. Some are weather-dependent too, but as the wind today was light and variable we could be allocated any runway.

They also use every inch of the available land for those pieces of tarmac, so one of the unique problems at Boston is shipping. Yes, I mean shipping as in boats. Shipping entering or leaving the harbour can cause a need to change a runway, to ensure there is no conflict to departing or landing traffic. You can imagine the situation where you need to reject a landing and find yourself taking off towards a ship sitting in the water, just a few hundred metres off the end of the runway. Then imagine that ship is an aircraft-carrier-sized container vessel. It would certainly focus the mind, and was probably best avoided, so I was grateful that, today at least, there was no mention of 'shipping'.

I was also keen to look over the landing performance calculations that had come with the forecast. These are in tabular form and are either generic for runway length, or specific to an airport. As we fly to Boston a lot, there are specific tables for the airport, one for each of its runways. This means we have very accurate information to draw on, rather than just having generic ones.

Today we were landing with a full passenger and freight load, and with the maximum landing weight for this aircraft being 269T, our 250T was quite heavy. This meant that of the four runways available to us, only three could be used without limitations; the other, Runway 27, was considered limiting. I duly did the calculations and once Steve had checked and agreed them we proceeded to brief for an arrival on Runway 27. Not my choice, obviously, since it was the shortest by far, but it is simple best practice to brief for the most challenging arrival – that way, if you are allocated a different runway, it will, by default, be easier to brief on the fly.

A little aside here, by the way, on runway numbering. At first glance, it can seem a bit random, but it's not. Runways are numbered according to their nearest compass heading, rounded up or down to the nearest ten. So a runway with a heading of 272 degrees would be rounded down to 270, giving it the number 27.

This applies at most airports, but there are exceptions. LAX, for example, has four runways, two on either side of the terminal complex, facing north and south, two stretching out over the Pacific, the other two towards Inglewood.

They are all parallel and, as such, all four have a heading of 251 or 071 degrees, depending on which way you are facing. It would be a bit confusing to have four Runway 25s at an airport, obviously, so LAX has retained convention on the runways to the south – they are Runways 25 Left and Right – but to the north they are Runways 24 North and South – a quirk in an otherwise clever and simple system.

Enough digression, though. Back to the approach briefing.

As this was a training trip, Steve wanted me to extract maximum value from it, so I would be briefing, flying the approach and landing the aircraft, something that may seem normal to most, but where I work, we usually do things a little differently.

Every approach is what is called a monitored approach, one where the pilot flying (PF), i.e. the one doing the take-off and landing, would normally not fly the approach to the airfield. When I started working for a commercial airline, I found it strange to do this, as in the military the landing pilot also flies the approach. To do it differently at first felt counter-intuitive, but I was quickly becoming a convert. I could see the value in having the landing pilot monitoring and, once comfortable and with stabilized criteria having been met, they can take control and land.

The key thing to note here is that while the landing pilot is always land-minded, the other pilot, the one flying the approach, is always planning for the go-around. I know it sounds confusing but, in reality, it is a great way to ensure both pilots are actively engaged and involved in the business of landing the aircraft safely.

Today, though, as I mentioned, I would be doing all of it myself, something I could only do because I was flying with a trainer. It would allow me to get as much exposure to the aircraft as possible – in using the automation for the approach, manually landing and then taxiing this behemoth around a relatively tight apron.

Briefing complete, it was soon time to start our descent and I felt the now familiar mix of excitement and nervous anticipation.

Steve pulled the transmit switch and made our request, and the reply, in an unmistakeable Bostonian accent, came immediately.

'Speedbird Two Thirteen descend flight level 290, cleared the OOSHN 3 arrival, AJJAY transition expect Runway 27, cleared direct AJJAY at this time.'

By the way, please bear with me on this. I know all this is a bit of a mouthful. But these five-letter codes refer to GPS 'waypoints', which we'll cover in more depth in a later chapter.

Meanwhile, Steve read back the clearance and I dialled 29,000 feet into the autopilot control panel, then pressed a button marked FLCH (Flight Level Change), and we started to descend.

We'd planned for the Ocean (OOSHN) arrival and to fly over AJJAY, a waypoint to the north-east of the airport on that path, so all was good. Well, apart from the fact I was sure he just said Runway 27. Typical! Runway 27 it was, then.

Steve duly made the necessary changes in the flight management computer, from Runway 33 (the longest) to Runway 27 (the shortest) and we began to descend along the Gulf of Maine. The view of Cape Cod out of the window was spectacular, with Nantucket and Martha's Vineyard, favoured havens of the super-rich, visible beyond. Although I was concentrating on flying, it was a bit of a wow moment. I was flying a 747 and things could not get much better.

My elation was short-lived. As we slowed and were vectored on to the ILS (Instrument Landing System), I got my first glimpse of Runway 27, and in doing so experienced an unexpectedly vivid flashback: me trying to land a C-130 on an aircraft carrier, back in my RAF days, albeit in a simulator.

'Wow,' I thought to myself. 'That is *short*.' It was going to take my A game to get us down safely. And not just on to the runway. If we didn't land on the marked touchdown zone, we would have to go around.

There is a clear rationale behind this. Even if the runway is 4 kilometres long, that touchdown zone is where the stopping figures are calculated from, and if you are out of it, your available stopping distance becomes guesswork. And in aviation, guessing is something we never do.

I was fully aware that I had less landings on the Jumbo than could be counted on both hands, but pride was at stake here. So I was going to do my darndest to get us in the zone the first time.

I got us descending on the ILS and we were now fully configured for landing. Using the automatics to their fullest, I had managed to keep the stress and workload to a manageable level, but that quickly changed.

'We are stable,' Steve said, 'so take the autopilot out and get a feel for her.'

I did so, and once the *whoop whoop* had sounded moments later I was hand-flying the aircraft towards the runway. When you are flying something that has 250 tons of momentum, small corrections are key, so as each took effect I continuously monitored and made further small corrections as they were needed. My focus now absolute, I was being measured and deliberate with everything. This wasn't a Hercules, a plane I'd spent thousands of hours flying. This was new, I was still learning, and I had to work very hard.

I was determined to cross the threshold at exactly the

point when the radar altimeter calls out '100 feet'. This was important; if I was late, I would be too low and need to go around. Too early, then I'd be too high and might land long. It was a virtual hoop I needed to jump through, like the ones you often see on simulators. Today, thankfully, I did, so we continued.

Now came the really hard part: judging the landing flare. This is where, just before you land, you lift the nose very slightly to arrest the rate of descent. All other things being equal, this makes for a light, comfortable landing. Conversely, if you don't flare you will land at a rate of descent of around 700 feet a minute. Not comfortable at all.

You may be forgiven for thinking that this last bit would be the easiest, because all the hard work to get to the runway has already been done. But you'd be wrong. It is anything but. At my airline's Cranebank training centre at Heathrow, there are two discs stuck on to the outside of the building. One, placed on the wall at the height of the second storey, represents a 747 pilot's eye-height during taxi. The other one, way up at the top of the fifth storey, represents their eye height at the flare. So, effectively – and it's best not to dwell on this right now – I was five storeys up, trying to put down sixteen wheels that were 100 feet behind where we were sitting on to a spot on a runway I could not see.

Simples.

The radar altimeter called out FIFTY and I started to lift the nose and ease back the power. Nothing too large, though. Just a trickle. FORTY, THIRTY, TWENTY ... then the speedbrake deployed, bringing the spoilers up. And we were down.

As the runway was short, we had already selected the maximum deceleration into autobrake, to come on at touchdown.

I placed the nose down and, having chosen idle reverse, I now pulled the levers up and back into maximum. There was a lot going on, but one thing was blindingly obvious. We were stopping. Really quickly as well.

'Seventy knots,' Steve announced as we slowed. I brought the reversers into idle power, then we came to a halt, and I was astonished to note that we had landed, and stopped, in a little over 1,500 metres. There was a *whole third* of the runway remaining.

'Howzat, then, for stopping performance?' asked Steve.

I didn't answer immediately. I was genuinely too gobsmacked.

I was still slightly in shock when it was time to do the debrief. Steve wasn't. He knew the 747's capabilities too well. While it was obviously essential to be cautious and to always do the maths, I had now learned about one of those capabilities for myself. This enormous Jumbo had the landing and take-off performance of a much smaller aircraft, in no small part due to the 747's triple-slotted flap. The three slots allow the air to be re-energized across the entire span of the flap, producing greater lift at slower speed (almost like having three individual wings). The resulting slower approach speed means less inertia and braking are required to stop this behemoth, thus reducing the landing distances compared to a similar-sized aircraft with more traditional flaps. In this it was, and still is, unique.

'Sutter really did design something remarkable,' Steve commented, having clearly read my thoughts. 'Now let's go toast both his and your success with a beer.'

I nodded my agreement but, in truth, I was still gobsmacked. No wonder they called the men who designed and built this machine The Incredibles.

*

I doubt anything as celebratory as a beer was on Joe Sutter's mind as he and his wife returned from their cabin on Hood Canal back in 1965. That would be some way off yet. But he was keen to get started. He was already giving some thought to what this new large aircraft might be like and had by now realized that his new job couldn't have come at a better time because, largely thanks to the people over at Boeing Defense, he knew he could think as big as he wanted.

Though Joe wasn't involved, he knew from his colleagues that the people working in that side of the business were designing a large transport aircraft for the US military. Named the C-5, it was to be complemented by a new type of jet engine – the high-bypass turbofan engine – from either General Electric or Pratt and Whitney.

Prior to the military C-5 project there was essentially only one type of jet engine in commercial use, the turbojet engines that were powering much of the world's jet fleets in the 1960s. These turbojets, the first of which was invented by British engineer Frank Whittle in 1930, typically identified by their thin cigar shape, pulled air into the front of the engine and compressed it, before mixing it with fuel in a combustion chamber, where it was ignited. These hot, high-pressure gases exploded out of the back of the engine, and then through several turbine blades. This in turn made the compressors at the front of the engine rotate, to suck more air in. The efflux produced thrust and you had yourself a self-sustaining combustion cycle.

The attraction of these engines was their simplicity and reliability, but they also came with challenges, namely noise, fuel consumption and slow acceleration. Think about jumping on a push-bike and setting off in tenth gear, which is pretty analogous to how these engines work in practice. Great once you're cruising, but pretty hard and slow getting there.

Turbojet engines were now beginning to be replaced by low-bypass turbofans, which produced thrust via a combination of the jet core and some bypass air. Although these jets were a little quieter, they offered no appreciable performance differences. The turbofans that had been developed for the C-5, however, were groundbreaking in that they took a turbojet engine and placed a much bigger fan on the front of it.

The first of these high-bypass turbofans, invented for the C-5 project, did two things. They passed a lot of air through to the engine core at much lower velocity, while also putting some compressed 'cold air' around the engine core, but never into a combustion area. This resulted in quicker engine acceleration, less fuel burn and, lastly, the bypass air mixed with the hot efflux and made the entire engine quieter too. Some magic.

And though Boeing ultimately lost out to Lockheed on the C-5 contract, for Joe Sutter the work they had done was a gift. Having previously worked on Boeing's smallest jetliner, he was now being asked to design their biggest.

I also feel I must clear something up here. For as long as I can remember, every time I've talked about the development of the 747, someone has always come up with the same line – that the design came directly from Boeing's C-5 bid.

This is an urban myth. Although I have been blabbing on about the C-5 engine for the last few paragraphs, I think we need to put everyone straight and clarify what that contribution was. And to do so, rather than tell you myself, I will defer to the words of Joe Sutter. 'Fostering large bypass engines,' he pointed out, 'was *all* that the USAF C-5 competition contributed to the Boeing 747, as my new airplane would be called. Time and again there appears in print the logical but false assumption that Boeing took its losing military C-5 bid and revamped it as the commercial 747. In fact, the 747 would be an entirely original design that owes nothing to the C-5.'

I hope that puts that one to bed for you.

Back in Seattle, as well as being able to think big, Joe was also coming to the realization that there was another reason he may have just been in the right place at the right time. Every single senior engineer at Boeing was clamouring to get on the supersonic project. After all, it was to be the future of air travel, wasn't it? So who wanted a subsonic large aircraft project? Joe knew that had the 2707 SST not been the biggest game in town, he'd probably never have even been considered for this project for Pan Am. 'I consider myself very fortunate,' he noted several years later.

As work got underway, the small team of twenty that Joe had been allocated soon grew to over one hundred. Though neither Boeing nor Sutter had any preconceived view on what this very large aircraft would look like, or how it would perform; these parameters would be coming from the lead customer, Pan Am.

As the premier airline of the US, what Pan Am wanted was extremely important, and their boss, aviation legend Juan Trippe, had a very clear idea of what he wanted. And even though it was generally agreed at the time that once the supersonic passenger jets reigned supreme it would become a freight carrier, this was as true for the 747 as for any other aircraft project.

Trippe had always been a visionary, and an early pioneer of the jet age, and his vision for the Jumbo was a bold one. He wanted an airliner that could carry more than 350 passengers and operate from regional airfields, while also having transatlantic and Pacific range.

The requirements to achieve this were mindboggling. The

Boeing 707, the then staple of the airlines, could carry 140 passengers. Trippe wanted this new aircraft at least two and a half times bigger.

Although Boeing obviously had a lead customer in Pan Am, they also touted the idea of this very large aircraft to TWA, BOAC and Japan Airlines, to name just a few. Perhaps unsurprisingly, there was significant interest. But these airlines had design ideas of their own, some of them equally specific. And while most of them embraced Pan Am's vision, a minority, rather than accepting the engineers' dial-in solution of a double-height 707, wanted variations, which also played a part in holding up progress.

At this time, if you asked an aviation engineer how they'd find seats for 350 passengers, their obvious solution would have been a double-decker, and this was one aspect in which most potential customers agreed, and the obvious point of departure for the development team.

Boeing formally launched their 747 programme in March 1966 and Pan Am signed a contract for the aircraft the following month. This made it the fourth aircraft development project they were working on, sitting behind the SST, the 737 and the 727-200, an elongated version of the 727.

Put together, this was obviously a big financial stretch. And when you added in the fact that Boeing also had the Saturn V rocket in first-stage development, reserves for this new Cinderella project were thin on the ground. After all, if supersonic really was the future of passenger air travel, anything Sutter came up with would have a limited lifespan.

This bothered Sutter, not least because it was becoming a very widely held view, so he was prompted to design something with a dual configuration in mind. An aircraft that could be used for both passengers and freight would have the economic viability and longevity these programmes needed, when, as was at this time widely expected, the SST project bore fruit.

Sutter and his team set about finding a solution to the myriad requirements of his dual-purpose vision, and this inevitably led them to design an aircraft with a large lower hold and two passenger decks. Sutter had concerns about its real-world use, however. Most freight organizations moved their stuff in large containers for ease of shipping and transloading. These would obviously be impossible to get up to an upper deck, plus the taper of the cabin would present space issues. Back to the drawing board, then. It obviously wasn't going to work.

Sutter had also looked at the configuration from a passenger perspective, particularly when it came to an evacuation scenario. The FAA for passenger-aircraft certification needed to see a full aircraft evacuated in ninety seconds, and Sutter just couldn't see how this could be done. The team had conceptualized and drawn hundreds of double-decker aircraft, but they just could not get a design that had the agreement of everyone.

Sutter then offered a new idea to the team, something that had never before been considered. Why not, he suggested, put a very wide single-deck fuselage on to the drawing board by way of comparison?

Joe's idea was met with incredulity, and also dismay. Everyone knew Pan Am wanted its new jet as soon as possible, and starting over with something completely different would scupper any hope of a quick build. Going double-decker, all were agreed, it had to be. It just needed a bit of maturing and fettling.

Sutter knew they were right about the challenges and risks of starting from scratch with the clock ticking. But committed as he was to the aircraft he'd imagined, he decided a 'quick and dirty' 'back of a cigarette packet'-style evaluation would at least give them an idea if his vision had legs.

Joe instructed Row Brown, one of his senior engineers, to look at the alternative. Row's rapid study of the new concept showed that Joe's single-deck model could indeed meet all of the requirements, though in doing so it was going to be enormous. Size aside, though, he could see that this was the obvious solution, so an unheard-of passenger configuration of ten abreast in economy was locked in straight away.

The freight solution was proving trickier, though, mostly because the side door of the aircraft – the usual point of entry for freight – might not prove large enough to allow it to carry outsize loads. So how about entry through an opening nose? It was the necessity for this that would go on to give the 747 its distinctive silhouette; having an opening large enough to allow loading of really big cargoes meant moving the flight deck *above* it – and so the 747's famous 'hump' was born.

As well as a distinctive fuselage shape, the 747 would also have a distinctive wing shape. With its sweep of 37.5 degrees, to facilitate the high-speed flight of Mach 0.85 (85 per cent the speed of sound), as required by Pan Am, this would be a huge improvement on the Mach 0.76 of the 707. This faster speed was also suited more to the Pratt and Whitney engine than the GE one chosen for the C-5, designed to cruise at Mach 0.70. Four of these engines would be placed on these swept-back wings.

That the number four was a theme was intentional. Sutter wanted to have redundancy in this aircraft-like-no-other and opted for four hydraulic systems, four flap sections, four elevators and four spoiler sections, all to ensure that no single failure could lead to an accident. Oh, and not forgetting four main gear posts each having sixteen main wheels which allowed the 747 to have a similar individual wheel-loading or footprint to the 707.

Sutter's thinking, that no aeroplane should have a single point of failure, was particularly pertinent when it came to an aircraft the size of the 747: the loss of an aircraft with almost 400 people on board, as well as representing a massive human tragedy, also had the potential to be corporately catastrophic and, as we'll see later, he was right to make those decisions.

For now, though, despite meeting all the requirements they'd been given, their big task was to convince customers firmly wedded to a double-decker that what they'd designed was the way forward. But how should that bombshell be dropped to Pan Am? After all, Juan Trippe wasn't known for his tolerance.

As Boeing continued to firm up contractual arrangements with Pan Am and others, Joe decided he first needed to call an internal meeting to broach the subject of his design change with Tex Boullioun, leader of Boeing Commercial Airplanes, and Joe's direct boss, Mal Samper, head of the 747 project.

To say the two men were dumbfounded would be an understatement. Joe left the meeting that day as convinced by his design as he had ever been, but also aware, having thrown several cats among the pigeons, that it might have been the last he ever attended as a Boeing employee.

Every department at Boeing was now nervous. Pan Am had expected a double-decker and, if the company was minded, it could easily go elsewhere to get its behemoth airliner built. Indeed, rumours abounded that Trippe had already tried to get Lockheed to make him a C-5-sized airliner. Lockheed had apparently declined, but that didn't mean he couldn't go back to them.

Boeing literally could not afford to lose this contract and, with the stakes so high, it needed the idea to be pitched by the best salesman it had. And Milt Heinemann, an articulate executive who was working on the 747 interior options at the time, seemed its best shot. Milt was, everyone agreed, a sales genius. He also understood that while engineering drawings were great for engineers, rarely did they sell aeroplanes in the boardrooms across the world. Sometimes you needed something simpler.

And a simple thing was what he came up with. Before heading to New York, and his showdown with Juan Trippe, Milt bought a piece of clothesline, measured and cut a twenty-foot length from it, coiled it up and popped it in his briefcase.

Always punctual, Milt arrived early for his meeting at the new Pan Am building on Park Avenue, to which the company had relocated only recently, and was ushered up to the main conference room. Finding himself alone, Milt wasted no time in using the situation to his advantage, pulling out his length of clothesline and quickly unwinding it so he could get a sense of where best to deploy it. To his surprise and delight, the length of line he'd so carefully measured turned out to be exactly the width of the meeting room. Milt felt a surge of confidence. Now he could really make his case.

Milt had just enough time to coil up the rope and pop it back into his briefcase before the Pan Am executives started to arrive, acknowledging Milt and talking among themselves as they settled into their seats.

Then, as if waiting for the perfect moment to make his presence felt, in swept Juan Trippe, with his chief engineer, John Borger. They sat down, and the room immediately fell silent.

Introductions were short, and Milt wasted no time in outlining the reason for his visit. As he began to justify the rationale for the change from double to single deck, the murmurs that had begun rippling around the room started to increase. He could also see several executives stealing glances towards their chairman, as if to establish whether he was on the same page – namely, 'Was this guy for real?'

Trippe himself was growing redder by the minute but, despite the painful lack of encouragement, Milt ploughed doggedly on to the end of his pitch, only to be greeted by a long and painful silence. Perhaps no one dared voice an opinion until Trippe had?

Perhaps so, because it was Trippe himself who broke the silence. 'You say you can get the full specified passenger load on to this single deck?' he asked pleasantly. It was difficult to gauge how he really felt.

'Yes,' Milt replied.

'*Comfortably?*' Trippe then added, and there was no getting away from it. His tone definitely sounded a little sceptical.

'Yes, sir,' Milt replied again, firmly. '*Very* comfortably.'

But these were just words. What Trippe needed was a visual. This was evidently the ideal time to deploy the clothesline.

Milt retrieved the line from his briefcase, gave one end to the executive sitting adjacent to him, and asked if he'd hold it against the wall. He then took the line to the other side of the room. 'This cord,' he explained as he did so, 'represents the inside width of the 747 passenger cabin.'

The shock on everyone's faces, Trippe's included, was good to see. None had ever really visualized a cabin of that width, and now they could imagine it for themselves, perhaps it didn't seem so bad after all?

Clearly not. As Milt had hoped, Trippe's interest had been piqued. He agreed to Boeing building two mock-ups for them to look at – one for the double-decker they'd thought they were getting, and one for Joe's alternative single-decker.

They wouldn't have to wait very long for them, either. Always one step ahead, Joe's team had already started building them.

Trippe's visit to Boeing HQ shortly afterwards was still a very high-stakes affair. This was a make-or-break meeting, and everyone at Boeing knew it. Bill Allen, Boeing's chairman and an old friend of Trippe's, accordingly dropped everything to meet them.

And despite the apparent success of Milt's pitch, the atmosphere when they arrived was less than cordial. Perhaps the extent of the change from what they'd asked for had sunk in? There was no doubt – it was a very big change indeed.

Joe was tasked to deliver an engineering briefing to explain why they had to change from a double- to a single-decker to make his vision work, but he knew – not least from the scowls and stony faces – that he'd put his own and his company's reputation on the line – definitely not a comfortable place to be. Everything now rested on the mock-ups.

On entering the mock-up department in the factory at Renton, Borger and Trippe made a beeline for the double-decker with which Joe's single-passenger-deck model was competing. He watched the men closely, noting that they seemed to be eyeing the cargo area with what appeared to be disappointment, which seemed to continue as they climbed the stairs to the lower passenger deck. They then climbed to the upper deck, and Trippe and Allen ventured to the front rail. Both seemed visibly shocked at the height from the floor – some 25 feet or so – but from up there, Sutter knew it must have looked like more. It clearly did – he could see the dismay on their faces.

The party descended the stairs and walked across to the

single-deck model. Once again, Joe followed them hopefully, but little was said as they took in the size of the single deck. Trippe then wandered over to the separate mock-up that represented the flight deck. He turned around to Borger. 'What's this for?' he asked, pointing to the open area in the 'hump' behind the cockpit door.

Borger didn't actually know. 'Crew rest area for long flights,' he improvised.

'*Rest* area?' Trippe scoffed. 'This is going to be reserved for passengers!'

Joe felt a wave of relief washing over him. '*Is* going to be'. Not '*would* be'. He'd said '*is* going to be'. And as if conscious that he needed to acknowledge Joe's achievement personally, Trippe walked over to have a word with him as they left the mock-up area.

'You made the right decision,' he said to Joe, smiling warmly. It seemed the world's first widebody airliner was go.

Juan Trippe was already widely considered the king of modern air travel. Now, with the help of Boeing, he was about to recruit a queen to join him. The new Queen of the Skies. The 747.

4. If You Build It, They Will Come

One of the challenges in trying to manufacture the biggest jet aircraft ever is you need to find somewhere large enough to build it. There was no existing Boeing factory that could accommodate such a massive aircraft and, since it also had to be sited close to an airport with a long runway, nowhere close to Seattle they could use either.

A team was duly gathered to consider Boeing's options and, over a period of weeks, various sites were assessed. Two main contenders were at least reasonably local. One was Snohomish County Airport, a former military airbase some 30 miles to the north, known to most as Paine Field, while the other was to the south, a little way past Tacoma, adjacent to an air force base.

Politics, however, had now entered the mix, with people in Boeing's senior management team arguing the case for siting the factory in Walnut Creek, California. There, the factory could benefit from the state's enormous political clout, and they would have more lobbyists to represent their commercial interests.

For Joe Sutter, though, this suggestion needed to be nipped in the bud. It would, he knew, be an unmitigated disaster, and when invited to share his views – quite a way down the line – he didn't hold back in telling them why. If 747 production were sent down there, he told the assembled committee, communication would slow, coordination would suffer, costs would rise, their overall logistical challenges would increase, and there was no way in hell they would meet their scheduled commitments to Pan Am.

The reaction to Joe's stance, and his bullishness in getting his point across, was one of shock and, from the Walnut Creek crowd in particular, pretty peevish. Who the hell did this lowly engineer think he was? But with Boeing now spooked about delivering – their commitment to Pan Am meant everything – Joe ended up getting his way. Not least because, by now, the 747 was his life. His commitment to his project, and to delivering it to the best of his ability, was equally as strong. Even if they fired him for his impertinence in putting his foot down so forcefully, he knew he had to remain true to it.

Within a matter of weeks, to Joe's great relief, it was announced that Bill Allen, Boeing's chairman, had opted for Paine Field at Snohomish, and in spring 1966 the ground was broken on the new 700-acre site. By the end of that year some two and a half thousand construction workers were employed there full time; this was, after all, a whopping $200 million infrastructure job.

It also became one of the first of the 747's clutch of world records. In order to deliver it, they were building something that, at over 470 million cubic feet, would become – and still remains – the planet's largest building. Indeed, so vast was the place that several Boeing workers reported that they could see rainclouds forming *inside* it.

I'm not sure that's true. I've been inside the factory many times, and I am yet to get wet from anything other than my own drool as I walk around this bit of aviation heaven. Though I'm obviously more than willing to be proved wrong!

Clouds, or lack of, were the last thing on most people's minds back then, though. All anyone could think about was how fast time was passing. The build schedule was so tight that, even before the actual work began, they knew they'd be finishing the aircraft while the factory was still being built around it.

This sense of jeopardy was not just due to the colossal scale of the engineering challenge they were facing. Boeing's very existence as a business was under threat. While Sutter's team were busy putting all their energies into delivering what they'd promised, the wider economic picture was looking grim. The company was, by now, frighteningly overextended. Having poured so much into the SST programme, which, by now, was stumbling, Boeing was already haemorrhaging money, and the 727-200 and 737 programmes, beset with engineering glitches, were not yet generating anything like enough cash. Boeing was also building the Saturn V Moon Booster for the Apollo space project, not to mention pulling engineers from the already troubled SST programme to get NASA's now beleaguered US space programme back on track.

There was now a general consensus that the only ace they had to play was the work going on at that site at Snohomish.

They were looking to the 747 to save them.

Joe Sutter, meanwhile, had a problem. A big one. While everyone was waiting on this game-changing new aircraft, back at the factory things weren't quite as rosy; the 747's wing wasn't passing the aerodynamic testing in the wind tunnel.

From the outset of the project, Pan Am wanted two distinct things from the 747. It had to have a high cruise speed to get people where they needed to be, fast, but also have as low an approach speed as possible, allowing pilots to do what I did in Boston at the top of the last chapter – approach a runway slowly, so they can stop quickly, which means they can land on shorter runways, making smaller airports accessible to big jets.

The wind-tunnel testing, however, was showing that aerodynamic loading across the wing wasn't distributed in a way that meant the underlying structure could support it appropriately.

Imagine a wing as a floor in your house. Beneath the floor is a series of evenly placed joists that support the floor structure and give it strength. If you want to put a heavier weight on the floor you put more support in that area, under the floorboards. A wing is no different. You can predict where the heavy aerodynamic load will be, so you put more strength in the wing at that point. On the 747, though, the paper predictions were wrong.

I feel I should pause here to consider that this extraordinary jet airliner was conceived, designed and manufactured at a time when there was no computer input, let alone any sophisticated algorithms. Every single detail was worked out by way of engineering and mathematics, using nothing more technological than slide rules and logarithms, plus pen and paper. So when I comment that the paper predictions were wrong, it's with one almighty dollop of respect.

But back to the problem itself, which turned out to be that the outboard portion of the wing was carrying too much load, causing the aircraft to pitch upwards. This was, to use Joe's own words, a disaster. Not only would they have to rethink, which would obviously take time, but due to the incredibly tight timescales they were working to they had already started manufacturing the wings.

This full-blown crisis threatened the entire project, and Sutter was once again under extreme pressure. And once the

Boeing board had got wind of the 'wing crisis', it convened what it colloquially named 'an engineering audit', an independent group of engineers that would work to solve the wing problem alongside Sutter's team. It would be led by Jack Steiner, the inspiration behind the 727 and 737, and he wasted no time in calling his shadowing team a 'black commando parachute operation'.

Boeing was, in short, hoping to find a 'quick and dirty' solution. These engineers, all at the top of their game, rarely agreed, but one thing that Sutter and Steiner *could* agree on was that the problem wasn't going to be fixed easily.

Both teams set immediately to work. Steiner and his team opted to start from scratch and redesign the wing based on the wind-tunnel tests, but as this would have required major design changes, they knew it wasn't ideal; it would blow both the schedule and the budget out of the water.

Sutter and his team, meanwhile, had found that by twisting the entire wing by 3 degrees from root to tip, along the longitudinal axis, they could, in theory, solve the problem less expensively, by decreasing the angle of attack on the outer edge, thus reducing the stress on the wing structure. This sounds like an easy fix, but when you realize that this twist would also change the way the wing joins the aircraft, there was obviously potential for the problems to get worse.

The strongest part of any aircraft is the centre section, sometimes known as the wing box; this is where the wing and fuselage join, and it is put under tremendous loads. This twist would mean a total redesign of the centre section, and that would be similarly catastrophic.

Now running out of time and options, Sutter's team were exhausted. They needed to find another solution to twisting the whole wing; it was just unworkable. And in realizing this, it hit Joe. They didn't *need* to twist the whole wing. Could the team not look at just twisting a part of the wing? Namely the outside of it, beyond the engines?

They trialled it, and although it wasn't a 100 per cent fix, it was a good 90 per cent – well beyond what was considered safe and acceptable. The 'Sutter Twist', as it is still known today by aerodynamicists, was born. The 'commando team' melted away as quickly as it had appeared, and Sutter pushed on to getting a flyable aircraft.

With the wing problems solved, everyone felt a good deal happier, but there was another stressful challenge keeping Joe up at night now – the 747's ever-increasing weight. (I know the feeling . . .)

Aircraft design is always an exercise in ultimate compromise, a fine balance between building an engineering marvel, meeting the needs of the customer and making it fiscally viable for the company. As Sutter neared the end of the design phase he was becoming more and more worried about the weight of the aircraft. While he wanted to create that engineering marvel, he also needed to leave some weight capacity left over for those two key elements – the passengers, and the freight. How else were they going to make money?

The more weight the engineers added, the higher the manufacturing cost and, crucially, the less weight capacity there would be to generate that all-important revenue.

Joe wasn't the only one worried about it, and the senior team at Boeing tasked a small group to carry out a weight audit on the aircraft. The audit team largely came up with the same ideas for weight-saving as Joe's team, but with one notable exception; they wanted to remove one portion of the flaps, and make them double-slotted, rather than the unique triple flap Joe had designed.

Joe was vehemently against this because losing one of the three flaps meant that to produce the same amount of lift to keep the aircraft airborne it would have to fly faster. This would increase the landing speed by 8 knots, which would mean the performance figures Boeing had promised Pan Am would be unachievable. While an 8-knot increase doesn't sound much (9.2mph), the stopping-distance increase using aircraft brakes is not linear.

In the real world, this would mean that many of the smaller runways Pan Am wished to open up to the 747 would be too short. Despite Joe's objection, Boeing decided to suggest the idea to Pan Am in any case.

Frustratingly for Joe, Pan Am had no investment in his triple-slotted flap configuration and was happy to see the extra weight lost, but on one condition: the approach speed stayed the same and the performance that was promised for landing was not compromised. Boeing came back to Sutter and the design for the triple-slotted flap was locked in. Needless to say, the double-slotted flap idea never surfaced again.

Joe got the Jumbo's weight under control without the need for using all the other measures that both his and the audit team had suggested. It goes without saying that Joe was immensely grateful to Pan Am (even if privately so) for sticking with its initial design performance figures and not being tempted to lose the weight. The triple-slotted flap, as we shall see, was to become one of the reasons the 747 has consistently been so safe in service.

The first Boeing 747 to emerge from the factory was pulled out of its hangar at Everett on the last day of September 1968. And the world, which had been waiting impatiently for this first-of-a-kind widebody jet to appear, was now watching. Unlike today, when new aircraft roll-outs don't tend to make headlines, the event was covered by most of the world's media, exactly as Boeing had hoped. And for those present it delivered the requisite bang for buck. There were audible gasps. A burst of spontaneous applause. Everyone who gazed up at the 747 was awestruck. And, to his own surprise, that included Joe Sutter – he who already knew the dimensions to the inch.

There was also a sense of relief in some quarters. While some marvelled at the scale, the sleek design, the aircraft's undeniably arresting beauty, others – namely the financiers who had bankrolled this project – felt mostly comfort. They could at last relax. They had an aeroplane for their money.

Except they didn't. Not quite. Though the roll-out was designed to calm any remaining jitters and show the world that no fewer than twenty-six airlines had already placed orders (twenty-six stewardesses, each dressed in their airline's uniform, lined up beside the aircraft to illustrate the point), the 747 itself, according to the engineering team, anyway, was only 78 per cent finished. (Always expect precise figures from engineers.)

Now they just had to reach the next stage in the process; getting it to a position where it could finally leave the ground, its maiden flight having been already pencilled in for early February of the new year.

Jack Waddell, Boeing's chief test pilot, was given the honour of taking on that task. An engineering graduate from Montana State University, Jack was also a veteran of the US navy and had served in the South Pacific during the Second World War. He'd joined Boeing after the war as a test pilot and, as he had already tested many of Boeing's aircraft types, there really was no better pilot for the job.

But, just like me that first time I rolled my first Jumbo off the stand at Heathrow, Jack knew that taking off and flying the aircraft were only two of the challenges to overcome. First he had to taxi this monster, the size of a tall building, to the end of a runway.

Quite reasonably (especially when you consider this was a first in every sense) he didn't fancy doing this for the first time in the aircraft itself. Could some kind of mock-up be made so he could trial it?

Heads were duly put together and the famous 'Waddell's Wagon' was created, essentially a truck pulling a trailer with a frame attached and a crude approximation of the 747 flight deck atop it at the same height as the aircraft would be. It looked utterly ridiculous. And was, of course, duly ridiculed.

Waddell didn't care. He was not about to compromise anyone's safety, and he knew it would be crucial, both to him and to the whole test team, to know how the aircraft would steer on the ground, not to mention getting used to taxiing when you were the equivalent of three storeys from ground level; it was incredibly easy to lose speed perspective when you were that high up.

The Waddell's Wagon having proved as useful as the man himself had thought, they then progressed to the test aircraft itself, and attempted some tighter turns on a large parking area. The jet wouldn't turn in the required radius, however, and needed more and more power to get around in the space. And when they eventually got it round – disaster: it turned out that they had completely ruined the tyres on the body gear.

Waddell called a halt to any more testing until the problem was solved. The problem was obvious to Sutter. During a turn, the wing gear, which are forward of the body main gear, are the pivot for the aircraft. The body gear sitting behind this are just scrubbed sideways on the concrete as they try to follow along in the turn, causing friction and sideways forces and ruining the tyres.

Sutter's team had foreseen this very problem several months earlier, but his solution had been rejected as part of a weight- and cost-saving exercise. However, Sutter, in his wisdom, hadn't cancelled the manufacture of the parts, so when the problem occurred, Waddell was astounded to find it was solved in a matter of days, not the expected several weeks.

Joe's simple solution was to have the body gear steerable to follow the turn, and as anyone who has ever had the privilege of piloting one knows, the 747 now turns on a veritable dime.

It was a wintry morning on 9 February 1969 when the first 747 took to the air. It had been snowing overnight and, under a still-overcast sky, remnants of snow were visible on the ground at Paine Field.

The grey blanket above could not dampen the enthusiasm of Joe Sutter as he stood and watched the aircraft being prepped for its maiden flight. Though he did not see an aircraft. He saw 75,000 drawings, 4.5 million parts, 136 miles of electrical wiring, 5 landing gear legs, 4 hydraulic systems, and 10 million hours of hard graft by his incredible team.

Not an aircraft, in Joe's eyes, but a piece of art, one that so many had worked so hard to perfect. And everything had been leading to this moment. In less than an hour the 'Three W's', as Sutter referred to them – Jack Waddell, fellow test pilot Brien Wygle and flight engineer Jess Wallick – would ascend the steps and take flight.

Sutter watched them climb aboard then positioned himself to get a good view of the take-off. The aircraft taxied, not unlike a lumbering whale, slowly and precisely to the end of the runway. It then taxied into position on the runway and held there for what seemed to be an age, before the engines spooled up and, finally, it was moving.

The Jumbo's size made it appear almost not to be accelerating, but then, when it seemed that it was travelling too slowly to do so, the nose came up, and the 747 was airborne.

Sutter stood there with a lump in his throat. He had done it.

But the day and its drama were far from over.

Sutter returned to the flight telemetry test room just in time to hear Wygle radio, 'The airplane's flying beautifully!' as they tested some of the low-speed-handling characteristics. This was cut short, however, when a minor structural failure occurred in one of the flaps.

For months, aviation experts across the globe had been peddling that the 747 was too big for any airline pilot to safely land, and now there they were, on the first attempt, trying to do that, with a flap problem, and with all the world watching.

Sutter crossed his fingers as he watched the aircraft line up on the runway for its final approach, but he needn't have bothered. Just some seventy-five minutes after he had departed the runway, Waddell kissed the tarmac with the 747's main gear and made it look effortless as they rolled out and stopped.

The 747 era had properly begun.

The punishing path to Federal Aviation Administration (FAA) certification was, however, just beginning. The fleet of test aircraft grew to five, the minimum number they felt necessary to cover the many different aspects of flight testing, from avionics to hot and cold, short field landing, stalls, flutter testing, engine and service checks, and system checks, to name just a fraction. There were also two further airframes which would be tested to destruction. To test absolute limits, in a world without computers, this was a necessary part of the process.

While all this went on, Boeing was selling aggressively; without a healthy number of orders in the book, their financial situation would be even more perilous. So while back at Everett the rest of the ships underwent all that rigorous testing, ship four, with Joe Sutter on board, attended the 1969 Paris Airshow so folk could drool over her undeniable magnificence.

And drool they did. And in a particularly sweet moment, particularly for Joe, they were parked beside Concorde – and, for all its speed, it looked dwarfed into insignificance. Everyone agreed: the 747 had stolen the airshow.

By late autumn that year the Queen of the Skies had proved her much-touted credentials. And, having exceeded even the best predictions from Boeing's engineers and sailed through all the developmental testing, flight test certification was complete in ten months. This remains a record for any commercial aircraft and is a huge testament to the original design.

It wasn't without last-minute jitters though. On 13 December, around two weeks before that precious certification was granted, Joe happened to find himself with time to kill at Boeing Field, as instrument problems had delayed the test he had been planning to run.

'Why don't you fly over to Renton on number 3 ship?' one of his team suggested. 'Observe a short field landing for yourself?'

This wasn't a test flight; number 3 ship had already finished with its testing. It was being flown to Renton to have its testing equipment removed and its airline interior installed, before delivery to a customer.

So why not tag along?

Joe decided he would. But little did he know that he was about to have a grandstand seat for the first ever 747 crash.

Compared to Paine Field's 9,000-feet runway, and Boeing Field's 10,000-feet one, Renton's runway, at only a little over 5,000 feet, was indeed short. Though not short enough to present problems for the 747. But when Joe came upon Ralph Cokely, the test pilot who'd be flying ship 3 over, it was to find him expressing concerns about its ability to land there.

Joe tried to set Cokely's mind at rest, calling for, and showing him, the performance charts and confirming what everyone in the team already knew – that the Jumbo would have absolutely no trouble landing there. Indeed, Joe highlighted that it could do so with a significant margin. Heck, he wouldn't be riding in the jump seat if he didn't think so, would he?

Cokely, however, still seemed unconvinced. Maybe he was superstitious about it being the 13th, or just wasn't happy to be working on a Saturday. Either way, they started up and taxied out, launching into the clear, crisp, blue afternoon sky over Seattle. Cokely then made a wide turn around Lake Washington and lined up for his approach into Renton.

Sitting behind Cokely, Joe could see that he was stressed; his knuckles were white on the controls. And as they descended Joe could see that he was approaching too short. 'By god,' he thought. 'We are not going to make it!'

They didn't. Seconds later, their right landing gear caught the lip of the concrete sea wall, shearing it clean off. The aircraft dipped immediately to the right, scraping the engines along the runway, and the grim sound of metal screaming against tarmac was, for several long seconds, all anyone could hear. Cokely fought to keep them straight, using reverse thrust and whatever directional control he had, and, moments later, the aircraft came to an abrupt stop – with some three quarters of unused runway still ahead of them.

It then dawned on them that they'd better exit the aircraft, and quickly, so they used the flight-deck escape rope – perhaps the only people who ever have? I suspect that might be true – and once on terra firma, glumly inspected the damage, while several rescue vehicles thundered towards them.

As it transpired, there was no fire, and, with the exception of the missing gear, the aircraft was only superficially damaged. Sutter was concerned that this accident would delay the FAA certification but, in the end, it was so clearly a case of pilot error that it was quickly discounted.

Certification happened as planned on 30 December.

Sutter must surely have allowed himself another moment of pride. His doggedness to make the 747 as robust as possible – designing the gear to shear off and not puncture the fuel tanks, for example – was all done in the pursuit of safety and survivability. But I'm betting he never in a million years imagined that he'd be the first person to be saved by those very features.

The aircraft was repaired and refitted at Renton and went on to be delivered to Pan Am, as N732PA Clipper Ocean Telegraph. As for poor Cokely, possibly knowing it was an error that he wouldn't live down, he left Boeing not long after the incident. He joined Lockheed, test-flying most of the L-1011 Tristar programme.

I think Cokely can be forgiven his trepidation. As Joe Sutter put it himself shortly afterwards, he was a good pilot who'd had a terrible day.

Believe me, I know how he must have felt.

5. The Jumbos Are Coming

Juan Trippe, born in 1899, was the type of character we rarely see in modern airline businesses. Something of an Elon Musk of his day, Trippe's charisma, his willingness to engage and his boldness in business – he simply was not deterred by the prospect of failure – are traits rarely seen by aviation CEOs in these risk-averse days. A graduate of Yale University, he was confident and suave, and by the time he and Boeing signed their historic 747 contract he already had the type of celebrity status that airline executives of today tend to shy away from, since shareholders don't like risk-takers or CEOs becoming the 'brand'. They want to make money – not fuel individuals' egos.

Though probably most famous for founding Pan Am, Trippe was, in fact, a serial entrepreneur. He's rightly credited with stirring up that insatiable public thirst for mass travel (and not just air travel, either; he also created the luxury hotel brand InterContinental Hotels Group), but Pan Am was not his first foray into the aviation sector. After a spell on Wall Street, which apparently bored him, in 1922 he set up an air taxi service for the wealthy called Long Island Airways. Shortly after that he branched out with Colonial Airways, a foray into the world of air freight. It's probably worth remembering how pioneering this was; this was a mere decade into the world of commercial air travel. These businesses gave Trippe the experience he needed to create Aviation Corporation of the Americas in 1927. This business, which saw him expand into the Caribbean and South

American markets, would eventually become Pan American Airways, but its roots, in the form of the flying boats they used initially, remained. All Pan Am's aircraft included the word 'clipper' in their names – a nod to the clipper ships of the mid-nineteenth century.

It was a tradition that the company would continue into the jet age, the first 747 delivered by Boeing being named *Clipper Victor*. Given Pan Am's undisputed place at the top of the US aviation tree, the second part of the nomenclature also seems appropriate. By this time, the airline epitomized everything people expected from the exciting new globe-trotting era, and the iconic logo that adorned the tail fins of its fleet, the famous blue globe, or, as it was colloquially known, the 'blue meatball', dominated the skyline at New York's Idlewild Airport, or JFK airport, as we know it today.

Back in 1966 when the 747 contract was signed Trippe had commented that the 747 would be 'a great weapon for peace, competing with the intercontinental missiles for mankind's destiny'. And where the Pan Am titan had led, many other airlines had followed, giving Boeing, still mired in the increasingly frustrating supersonic race, good reason to feel positive about the future. But for all the wealth these behemoths were sure to deliver down the line, by the time the first aircraft were in the latter stages of production, the Boeing Company was struggling with cash flow. There would be no globe-trotting on the horizon – either for the public or the manufacturer – if the planes weren't delivered, and quickly.

Just when jets were beginning to emerge from the factory, however, Pratt and Whitney defaulted on its contracted delivery schedule for the JT9D engines. The timing could not have been worse. With the 747 production line going at full tilt, and no room at the proverbial inn, they were having to pull finished aircraft out of the building with 5,000-pound concrete blocks hanging from the wings, just to stop them tipping back on their tails. Were it not such a crisis, it would have been almost comedic; all these 'finished' aircraft, looking so fine with their shiny new livery, yet lacking the very thing that is central to an aircraft's USP. Until the engines turned up, they were flying precisely nowhere.

It would be a month before the engines finally began arriving and Joe Sutter could at last see his endeavours bearing fruit, as the finished jets began flying away to earn their keep with their new owners.

With aircraft now delivered and Boeing's financial pressures abating, Pan Am wasted no time in launching its flagship 747 service from New York's JFK Airport to London Heathrow, perhaps the most iconic of the transatlantic routes. But Joe Sutter wasn't the only one who was suffering engine troubles. The inaugural flight had been scheduled for 21 January but, at the eleventh hour, a mechanical issue left Pan Am with no choice but to hastily rearrange things, bring in another aircraft and reschedule the maiden flight for the following day.

Though this might not appear to be ideal in terms of optics, these kinds of hiccups weren't uncommon back in those days, though a little sleight of hand was still deployed. Though *Clipper Young America*, the intended plane, was substituted with the *Clipper Victor*, the latter aircraft had a tactical, if temporary, change of name.

Fortunately, with none of the passengers seeming too bothered about the delay, all went to plan on 22 January, and *Clipper Young America* (well, at least as far as most people knew) touched down in London as scheduled. It was met with a rapturous reception. British Pathé News, reporting on the arrival at Heathrow Airport, led its film by announcing 'The Jumbos are coming!', and even the crisp British tones of the narrator couldn't disguise the feverish excitement which greeted it. 'It seemed as if the QEII had taken to the skies!' observed one of the lucky journalists present.

For Pathé, and, it seemed, everyone involved, this was every bit the game-changer Boeing had promised and marked 'a revolution in the future of civil aviation'.

With that revolution now endorsed and very much underway, you might be forgiven for thinking Joe Sutter could at least pause to draw breath – certainly to take a little time to rest on his laurels. But as anyone who works in aircraft engineering already knows, this was far from the case. Right away, once the aircraft was in service and the airlines were sending feedback, there were engineering tweaks and improvements to be made.

But if the work was ongoing, and it would be for years, there was at least one special moment when Joe had no choice but to reflect on the contribution he had made. Not long after the first of the aircraft had been delivered, Joe and Jack Waddell were invited to the Pan Am Building to discuss the design changes that would potentially be made and incorporated in those aircraft yet to be delivered.

During the lunch Joe and Jack were standing eating their sandwiches when another attendee wandered over.

'You know,' he said to Joe, 'this is one of the great ones.'

The attendee in question was no less than Charles 'Slim' Lindbergh, one of Joe's childhood heroes. Were that not enough, he then went on to tell Joe that he considered the emergence of the 747 to be one of the most significant milestones in the history of flight.

As Lindbergh moved away, Joe found himself lost for words. Lindbergh, the first aviator to fly solo across the Atlantic, was indisputably one of the world's greatest aviation pioneers. To hear such a positive affirmation from someone of that stature would be something Joe would treasure for the rest of his life.

Meanwhile, Pan Am was embarking on a massive recruitment drive. As well as hiring and training crews, the airline needed to find lots of stewardesses. Each 747 would have a complement of fourteen, who would be highly trained in all aspects of safety but with a clear focus on beauty and intellect – a drive for excellence in service in which Pan Am was clearly leading the way.

Nobody knows this better than Dr Sheila Nutt, who back in 1970 joined Pan Am as one of the first African American stewardesses. Competition to get the gig was fierce; it was widely known at the time that it was harder to get a stewardess job at Pan Am than it was to get into Harvard – where, coincidentally, Sheila worked after leaving Pan Am, up until her retirement aged seventy-six, in 2020.

For Sheila, what Pan Am offered was opportunity. The airline company incentivized education, with a financial benefit and flexible schedules. Many of Sheila's cohort studied while they worked, attended Columbia, Pace, Harvard and went on to have successful careers as diplomatic ambassadors and lawyers. Sheila herself earned a doctorate in education from Boston University, her dissertation being on the effect of prolonged stress on flight attendants. And, after BU, she went on to attended Harvard and earned a master's degree from the Divinity School. As far as Sheila is concerned, Pan Am was a 'launch pad for greatness'.

Growing up in Philadelphia on a pretty tree-lined suburban street, Sheila came from a loving and supportive family and had plenty of ambition. She took to the arts, ballet especially, and went on to model – she was first runner-up in the Miss Philadelphia pageant, an official contest of the

Miss America franchise. It was a fellow contestant who told her about Pan Am, and when Sheila saw an ad in the newspaper for interviews at a hotel in downtown Philadelphia she quickly applied. Coming from the suburbs, she was keen to start broadening her horizons and the idea of travelling the world as an airline stewardess was compelling.

Sheila was also no stranger to the world of aviation, or, indeed, the circles in which, as a Pan Am stewardess, she might find herself. Her grandfather attended Harvard Law School in 1916 – a major feat for an African American at the time – and her uncle Ambrose was a notable aerospace engineer, one of the youngest students to matriculate into the School of Engineering at the University of Michigan, to study aeronautical engineering. He went on to work as the Head of Special Projects at the Wright Aircraft Laboratory, where he was instrumental in designing ejector seats for jet planes which went on to become standard in fighter jets.

Sheila also spoke fluent Spanish, which would enhance her application, though to become a stewardess she would need to get herself a passport. (At the time, many Americans did not have a passport.)

She applied to become a Pan Am stewardess in late 1969 and after a very thorough interview, which included testing her second language, she was offered the job via a Western Union telegram.

She felt as if she had won the lottery. Though it was a lottery win with conditions attached as, before being allowed to don that iconic even then powder-blue uniform, she had to earn the right by going through a rigorous training course.

While Pan Am already had well-established training processes, nothing on the scale of the Jumbo had ever been seen before, so the new recruits' training programme was 747-specific. The successful candidates were grouped into classes of around twenty-five and, to give you an idea of what a very different time this was, several in Sheila's had never interacted with a black girl in person before.

The training programme included dining and how to cook a steak to perfection – they served food on china, at that time, with silverware. The recruits also learned fine-dining staples, such as how to prepare a baked Alaska dessert and set it aflame beside a passenger before serving – which might sometimes come with a side order of turbulence.

But, for all the service aspects, the priority was always safety. How to exit the aircraft, and how to do so in ninety seconds. At their Miami training school, they even went to a nearby pool to practise saving passengers under water.

Pan Am demanded that its stewardesses maintain the very highest standards, and not just in terms of the non-negotiable physical attributes, such as being within strict height and weight parameters, and not needing to wear glasses, and directives about grooming and hairstyles and so on that many would probably blanch at today. The company was equally prescriptive, if not more so, about the kind of personal qualities it wanted to embody in its cabin crew. As well as a passion for both people and travel, Pan Am wanted grace, dignity, professionalism and elegance; girls (as if anyone would say *that* now . . . and rightly so) who were educated, knowledgeable, open-minded and warm, and always finely attuned to their passengers' needs. Perhaps above all, Pan Am wanted its stewardesses to show genuine interest in those customers and have empathy; a quality Pan Am stewardesses were rightly famous for and central to Juan Trippe's vision of bringing air travel to the masses.

To fly Pan Am was to be enveloped not just in physical luxury, it was about being made to feel special, to a degree rarely seen in mass transportation before, and this was as true back in coach as in first class. Where air travel had previously been the preserve of the white and privileged, it would quickly become not just *for* the masses, but *of* the masses. It would be properly democratized. They would not only find out how the 'other half' lived, but live it alongside them (well, for most people, behind them) and experience service the like of which many had never encountered before.

Trippe's ethos did not just extend to the passengers, however. Though Sheila never met him personally, she held, and still holds him, in the highest regard, and credits him with no less than changing her life, opening up the world to her and giving her opportunities that, at the time, many African Americans could never dream of, particularly women.

Indeed, such was Trippe's influence and presence that she didn't need to meet him. Trippe was obviously regarded as an innovator, but his forward thinking didn't end with championing new aircraft. He was also a proponent of the then newly emerging business style of 'servant leadership', the guiding principles of which rippled down through the entire company, empowering his employees to do their best, fostering a culture of loyalty and inspiring staff to feel valued, that it was an honour to serve, to feel pride and contentment in their work.

Although, with the Civil Rights Act of 1964 mandating diversity in corporations, there was already regulatory pressure on businesses, in terms of employment practices Trippe was still ahead of his time, making it a point of principle, and also pride, to employ cabin and flight-deck crews with roots in every single one of the countries the airline served. Some of the travelling public, however, were slightly slower to catch up, so, in the early days – and Sheila is clear it was her fellow Americans who were the worst culprits in this regard – she did experience a little racism. However, she never paid it much attention. And not only because she'd been brought up in a family where she was constantly reminded that she was as good as anyone, it was also because she was part of the Pan Am family too, a family she knew would always call it out and do right by her.

'We were,' Sheila explains, 'de facto ambassadors of the American ethos. We represented America to the world. We were also pop culture figures and given special treatment outside of work once we said we worked for Pan Am, the world's most experienced airline. We were considered glamorous, and glamour transcended race.'

On so many levels, Pan Am had nailed it. And the world, as it and Boeing had promised, was really now beginning to shrink. The route between New York's JFK Airport and London Heathrow was not chosen by random by Trippe to launch his Jumbo service, however. This city pairing was quickly becoming the most popular for business and, with a promised revolution in personal travel fuelled by easy-to-access credit, the route soon became worth hundreds of millions of dollars.

By the time I made my first visit to JFK as a 747-400 pilot in 2008, my employer alone had eight 747s travelling between the cities almost *every single day*. As Trippe had predicted, it had become a billion-dollar route.

6. Carrying the World

'The airplane became the first World Wide Web, bringing people, languages, ideas, and values together.'
— Bill Gates

You're right, of course. Bill Gates is referring to the Boeing 747. But if you'll forgive a bit of backtracking, I should first make it clear that this historic aviation milestone only happened after the protracted, and very costly, false dawn you may recall me alluding to a couple of chapters ago.

Back in September 1966, while Joe Sutter was busy making progress on his subsonic project, proposals for the SST aircraft everyone *thought* was going to change the world were ready to be submitted to the US government for consideration. Both Lockheed's L-2000 and Boeing's 2707 (the only two designs left in the US race) were then subject to a tortuous review by various experts.

Their findings were extensive and, thankfully for Boeing, conclusive. Though the Lockheed L-2000 would be both easier to produce and less risky as a holistic proposal, Boeing's speed performance was superior and its noise footprint much smaller, so on New Year's Day 1967 it was announced that, paired with General Electric's GE4/J5 engines, it would be Boeing who would have the privilege of building the US's first supersonic transport aircraft.

Boeing now had a lot of ground to make up. By this time, with their construction having begun as long ago as February 1965, six prototypes of the UK/French Concordes were nearing completion. Plus, the Russians, though a little behind their Western European competitors, were also getting close to their first test flight.

Boeing, on the other hand, were experiencing design challenges. The project's aerodynamicists had decided that canards were needed to add controllability, which added weight, while the engineering team faced insurmountable problems with the complexity and weight of the swing-wing design, reducing range to well below the specification. It was October 1968 now, and with a huge rethink and redesign required, Boeing's SST was headed nowhere apart from back to the drawing board.

The news didn't improve. Two months later the supersonic transporter era had properly begun, with the Soviets leading the charge and flying their SST, the Tupolev 144, from Zhukovsky Airport, and some three months after that, in March 1969, Concorde lifted away from Toulouse.

Meanwhile, having dispiritedly returned to its own SST drawing board, Boeing had adopted the delta fixed wing that featured in both Concorde and the Tupolev, and had gone for a smaller 234-seat aircraft design that was to be designated the Boeing 2707-300.

The design was approved in September and work on two prototypes, plus full-sized mock-up, was finally – *finally* – to begin in earnest.

Glad to have arrived at the party, even if a little late, industry met the news with much excitement. Airlines flooded to Boeing to buy options for the larger SST, with sixteen of them accounting for 122 SST orders – almost three times as many for Concorde. However, during all this excitement in

Seattle, in June 1969, the Tu-144 had flown supersonic, being the first aircraft to pass this key milestone, with Concorde following four months later.

When in the spring of 1970 the TU-144 was the first to exceed Mach 2, twice the speed of sound, interest in the SST was already waning in the US. It was obviously too little too late. The supersonic ship had sailed.

Having sunk so many dollars into what had been anticipated to be the next aviation breakthrough, the US government responded suitably robustly, creating and funding a promotional campaign extolling the benefits of supersonic travel over subsonic. But while the airlines still seemed equally committed to the whole supersonic project, the public mood continued to turn against it. There were many reasons for this. As well as the prevailing economic climate becoming gloomy, there was also the ongoing and increasingly controversial war in Vietnam, plus the Apollo project was competing for ever more of the American people's attention; the moon, it seemed, just felt a lot sexier.

The final nail in the coffin came from the now highly driven and very vocal environmentalist lobby, which had rallied both public and political support over the negative impact that the use of SSTs overland in the US would have. This ranged from the noise footprint of supersonic speed and its detrimental human impact to the increase in stratospheric water content which would potentially 'envelop the earth in a deathly cloak'.

So, amazing as it is to contemplate in the twenty-first century, the Boeing 747 became the most acceptable method of air travel for the environmentally conscious.

In short, it slammed the lid on that SST coffin, and by the time a funding review came to the Senate in March 1971 the coffin was almost sealed. The Tu-144 had beaten everyone.

It had been first to fly, first to go supersonic, and first to exceed Mach 2. The Concorde, too, was well established in its flight-test programme and was exceeding the expectations of the UK/French consortium. Boeing, meanwhile, was yet to finish its prototypes and all it had to show for the nation's efforts to enter the SST family was the single full-size mock-up – only a part of which, as we've seen, still exists today.

By this time, many believed the SST race to be already lost. Despite significant concern that the aftermath of the Vietnam War, the scaling back of the previously feted Apollo missions and the loss of the SST would be too much of a burden for an already ailing industry, the Senate voted to reject any further funding.

It was generally agreed that this would probably spell the end of it, but it didn't. At least, not quite. A group labelled the 'National Committee for an American SST' urged the public to support the threatened development by sending in a dollar to the project and, with layoffs on the horizon, the unions supported it too. But despite gaining almost a million dollars, it was never going to be enough and, when the House of Representatives voted to stop the funding in May 1971, that truly was the end of the Boeing SST dream.

It was also, many agreed by now, likely to be the end of Boeing. The company that William E. Boeing had set up in 1916 was by now one of the USA's most iconic – not to mention most innovative and profitable. For it to find itself on its knees seemed unthinkable. After all, this was the company that had built the legendary Flying Fortress, mass-produced bombers for the Second World War, invented the large swept-wing jet, with the B-47 Stratojet designed the mighty B-52 Stratofortress, introduced the first successful commercial jet, the 707, and even helped to land astronauts on the moon. Surely it could find a way to survive?

But the loss of the SST contract, alongside other defence projects, plus a general downturn in the civilian aviation market, saw Boeing having to lay off more than 60,000 employees, which had a devastating wider impact on the business and the local economy as many left the Pacific Northwest with their families to seek employment elsewhere. So there was truth behind the moniker then affixed to the SST: 'the airplane that almost ate Seattle'.

To rub salt in an already gaping wound, someone with a warped sense of humour (was it Lockheed? The unions? We may never know) rented a billboard, emblazoned it with 'Would the last one out of Seattle turn the lights off?', and strategically placed it on a major highway near Sea Tac Airport, where the travelling public would be able to see it every day.

They had a point, too, because the SST really did almost eat Seattle. All Boeing had left was its stalwart 737 (still the most successful airliner ever, to be fair) and the aircraft that had emerged triumphant from that rain-making factory – the new kid in town, that 'stopgap' 747. Just as well, then, that its shoulders were so broad.

Enough of the gloom, though. Back to Bill Gates and that quote. He was obviously referring to the invention of the aircraft as a vehicle, but as I am sure you are already beginning to work out, no other aircraft has made such an impact on expanding the worldwide *human* web than the Boeing 747. As with pilots' seniority, it's a numbers game. In both capacity and range the Queen of the Skies had no equal, something that would not only see Boeing over the biggest financial crisis it had ever suffered, but also, with the supersonic dream dead and buried, assure the company's dominance for many decades.

Dr Sheila Nutt has shared her first-hand experience of how it expanded the horizons of so many passengers who, due to the prohibitive cost, had previously been excluded from much international air travel. And that democratization of air as a means of transport was indeed driving the cultural revolution Pathé News had so breathlessly promised. Thanks to the 747, that ancient dream of flight was fast becoming a reality for much of humanity. For the first time in human history, the 747 made it possible for almost anyone on earth to travel anywhere; it was beginning to shrink the world.

If you'll bear with me, I think now is a good time to talk some numbers, to give you an appreciation of the scale of the Jumbo Jet's impact across the globe.

Since the first one was delivered to Pan Am back in January 1970, history records that Boeing's 747 fleet has logged 118 million flight hours and carried some 7.5 billion passengers, almost the equivalent of every human on the planet.

Of the 1,574 aircraft the company has manufactured, 1,227 were passenger variants, with only 347 being the dedicated freighter version at the time of manufacture. Though it must also be remembered that the passenger aircraft didn't just carry luggage. It had room to carry freight, and rather a lot of it, in its enormous holds.

Talking about human capacity in particular, Pan Am's first aircraft, a 747-100, carried 335 customers in a two-class configuration. In 2024, the Lufthansa 747-8 intercontinental (747-8I), in a three-class configuration, carries 365.

Not much has changed, then, in terms of passenger

capacity, but Boeing maintains that the Jumbo *could* be configured with up to a whopping 605 seats. With the exception of one record-breaking event, which we'll be returning to later in the book, no airline has dared squeeze more than that in. Japan Airlines (JAL), however, did have several 747s configured for domestic flying, which carried an almost as unbelievable 568 souls.

Mike Lombardi, the Boeing Company historian, shared with me another mind-blowing fact. 'The interior space on a 747-8I is something like 31,000 cubic feet. The *air alone* in that space would weigh 2,500 pounds.' The weight, for example, of a small car. Can you get your head around that? I'm not sure I can.

The freighter versions of the same aircraft can also carry some 292,400 pounds (132.6 tons) of cargo. Or, as Mike describes it, 'about 19 million ping-pong balls'.

I'm not sure a 747 has ever needed to carry 19 million ping-pong balls anywhere, but it certainly concentrates the mind. The main point, however, is that the 747's capacity was far greater than any competitor's, hence its capacity to really change lives.

Its other key strength is its range. When the first Jumbo took off in 1970 it could span 5,320 miles without refuelling – a 23 per cent increase on the Boeing 707 that it replaced. This later increased – and by rather a lot. In August 1989 a Qantas Airlines 747 travelled non-stop from Sydney to London, a flight that took some twenty hours and covered a record-breaking 11,185 miles. It was a glimpse into the future of truly long-haul air travel.

A lot of numbers to digest, I know, but they are not even the most important. As most know, there are two key numbers that tend to drive every business: costs and revenue.

When Pan Am started its Jumbo journey back in 1966, Juan Trippe had recognized the enormous potential the 747 could deliver. Unlike today, where airlines compete largely by tweaking the ticket price/operating cost relationship, back in the 1970s the price of an airline ticket was regulated by the government, so generating profit was all about selling more of them.

This was where the 747 really came into its own. At an operating cost that was comparable to that of the aircraft that dominated the skies at that time, the Boeing 707, the 747 carried two and half times its capacity, which is pretty extraordinary, when you think about it. Profit-generating manna from heaven.

But that only applied if you could fill all those seats, and doing so, via marketing, was where Pan Am excelled. The company launched an advertising campaign that was bold, and truly global; in ninety different countries, and thirty different languages, people were encouraged to share the airline's thrilling vision for its potential new passengers. 'The world is a stage,' went the slogan. 'And you put on the show!'

It was not about price. Its key message was luxury. Flying, they stressed, was all about 360-degree glamour, and for the first time that luxury and that globe-trotting lifestyle were within the reach of ordinary people. And it worked. In 1970, the year the 747 was launched, Pan Am flew 11 million passengers to eighty-six countries across the globe.

They were soon to be helped by a change in the law, too, when the Airline Deregulation Act in 1978 removed governmental control on things such as air fares and the resulting free market led to a decrease in ticket costs. And though the income per ticket dropped, it was more than compensated for by the even greater increase in passengers. And who was best placed to serve those passengers? Airlines who had Jumbos.

Jumbo Jets had delivered exactly what they'd promised: that ancient dream of flight was now a reality for all of humanity. The 747 had shrunk the world.

More than any other aircraft, the 747 could *carry* the world.

7. Delivering the World

The 747 quickly grew in popularity as the first choice of aircraft for the aspirational traveller, bestowing impressive profits on all the airlines that had bought them. But those profits weren't just generated from humans.

As well as some 335 revenue-raising seats, the passenger-variant 747s also had enormous holds, sufficient not only for passengers' luggage but also freight, and plenty of it, too.

Delivering freight was of course another whole revenue strand, but it happened largely unobserved by the passengers, who were probably entirely unaware that the aircraft that was taking them to, say, Boston, might also be delivering six or seven tons of langoustines on ice, direct from Scotland. (Quick aside – incredibly, this is cheaper than sourcing them locally.)

The enormous capacity of the 747 made it the obvious choice if you needed to take a great deal of stuff to a faraway place and needed to get it there fast. This is as true today as it ever was, and the skies are still criss-crossed by Jumbo Jets doing just that, while the world goes about its business, largely oblivious.

As with passengers, the size of Jumbos really matters. And something many people won't have realized – or, perhaps, even thought about – is that priority freight makes more money than passengers, due to the nature of our modern just-in-time economy, which sees businesses engaged in a constant, carefully choreographed, commercially driven dance, in order to keep production chains moving.

But the 747 didn't just help oil the wheels of business, it played a key part in both creating them and growing them, in economies right around the world.

Mike Lombardi, Boeing's historian, sums up the role the 747 played perfectly. 'The great story about the 747 is that this airplane shrank the world. Bringing goods from one part of the world to the other, increasing the livelihood of countries around the globe. Farmers in East Africa, who are growing flowers to be sent to Europe for Mother's Day – they have a livelihood *because* of this airplane. In South America, fruit and vegetables are sent to North America so that, in the dead of winter, you can go to the market and pick up fresh fruit. All of this because of this magnificent airplane.'

Joe Sutter's vision, as we know, had always been of an aircraft that excelled in both passenger and freight roles. And his insistence on a design that made loading freight so simple meant that as soon as the first dedicated cargo aircraft, the 747-200 Freighter, rolled off the production line at Everett it was, in Joe's own words, already 'light years ahead of the competition'.

There was also great interest in the 747-200 Combi, which was half passenger jet and half freighter on the main deck – a variant helped into being via geopolitical forces. It was ordered by a single airline – Sabena, Belgium's flag-carrier, which was doing well filling its holds with freight but rather less well when it came to attracting sufficient transatlantic passengers to make it profitable.

That they had their two 747s in the first place was, in fact, something of a mistake. Until the 1960s, when it had won independence from Belgium, Congo was a country with which Belgium had done a brisk trade, in both freight and in tourism. This had naturally dropped off once the colony had become independent, but the Jumbos had been ordered before the inevitable marked drop in business became fully apparent.

Boeing stepped up and thought about what they could do to make its client's costly purchases more profitable. The solution was to redesign the vast passenger cabin to make the rear part suitable for freight – changing the interior, strengthening the freight section floor and installing a huge cargo door aft of the wing. After the modifications were made, back at Everett, the two aircraft were then returned. The 747 Combi was born.

With the Combi-200M so successful, particularly among airlines in countries that would struggle to regularly fill the passenger cabin, Boeing ended up making seventy-eight of them. KLM and Iran Air became the largest operators of these hybrids, but dedicated freighters soon became the go-to for those airlines whose job was mostly to deliver cargo. And it's easy to see why it made such an impact. According to Captain Kelly Lepley, with the global giant UPS, 'as a cargo plane, the 747 has excelled. It has a huge fuselage, and the cockpit sits above it, so you can load directly into the fuselage itself. It's easy to manoeuvre, and it can carry prodigious amounts of weight. They can also,' she adds, 'actually take all the cargo out and bring the new cargo on in less than two hours.'

While freight companies spend a lot of their time ferrying fresh produce and other staples around the world, they can and do transport pretty much anything you can think of. Anyone for a pair of Beluga whales? Back in 2019 a pair of 12-year-old female Belugas – Little Grey and Little White – took a trip aboard a 747 to complete the penultimate leg of their journey from an aquarium in Shanghai to their new home at a sanctuary in Iceland. Herring, I'm told, was provided as an in-flight snack . . .

*

If we were to be shown the logos of the world's largest and most famous passenger airlines, even the non-aviation fanatics among us would recognize those of American Airlines, Delta, even perhaps some of the smaller ones such as JAL. However, how many of us could hand on heart say we could name the largest of the dedicated air-freight operators? I'll wager very few. You would maybe guess FedEx and UPS, but who else would you be able to identify? Be honest. Had you even heard of Atlas Air Worldwide? No? Well, you might be surprised to know that it currently ranks second, and is consistently in the top three.

Despite its low profile, Atlas Air has played a huge part in the history of the Boeing 747, with businessman Michael Chowdry launching the cargo airline in Golden, Colorado, in 1992, with one single 747-200 converted freighter aircraft. Within a year the success of the operation meant they had added another 747, and within two they had grown to a fleet of six. This venture was, if you'll excuse the pun, really flying.

By the end of 1996 the operation had fifteen 747s, all working for major airlines in what is called an ACMI (Aircraft, Crew, Maintenance and Insurance) operation. (ACMI essentially means that Atlas Air provides aircraft and crews for a third party, but the branding is that of the buyer.) And by the end of the millennium, it had grown its fleet to thirty-one Jumbos, gaining that spot right behind FedEx and UPS.

Rick Ruiz, who's been a professional pilot for twenty years, has now worked for Atlas Air for a decade. A typical day for him starts at around 4 a.m. in Miami, the air humid and laced with the smell of jet fuel. Like pretty much every 747 pilot I have ever spoken to (and I've spoken to a lot) Rick still gets butterflies every time he sees the aircraft standing on the apron, and never fails to acknowledge both the scale of it and the truly awesome responsibility of being entrusted with flying it. He's a captain and he takes his role very seriously.

Once on board, and with his bags stowed, Rick climbs the stairs to the hump and settles down in the left-hand seat. It's at that point that size becomes completely academic, forgotten. Cocooned in front of controls that are like bodily extensions, flying the Jumbo is, he explains, 'like putting on a well-worn pair of blue jeans'.

Rick is very much at the sharp end of delivering the world, as much of what he carries is perishable, from flowers, fish and asparagus to temperature-controlled pharmaceuticals, all frequently loaded and unloaded in very hot conditions. He's also carried livestock, including flamingos. And when a zoo in Zaire was closing down a few years back he delivered their elephants to a zoo in Mexico.

Atlas Air CEO Michael Steen is similarly proud of the company's record when it comes to getting flowers where they are needed. 'We take a lot of pride,' he tells me, 'in being a part of people's lives. But we're never seen, we're never visible. But take when we're celebrating Valentine's, or Mother's Day. A significant proportion of the flowers sent are flown by us. In fact, half of all the flowers flown around the world today,' he adds, 'are flown by Atlas Air.'

Both Rick and Michael are clear about the 747's unique strength as a freighter, citing its unique nose-loading capability as a game-changer, allowing complicated freight to be safely loaded and unloaded. And they do see a lot of complicated freight. They have been the proud carriers of Taylor Swift's stage – everything that's needed to put on a massive arena show. Atlas Air is also responsible for many of the Formula 1 flights around the world, carrying all the cars, and their associated parts and equipment, plus the media centre and all the broadcasting telemetry, which, in all, takes eight 747 equivalents, for every race.

Over the years, Atlas Air has expanded its operation to include specialist passenger flights too, including those for sports teams and the military. It also has its own flight and cabin-crew training facility in Miami, and they have the honour of training all the pilots who fly the 747s with the callsign Air Force One, the two US presidential aircraft.

But why the emphasis on Atlas Air, I hear you ask? Well, it's because, in 2021 the company made the historic decision to order four brand-new 747-8F aircraft. And, after fifty-four years of continuous production, these will be the last off the production line at Everett. Altas is therefore carrying the last baton in the 747 relay.

This makes Atlas, with a global Jumbo fleet of 60, out of its 121 aircraft, the largest current operator of the Boeing 747 family, and, as Michael Steen observes, 'Without Joe Sutter's innovation, and his engineering prowess, where would we be as a company?' As it stands, with the aircraft still the biggest and best freighter the aviation industry has to offer, it will be a mainstay of its company well into the coming decades.

No chapter on the way the 747 has delivered the world would be complete without mentioning the special role it played during the 2020/21 global pandemic. Prior to Covid-19, many of us rarely gave thought to the wider implications for the developing world once they could get their fresh produce on to our plates. We would just see stuff we wanted in the shops and be happy. But the Covid-19 pandemic brought the entire world into everyone's living room, making us sit up and take notice of just how connected we are; how everyone around the world, at that time, was in the same situation.

And 747s, still circling the planet while those on the ground were holed up, played a vital part in maintaining those connections. I have a little personal experience of this watershed time myself – although not in a Jumbo. At this time I was flying an Airbus, carrying oxygen and ventilators to Bengaluru in India. It was a round-the-clock operation to get help where it was so desperately needed.

Some avgeeks, like me, will be aware of Sam Chui, a fellow devotee of the Queen of the Skies – his first love and favourite aircraft. With some 4.5 million followers on various social media channels, Sam's turned his passion for flying into a successful career as an aviation influencer. It's also given him a great insight into the complex logistics of carrying out a 747 humanitarian aid mission. In the summer of 2021 he joined a National Airlines B747 which delivered 80 tons of US aid to Islamabad and Nepal to help them through the aftermath of the pandemic.

The trip took a whopping forty hours in total – dark to light to dark again – with the crews, for whom this is very much all in a day's work, setting up sleeping bags and pillows on the floor of the upper deck in order to get some rest. Though, from Sam's point of view, that was actually a bonus. 'The space was great,' he says. 'Better than most of the current business class cubical seats!'

Though I wouldn't necessarily agree with Sam about sleeping on the hard floor of an aircraft not kitted out for paying passengers – having done that more than once on a Herc – I think it's great that he's able to have these experiences and share them with so many. Without missions like these, an already desperate situation could have been so much worse.

But perhaps one of the most notable jobs 747s helped to carry out during the pandemic was the transportation of many millions of coronavirus vaccines, helping to save lives and curb the spread of this global scourge. For this reason alone, arguably, the 747 is still the queen of the cargo industry, and, for many years yet, likely to remain so.

8. Tragedy on Tenerife

It's often said that the progress made in safety in the airline industry has been written in the blood of those who went before us, and for good reason. I know from personal experience during my time in the RAF that in many cases that is exactly what it has been.

This is obviously why risk needs to be mitigated, as far as possible. And why Joe Sutter, in designing the first 747, built redundancy into systems in every way he could. Now that so many people could be carried in a single aircraft, there was potential for tragedy on an unprecedented scale.

But there is one thing engineers cannot design away completely – the capacity of humans to make mistakes. Which is why, as people working in such complex and potentially life-threatening environments, it's the responsibility of all of us to learn from them.

In aviation, as I've already mentioned, guesswork plays no part in what we do. It's why pilots in all the airlines I have mentioned are continually trained and checked. I'd even go so far to say that ours is among the most tested and regulated professions in the world. Which, given the responsibility, is exactly as it should be.

This doesn't stop when a pilot leaves the simulator. After all, there is no point in managing a non-normal situation well – saving the day by getting the aircraft safely back on to the ground, say – and then failing to evacuate the customers and crew. In an emergency situation, in fact, the *primary* role of the *entire* crew (the italics are there because I very much want to stress that) is to ensure everyone is taken care of until they are out of the aircraft and away from any threats to their safety.

Part of every pilot's continuous training, therefore, involves joining their flight attendant crew colleagues for a portion of their annual retraining in Safety Equipment and Procedures, or SEP.

For the cabin crew, this annual check of proficiency is just like our simulators, in that it involves an element of jeopardy, and anyone who doesn't meet their airline's exacting standards will not be going flying again until they do. The course is a blend of learning and confirmation, the aim being to practise and practise again, until every single aspect of the evacuation and emergency procedures are so familiar they become muscle memory. Cabin crew these days have also been empowered. As a result of prior tragedies where lives might have been saved, they are now trained, and expected, to start an evacuation without command from the captain.

Los Rodeos Airport, Tenerife, 27 March 1977

With over 20,000 hours of flying time under his belt, Captain Victor Grubbs, a highly experienced Pan Am pilot, along with First Officer Robert 'Bob' Bragg and Flight Engineer George Warns, was on the last leg of a pretty lengthy journey. Initially departing from Los Angeles, the aeroplane had stopped over in New York and now, after several further hours of flying, was close to its destination of Las Palmas in Gran Canaria. Throughout the flight his efficient cabin crew – thirteen in all – had been providing for every whim of the 380 passengers.

Clipper Victor, their aircraft for the trip, was already a bit of a legend. It had been, as we've seen, the first 747 ever delivered, and was also the first ever Jumbo to be hijacked, having been forcibly re-routed to Cuba in August 1970. As the final leg of the journey neared completion, everyone was hoping that tonight wasn't going to bring any more firsts. A nice routine flight, a short rest, and then home.

Their nice routine flight, however, was to become anything but.

Just as they were approaching Las Palmas there was a transmission from air traffic control.

'A bomb has exploded in the terminal,' they were informed. 'The airport is closed due to the possibility of another device. All aircraft are to divert to Los Rodeos.'

Los Rodeos, a small airport on the island of Tenerife, was not generally graced by 747s, as parking was tight at the best of times and Jumbos took up a lot of space. Today, however, they were about to be visited by two. As well as *Clipper Victor*, Pan Am flight 1736, there was another Jumbo incoming, also with blue-and-white livery – KLM flight 4805, the *Rhine*.

While the KLM aircraft asked for a routing to the airport, Captain Grubb, looking at the fuel situation, asked for a go-around. It was obviously an ongoing situation, but they had a couple of hours' leeway with the fuel, and the flight crew were agreed that they would rather fly around for a bit than divert to Tenerife.

They did so, to be greeted by a few moments of silence. Then, just as they were about to transmit a second time, back came the response, which was negative: they must divert.

Grubb called cabin crew member Dorothy Kelly up to the flight deck. Though only the junior purser, 35-year-old Dorothy was acting-up on this flight, as her colleague, Senior Purser Françoise Colbert de Beaulieu, felt self-conscious about her French accent when making announcements. It would be tough on the passengers, who were tired, plus many of them were elderly; a proportion had travelled many miles to join a cruise ship on Gran Canaria. But it was what it was, and hopefully the delay wouldn't be too long. Grubb told Dorothy to let them know they'd be on the ground on Tenerife in thirty minutes, then changed course.

The bomb at Las Palmas, which had been planted by Canary Islands separatists, was already creating problems at Los Rodeos. They were struggling to accommodate the extra aircraft and passengers who'd been diverted there, and the arrival of two enormous Jumbos was the last thing they needed. It would be a squeeze to find room for them both.

The regional airfield had just the one runway, with a parallel taxiway and a small parking apron at the terminal. The diversions from Las Palmas meant that the apron was full. So the taxiway was now being used to park aircraft.

After a smooth, unremarkable landing, *Clipper Victor* ended up being parked very close to the KLM flight they had come in behind. While the cabin crew on the Dutch aircraft were already de-planing their passengers, the Pan Am Jumbo was not allowed to let theirs off the aircraft – with several diverted flights having landed and let their passengers off already, the terminal building was full.

Dorothy and the cabin crew therefore set about providing what little food and drink they had left for the passengers, who, in some cases, were tired and becoming irritable about the delay.

Victor and Bob, meanwhile, up on the flight deck, listened to the air traffic control radios. They were hopeful that they might get an update on the situation, but all they could hear was the constant badgering of the ATC controller by the KLM captain Jacob Van Zanten.

Van Zanten, also a highly experienced pilot, was something of a celebrity with his airline. He'd flown the first KLM Jumbo from the factory back to Amsterdam, and his smiling image graced many of the airline's glossy adverts. He was also clearly tetchy, and very anxious to get airborne – if they didn't depart soon his crew would run out of flying hours.

He was piling on the pressure, but ATC was powerless to help. Who knew when Las Palmas would reopen? Van Zanten, along with First Officer Klaas Meurs and Willem Schreuder, the flight engineer, could only sit impotently and wait. But as the time ticked on, and with nothing in the way of further information, Van Zanten came up with a plan. If he used the time at Los Rodeos to fully refuel the aircraft, it would cut down his time at Las Palmas.

Just ten minutes after he started refuelling, though, a new transmission came in from air traffic control.

'All aircraft,' the ATC said, 'Las Palmas is now open. We will be able to depart the aircraft as soon as you are ready.'

Van Zanten now had to get his passengers back from the terminal and finish the refuelling before he could depart. Frustratingly, he had played the odds and lost.

Aboard *Clipper Victor*, Captain Grubb and his crew had also heard the welcome news. And with the passengers still on board, they were in a position to get away as soon as they could close the doors. There was a problem, though; the KLM aircraft was parked awkwardly ahead of them and they weren't sure if they could get past them to the runway.

While he prepared the aircraft for departure Grubb despatched Bob and George to go down on to the ground and assess the amount of space available for manoeuvre. They duly paced out the taxiway space adjacent to the KLM 747 and met at the edge of the tarmac.

'What do you think, George?' asked Bob.

The flight engineer shook his head. 'I think we're about twelve feet short,' he replied.

There was nothing for it. Before they could leave Los Rodeos Airport, they would have to wait for the KLM aircraft to recover its passengers, finish refuelling and depart.

But now another problem had emerged. In the time it had taken the *Rhine* to be ready for departure a thick bank of fog had begun rolling down off the nearby hills and was beginning to substantially restrict visibility. If they didn't get away now, they would all be fogged in.

The KLM captain was obviously thinking the same thing. The Pan Am crew could hear him call for taxi clearance, and the ATC's response: 'KLM 4805, enter runway 12 and back track to do a one-eighty to get into take-off position for 30.'

The one eighty, also known as a back taxi, involves an aircraft taxiing the length of the runway and turning around before taking off in the opposite direction. It was a rare thing to have to do at a commercial airport, and rightly so, because it's never optimal to have taxiing aircraft on the same runway as planes landing and taking off. But with the congestion, there simply wasn't an alternative.

The instructions were read back by the KLM co-pilot, Klaas Meurs, and moments later, *Clipper Victor* was also instructed: 'Clipper 1736, enter runway 12 and exit third taxiway on left, join taxiway going east and hold short runway 30.'

Confused about the taxiways, the Pan Am crew double-checked their instructions. 'The third one, sir,' came the reply. 'One, two three; third, the third one.'

They began to taxi, the visibility now getting poorer by the second – it was down to less than 200 metres, if that. And with the exits to the taxiways unmarked, they were struggling to see where to turn off.

At the other end of the runway the KLM aircraft, still in clear conditions, had performed its one-eighty and was ready for departure. Seeing the clouds rolling down the runway, Van Zanten was even keener to get going, so he edged the 747's thrust levers forward, prompting a 'we aren't cleared to go yet' from Klass.

'No, I know. Go ahead and ask,' replied the captain.

'KLM 4805 ready for take-off,' said Klass. 'Waiting for our ATC clearance.'

The controller read out the route and the altitude they were cleared to but, crucially, did not clear them for take-off.

Klass then read back the clearance, adding, 'We are now, uh, at take-off.'

'Let's go,' announced Van Zanten, releasing the brakes.

Inside *Clipper Victor*, the fog was already causing problems. Bob had spotted the first two taxiways, but they had inadvertently missed the third. Having heard the *Rhine* telling ATC 'We are at take-off', they transmitted to ATC, 'And we're still taxiing down the runway'.

Unbeknown to them, however, that transmission to ATC had blocked another crucial message, which should have reached Klass on board the *Rhine*: the one sent by the controller, at almost exactly the same moment, saying, 'Okay, stand by for take-off. I will call you.'

As communication at this time was done via two-way radio, the two communications almost cancelled each other out. All Van Zanten heard of the ATC's transmission was the first word: Okay. Which it clearly wasn't – not only did that one word not constitute an instruction, but hearing nothing but a squeal after it, the crew of the *Rhine* had no idea the *Clipper Victor* was still on the runway.

Meanwhile, the Pan Am Jumbo was still looking for the elusive taxiway.

'Clipper 1736, report runway clear,' instructed the controller.

'Okay,' confirmed Bob. 'Will report when we're clear.'

It was a transmission that, though missed by Van Zanten and Klass, was heard by Willem, the second officer. 'Is he not clear, that Pan American?' he asked.

'Oh, yes,' Van Zanten answered, as he continued with the take-off.

They were now an unstoppable force, racing towards disaster.

Still shrouded in thick fog, the crew of the *Clipper Victor*, which was indeed still on the runway, were shocked to see the lights of a 747 appearing from the murk ahead of them. It was immediately obvious that the KLM aircraft was closing in on them, and fast.

'There he is!' Grubbs shouted, pushing the thrust levers to full power. 'Look at him! Goddamn, that son-of-a-bitch is coming!'

He pushed the thrust levers to max power and hauled over the tiller, trying desperately to get the 747 on to the grass and out of the way of the fast-accelerating aircraft.

But there was little they could do. The *Rhine* was travelling much too fast and was still, it was obvious, way too low. And try as Van Zanten might, once he realized what he was seeing, no amount of pitching or thrust would prove enough. He felt the nose lift into the air, and then the main wheels come up, but the Pan Am 747, still slewing away from them, was too big an obstacle to clear. Unable to achieve sufficient height even with the tail dragging on the ground, the undercarriage and engines of the only partly airborne KLM aircraft sliced straight through the top of the *Clipper Victor*.

The Pan Am crew, looking out in horror, could only close their eyes, and duck.

Dorothy Kelly, sitting in her jump seat at the rear of the first-class cabin, had no window to look out of and, cocooned as she was inside the cabin, no more idea of the unfolding tragedy than had any of the passengers. Indeed, many were asleep, having been awake for most of the night. One minute she was chatting to her colleague, sipping a welcome coffee and expressing her relief that they'd be on their way soon, the next it was as if a bomb had exploded. There was an ear-splitting noise and things started flying around the cabin, something hard hitting her sharply on the side of her head. And as the floor collapsed beneath her, she found herself falling.

Dorothy came to in the cargo hold, where, disorientated among the baggage, and now in total darkness, she was unable to orient herself in space. The one thing she could see was a tiny pinpoint of light. Light surely meant outside, so she decided to clamber her way towards that, hearing multiple explosions happening all around her.

The climb led her finally to the cabin behind the cockpit, normally used as a lounge area. At first it seemed empty. No passengers. No nothing. Just a big empty space. And, she realized, completely open to the sky.

Dorothy then saw a few passengers and, instinct kicking in, she tried to lead them to a place from where they could jump. Not that Dorothy fancied their chances. It was like looking out from a second-floor window, and below them, on what had previously been grass, was a sea of vicious-looking debris, including shards of jagged plastic and metal. She had also, at some point, lost her shoes. There was no choice, though. Smoke and fire were racing towards them through the aircraft; it was either jump or certain death. So those that were too scared to do so, she had to push, all the while trying to block out the sounds coming from aft, of passengers who were trapped and had no hope of escaping banging on the windows and screaming.

Once the last passenger, an elderly man, was safely out, Dorothy jumped from the aircraft herself. She landed hard, scrambled up and, seeing three cabin crew colleagues who had also jumped out, ran away from the aircraft towards them. She was now struggling to see, and realized that blood from a head wound was pouring into her eyes and congealing. Despite this, always conscious that there could be another huge explosion at any moment, she kept running back and herding passengers away from the heat and the danger. In shock, many were just milling around, some even chatting, seemingly oblivious to the fact that the aircraft, already creaking as it started to fall apart, could come crashing down on them at any moment.

Gathering his wits, up in the cockpit Bob Bragg thought they might have got away with it. There had been no big crash – could it be that the other 747 *had* managed to clear them? But then he sat up and realized the flight deck windows were all gone and, looking out to the right, that the right wing was engulfed in flames. Looking behind and to the left, the entire upper deck area had vanished, from just behind his seat. He could see all the way to the tail.

The lessons drummed into Bob over many years of training had him instinctively reach for the fuel cut-off switches in the hope that the engines would stop and make any evacuation – which there surely would be – that much safer. But the engines didn't stop. They were still running at what sounded like full power, so he reached up to turn the four fire-control handles, which would hopefully shut everything off to the engine. It was then that he realized there was no longer a roof on the flight deck, and very little of the sides remaining either. There was nothing else for it but to jump the 50 feet to the ground down below.

In what remained of the first-class cabin roof, still strapped in, the flight engineer and the crew in the jump seats were hanging upside down. They managed to unshackle themselves and were able to slither down to the main cabin floor then leap to safety.

Captain Grubb had opted to jump down into the first-class cabin, and, like Dorothy, tumbled straight down into the hold and out through a hole in the bottom. Though in his case he was propelled by the passenger oxygen tanks, which simultaneously exploded.

When he came round, finding himself sprawled on the grass beneath the aircraft's nose, he heard a voice speaking urgently. To him.

It was Dorothy, the purser. 'Captain, we have to get out of here. Can you move? Are your legs broken?'

Disorientated after the fall, and badly burned by the exploding oxygen tanks, he couldn't take in what she was saying. Why couldn't they just stay put, where it was cool?

'No, we need to get away,' Dorothy told him firmly. Seeing his confusion, she rolled him on to his back, looped her arms beneath his armpits and began dragging him away from the burning aircraft as quickly as she could.

She was right to be frightened. She had only managed to

pull Grubb 40 feet or so when the right inboard engine disintegrated with a blinding flash and threw white-hot shards of metal in all directions. Was that it for them? Dorothy thought. After surviving the crash and the fall, were they both going to die now?

But the maelstrom subsided and, as they seemed to have suffered no further injury, she decided they must still have some luck left between them. Redoubling her efforts, she dragged the captain to safety.

'Stay here,' she told him. She then turned and, once again, ran back towards the aircraft, where she and Bob Bragg, who was very badly burned, did all they could to herd people to safety. This was a not inconsiderable task: most were elderly, some were confused, wandering around in a daze, some were barely clothed. One passenger had also been seriously injured. Having been one of the first to jump, she'd then had several other passengers land on top of her. They could also see passengers trapped far above banging on the windows and screaming for help, and tried to indicate that they should try to get to the left wing, where there was a hole in the aircraft.

Five minutes had now passed since the crash and, incredibly, there was not a single fire truck at the scene to help with the inferno or the evacuation. Bob and Dorothy could only look on in despair as the screams they'd heard from inside the cabin were replaced by the eerie sound of groaning metal as the aircraft fell apart and began collapsing in on itself.

Airport service trucks were now arriving, as well as random airport workers' vehicles, and the surviving crew set about getting the injured into them and, hopefully, straight to the local hospital. Fifteen minutes later, after a walk-around over on the other side of the aircraft, and finding no other passengers, Grubb and Dorothy climbed into vehicles themselves.

They would not be rescuing anyone else that afternoon.

That no fire trucks attended the *Clipper Fortune* during those first vital minutes was a tragedy, because had they been there fires could almost certainly have been extinguished, and more lives saved. That none came was because they hadn't seen it: they hadn't realized two aircraft were involved.

The *Rhine* had travelled some way up the runway on its belly after the collision, and was being consumed by the fires of multiple explosions before it had even come to rest. Its left main gear had been mangled in what remained of the *Clipper Victor* but momentum had carried it a full 1,500 feet, placing it closer to the Los Rodeos air traffic control tower, and clearly visible as a huge and growing fireball.

Seeing the inferno, ATC had immediately dispatched all the airport's emergency vehicles and though, for the KLM aircraft, it was already too late, their focus was entirely on the fireball and attendant smoke. No one had realized that, a little further down the runway, a desperate evacuation was ongoing. By the time the last survivor of *Clipper Victor* had left the scene, no emergency services help of any sort had come to help them.

Just sixty-one people had been able to escape and survive. With 583 people losing their lives, the number of fatalities at Los Rodeos remains the highest ever in an air disaster. How on earth could something like this have happened?

The investigation launched by Spain was exhaustive and involved a multinational group of some seventy people. The first of its kind to include an assessment of the human factors at play, its report highlighted a number of failings, any of which, they concluded, could have been avoided.

As far as the Spanish were concerned, the main cause of the accident was that Van Zanten had attempted to take off without a clearance. The investigators suggested that the reason for this was a desire to leave as soon as possible to comply with KLM's duty time regulations and before a further deterioration in the weather.

The Dutch authorities, perhaps reasonably, were reluctant to accept the Spanish assertion that the KLM captain alone was to blame, citing the fact that the Pan Am aircraft had taxied beyond the clearance of the third exit and that the controller's clearance had been ambiguous.

Despite this reluctance, KLM ultimately accepted responsibility for the accident and paid compensation to the families of the victims.

There is always much to learn during an air crash investigation and the opportunity to do so following what happened in Tenerife was not squandered. It led to an international requirement for standard phraseology to be adopted across aviation and for there to be a greater emphasis on English as a common working language across the industry. It also led to the requirement for all air traffic instructions to be read back – not just acknowledged with a 'roger' or an 'OK' – neither of which implies understanding of the instruction.

The hierarchical relationships in the flight deck and beyond were also examined, leading to the introduction of Crew Resource Management as a concept, something that places greater emphasis on team decision-making by mutual agreement, rather than top-down imposition. Had this been in place prior to this incident, the KLM flight engineer, Klass Meurs, might have felt empowered to question the captain more robustly when he noticed the Pan Am 747 might still be on the runway. This training has been mandatory for airline pilots since 2006 and is now widely used across the aviation industry and in other professions.

As part of the wider investigation, all the surviving cabin crew and passengers were interviewed. Though most of those who lost their lives never had a chance to escape their aircraft, most of those that did, all aboard the Pan Am 747, had one thing in common. They knew how to get out because they had taken time to read the safety card.

Anyone who flies these days will know the drill. Either the pilots or the cabin crew, or both in some cases will ask you to 'give a few moments of your time to watch the safety demonstration and familiarize yourself with the safety card in your seat pocket'. I include this very line in every welcome on board public address (PA) I give to passengers. And for good reason. Both could save your life.

The safety card and briefing that any flyer will (hopefully) be familiar with has been around for almost a century. But the cost of its introduction was also paid in lives. Back in 1928, a KLM Fokker F.III aircraft crashed in Waalhaven, in the Netherlands, and all the crew and passengers perished. The investigation concluded that though they survived the initial crash, the passengers died because none was aware of the existence of an emergency escape hatch in the roof.

The tragedy highlighted the need for passengers to be briefed on exits and safety procedures before departure and was the origin of the passenger safety briefing we know today.

Imperial Airways, one of the first UK airlines, was one of the early adopters of the concept and gave everyone a pamphlet entitled 'Notes for the Comfort and Convenience of Passengers'. The booklet was mostly about the journey, and the comfort aspect. Tucked away on the back page was at least some information about the emergency exits and instructions on how to put on and use a life belt, if required. Not ideal, perhaps, but at least it was a start.

This less than perfect situation took a long time to improve. It wasn't until the early 1960s that it was generally agreed that passenger safety should be given greater prominence than all the puff. And this only happened because two accident psychologists, Dr Daniel Johnson and Dr Beau Altman, noticed that while air crashes were becoming considerably more survivable, post-crash survival was not keeping pace. Yes, you might survive the wild ride down to the ground largely unscathed but then die anyway because you couldn't escape the aircraft before being overcome by smoke or fire.

Incredible as it may seem today, this was a revelation to the industry. But, to their credit, the Douglas Aircraft Corporation, forerunners of McDonnell Douglas and the makers of the famous DC-3 airliners, engaged Johnson and Altman immediately to see what could be done. They assembled a team and it embarked on a comprehensive study of human behaviour, through interviewing air crash survivors and simulating hundreds of evacuations. To instil some genuine panic, to better simulate a real and scary emergency, they would turn out the lights and sometimes throw in the odd smoke grenade, just to motivate their pretend passengers to get out. They also looked at the use of seatbelts and lifejackets *after* passengers had listened to a safety briefing, to see if they were being deployed correctly.

They weren't. At least, not by many.

The main takeaway, however, from this massive undertaking was that they learned that to have the best chance of surviving an air crash, you needed to get out of an aircraft within ninety seconds of it stopping, and that the addition of safety cards, as well as the safety briefing, markedly improved survivability.

As a result of the work done by Johnson and Altman, the safety card became the norm on board aircraft in the mid-1960s, but the format we know today was mandated only in 1978, directly as a result of the Tenerife disaster, when Johnson and Altman pushed Congress to adopt a new standard, swapping the earlier text-heavy cards for a story told in pictures. This moved the emphasis from reading to recognition, making the cards universal and understandable by everyone, regardless of language barriers. Johnson and Altman also found that depicting people of various genders and races on the cards resulted in the information being retained longer, proving their theory that if people could see themselves reflected in the images the information contained in them was more likely to be retained.

Larry Bruns, the talented artist who designed those first story safety cards with Johnson and Altman, still produces them today. His business, Aviation Safety Art International, creates them for every single aircraft type in operation – yes, that laminated card you find in every airline seat's back pocket – in the hope that you will pick it up and digest it. Do you? If you don't, it might help to remember that, chances are, you will have just ninety seconds.

The safety briefing, on long-haul especially, has also moved on. Many airlines seem to be engaged in a rolling contest to see whose creates the biggest passenger buzz. Some use cartoons, others A-list actors, or other celebrities; when New Zealand Airways launched a new one to celebrate the final instalment of the Lord of the Rings trilogy, it was greeted with almost as much fanfare as the movies themselves.

Though I don't know which is the chicken and which the egg here: it seems science has backed up the trend. Though a recent evacuation on a JAL aircraft bucked the trend by successfully getting everyone out without the use of A-listers and gimmicky videos, research from the University of New South Wales found that videos containing celebrities and/or humour to get the safety message across were significantly more effective than those that didn't, with 50 per cent retaining the information in these mini-movies, as opposed to 32 per cent with the control. Personally, I suspect that in the Japanese evacuation there were cultural influences at play which affected the eventual outcome.

As I mentioned at the start of this chapter, operating a passenger airliner is very much a team sport. In simple terms, pilots do the driving and the cabin crew take care of the customers. It is obviously not quite as simple as that, but it's worth restating that the tragedy at Tenerife directly contributed to the development of that Crew Resource Management training I also mentioned earlier. And it's not just about familiarizing ourselves with other colleagues' roles. It's also about accepting that making errors is something we all do, and being encouraged to challenge actions and behaviours. If challenged ourselves, we're trained not to take it as a criticism but as a chance to clarify, to discuss, to be *safe*. Few initiatives have contributed to aviation safety in a more widespread way.

One last thing to note. As you will no doubt have heard pilots say in hundreds of welcome PAs, the cabin crew really are 'primarily there for your safety', and your safety will always be their main focus. Whether it be dealing with an inflight cabin fire from an iPhone or delivering emergency medical care, they have the skills to step up to the plate, and, in 'the unlikely event of an emergency', will do what's required to ensure a timely evacuation can take place. For passengers to get that, and to *respect* that, seems only fair.

Perhaps the greatest legacy of the crash at Tenerife is the

spotlight it shone on the professionalism, skill and training of cabin crews. It was particularly personified in that courageous junior purser, Dorothy Kelly, whose commitment to her job did not end that day. Despite having fractured both her elbow and her skull, she remained in Tenerife for several days after the accident and, along with Bob Bragg, helped care for the injured passengers who had survived. Their captain, Victor Grubb, would remain in hospital in the US till the end of April.

Dorothy returned to flying for Pan Am eighteen months later, but would go on to admit that the tragedy changed her for ever: from then on, she found herself slightly intolerant of passengers who only wanted a pretty face to serve them a drink or a meal. In her own words, 'It's not about what you're going to get fed or how quickly you're going to get a glass of champagne. Our main task is to get you on and off the plane and to your destination as safely as possible, something that is never emphasized enough and something maybe to remember next time you take a flight.'

Oh, and from me, if it's not too much bother:

Take note of the nearest exits.

Watch the video.

Read the safety card.

9. The Galunggung Glider

Iceland, 17 December 2023

It is the run-up to Christmas and with a couple of days' leave in the offing I am in a buoyant and festive mood, only heightened by the fact that I'm unexpectedly in Iceland – only a short sleigh ride to the home of Santa and his reindeer.

The reason I've found myself here is the subject of a whole other story, but what feels particularly pertinent is that I've been flying alongside my friend and colleague Iain Moody, who is captaining our Airbus A350. And since our unexpected layover is in the land of ice and fire, talk in the hotel bar naturally turns to volcanos – specifically Eyjafjallajökull, a volcano near Iceland's southern tip, whose eruption in 2010 grounded both of us. And not just us; the ash cloud Eyjafjallajökull created was so vast and far-reaching it led to a total ban of air traffic over large swathes of Europe and left thousands of aircrew and tens of thousands of passengers twiddling their thumbs for almost two weeks.

Most people these days are familiar with the threat to air traffic that can be caused by volcanos. But you might be surprised to know, given that powered flight has been with us for around a century, that for most of that time the potential danger to aircraft was unknown. It had certainly never been recorded.

That was, until 24 June 1982, when another Captain Moody,

who happens to be Iain's father, found himself something of an unwitting test pilot.

The majority of flights pass entirely without incident, and of those that don't – well, as we've already seen in this book (and will see again), most go wrong in largely predictable ways, involving recognizable patterns and events. But an experienced crew always know to expect the unexpected, even if they think they've seen all there is to see.

Eric Moody, Iain's dad, was a very experienced pilot, having passed his flying scholarship in 1958. Since his young years as a cadet at the BOAC college in Hamble, flying had been in his blood, and he was an early convert to the 747.

BA009, a 747-236B named the *City of Edinburgh*, was in the middle of a multi-sector journey. Having originated in London, it had first made a stop in Bombay and, from here in Kuala Lumpur it was going on to travel to Melbourne before reaching its final destination of Auckland.

Eric and his crew, Senior First Officer Roger Greaves and Flight Engineer Barry Townley-Freeman, were looking forward to their leg of the journey. They were well rested and with nothing of note showing up on the weather forecast were not expecting any problems during the upcoming five-hour flight.

Once the customers had been welcomed on board, they departed Kuala Lumpur into clear skies, turning south and starting their climb towards the cruising altitude of 37,000 feet. Levelling off, with all well, they wasted no time in having dinner; it was just approaching 20:15 local time and they were ravenous.

Dinner finished, Eric decided to hand control to Roger so he could go to the bathroom and freshen up. But with the upper deck WC adjacent to the flight deck engaged, he went downstairs to the first-class cabin in the nose.

Coming out of the bathroom, Eric had just started chatting with one of the crew in the galley when he noticed something odd – the seatbelt signs had come on. Almost immediately they were joined by a crew member from upstairs, saying Eric was needed back on the flight deck.

Wondering what could be wrong, Eric headed back up the stairs and as he did so noticed that there seemed to be puffs of smoke coming out of the air-conditioning vents, and an acrid, almost electrical smell. That must be it then, Eric thought. Something electrical had overheated. But when he got back to the flight deck he was stopped in his tracks.

'Come and look at this,' Roger said, motioning towards the windows. 'Isn't it beautiful?'

It was indeed, he agreed. And Eric knew exactly what they were looking at, too: a phenomenon known as St Elmo's Fire. Though fairly rare, most, if not all, long-haul pilots would have seen it at some point, as they tended to travel through the bigger weather systems. It was created by the electrical field around an object being charged, causing the air to become ionized. The result was what looked like a violet or blue fork of lightning, due to plasma being discharged, and the windscreen became the lightning itself.

St Elmo's Fire wasn't dangerous, but it usually meant that the aircraft was flying near thunderstorms. So with that in mind, as well as switching on the seatbelt signs, Barry had already taken precautions, placing the anti-icing system for the engines on and switching the ignitors to continuous ignition. As Eric strapped back into his seat, he was simultaneously flicking the radar controls to ascertain the whereabouts of the weather; it seemed clear that they must have inadvertently flown into something.

Roger then brought their attention to the leading edges of the wings and the front of the engines. All were now bathed in an unearthly glow, almost as if covered in some bioluminescent alien life form. The inside of the Rolls-Royce engines looked even weirder; something was creating a stroboscopic luminescent spiralling effect in front of all the fans that was equally mesmerizing – a bit like the eyes of Kaa, the snake in *The Jungle Book*. The view out of the front window then changed. No longer was St Elmo's Fire only on the windscreen; to them it felt like they were accelerating to lightspeed in their Jumbo Jet version of the *Millennium Falcon*, or driving a car through a snowstorm with the headlights on – tiny shards of light seemed to be coming straight at them.

This array of odd phenomena was becoming quite concerning, and Eric's thoughts returned to the smoke he'd seen while climbing the stairs. He was just trying to think what the connection might be when Barry called out, 'Engine failure number four!'

Eric called for the engine failure checklist and Barry and Roger ran through the immediate actions that were always done from memory. They were just about to confirm that they had all been done correctly when Barry called out again. 'Engine failure number two . . .' Then '. . . number three . . .' Finally, in a voice that suggested he couldn't believe what he was seeing: 'They have *all* gone.'

Stunned, Eric looked down at the array of engine instruments. The picture was very confusing. Recalling a recent simulator check that had involved an all-engine failure, he knew, because no engines equalled no electrical power due to the generators being off, that all the lights should be off in the aircraft. Yet they weren't. Some instruments were frozen showing normal indications; others were showing failures. Everything was still on, including the autopilot.

It was a scenario that didn't match up to anything the three pilots had seen before. They had no idea what was going on.

With the 747 now effectively gliding unpowered, Eric could

only fall back on the fundamentals that all pilots have drummed into them from day one of flying school: aviate; navigate; communicate. The speed was now decreasing so, to keep the aircraft safe, he decided to initiate a slow descent. It was as he was doing so that he noticed another worrying oddity: his airspeed indicator was showing different numbers to Roger's, something that might also point to their proximity to thunderstorms, causing icing or other extreme weather. Figuring that his indicator showed what was probably the closest to their true speed, he used that as his medium to set the descent.

Four minutes had passed. And now flying safely again, at least for the moment – they were by no means out of jeopardy – Eric turned back towards Jakarta, the nearest piece of tarmac, and directed Barry to have a go at restarting the engines while Roger transmitted a mayday call.

'Jakarta, Jakarta,' Roger transmitted, 'Mayday, Mayday, Speedbird nine. We've lost all four engines: we're leaving flight level three seven zero.'

The static on the radio and interference made the reply from Jakarta almost unintelligible, but one thing was clear: they didn't understand the gravity of the situation, believing that the aircraft had only lost the number four engine. Roger tried again, but with the language barrier and awful radio interference he just wasn't getting through to the controller.

Luckily, there was a Singapore Airlines 747 nearby, and, understanding the situation, its captain was able to intervene and relay the full facts to the controller on the ground. While this was going on, Barry was trying to restart the engines and had undone some of the previous actions they had taken to shut down number four engine, to allow for it to be restarted, or at least for an attempt to be made.

Things weren't looking promising. Eric now turned his thoughts towards his glide ratio. He knew that for about every

15 kilometres he travelled forward he was losing about 1,000 metres (3,500 feet) in altitude. If they were to safely make it over the mountains that lay between his aircraft and Jakarta, he would need 10,500 feet of altitude by the time they got there. But he wouldn't have that. They were descending too fast.

Passing 26,000 feet, another alarm sounded in the flight deck – not engine-related this time, it was the cabin altitude alarm, which activated at 10,000 feet cabin altitude, the limit at which humans can reasonably function without supplemental oxygen. Bleed air from the engines worked to keep the cabin pressurized, allowing everyone to breathe normally. With none of that air incoming, the air in the cabin would gradually leak out, lowering the air pressure, meaning, weirdly, that the cabin 'altitude' would gradually be climbing relative to the aircraft, which was descending.

Eric ordered the team to put on their oxygen masks and grabbed his own from the stowage to his left. He looked around to see Barry had his own safely donned, but Roger's had come out of stowage unusable.

With the cabin altitude still rising, Eric now had a choice to make. To preserve the altitude and thus airborne time, or start an emergency descent and keep Roger conscious and a working part of the team.

Eric opted for a halfway house, deciding to increase the rate of descent but not go all out and lower the gear, which would create maximum drag and a huge rate of descent. This was partially driven by Eric's encyclopaedic knowledge of the 747's systems. He knew that selecting the gear down would place a huge demand on the hydraulic systems, which also powered the flying controls. He had no idea if there was enough pressure in the system to do both, and there was no point in having their gear going down if they'd have no power to be able to manoeuvre the aircraft: everything else would become academic at that point. There could only be one outcome. And he had the lives of 270 passengers and fifteen crew in his hands.

Passing 20,000 feet, Roger managed, by some miracle, to fix his oxygen mask, which allowed Eric to immediately ease back on the rate of descent, to preserve that precious altitude. Having by now done the maths, however, as they were passing through 15,000 feet, he shared the reality of their situation with his crew.

'If we don't get them started by 12,000 feet,' he told them, 'I will turn us towards the sea and we can prepare for a ditching.'

Everyone nodded in understanding and resignation. They all knew that, even in daylight on a calm sea, ditching a 747 was a marginal affair. At night, the outcome was likely to be catastrophic. At least he hadn't put the gear down, he thought, which provided a small shred of comfort. Ditching with the gear down would only ever have one outcome.

Having assessed the situation and aware that the passengers must by now be terrified, Eric reached for the button and composed himself to make a PA.

'Ladies and gentlemen,' he said, 'this is Captain Moody again. We have a small problem, in that all four engines have failed. We are doing our utmost to get them back going. I do hope that you are not in too much distress . . .'

He finished off by giving the verbal signal used by pilots to alert the senior crew member that all was not well, and that Eric needed to speak with them face to face immediately.

The cabin manager entered the flight deck to see all three flight crew wearing their oxygen masks and working to get the engines re-started. They looked Eric in the eye and all they could understand through the restrictions of Eric's mask was the word 'ditching'. That was all they needed to know, and they left immediately. None of them could understand why the engines weren't starting. Every time Roger tried, they were getting fuel and igniting, and then just as quickly any hope of fully starting up ceased. It was looking hopeless.

The aircraft had by now passed below 12,000 feet, not much higher than the mountains they would have needed to avoid. It was time to make the turn out to sea, and the narrowing of their remaining few options.

All the while, Barry had been trying everything he could, frenetically moving between 'by the book' and 'not by the book' in the vain hope of getting something started, while Eric and Roger were contemplating a water landing and trying to accept that their fate was probably sealed.

Then Barry said something no one by now expected to hear.

'Number four is starting.'

Eric and Roger were so relieved they were almost jubilant; this meant Eric could ease the rate of descent further. And then another engine started, then another, and then the last. As inexplicably as they had failed minutes earlier, all four were once again running and what looked like being an inevitable crash was now a situation with hope.

Eric reassessed. They were too low, and needed to climb, so he instructed Roger to inform Jakarta. At 20:57, some seventeen minutes after the first engine failure, Roger did so. 'Jakarta Speedbird nine,' Roger transmitted, 'we are back in business. All four engines operating.'

But not knowing why the engines failed, they had no guarantee it wouldn't happen again, so Eric was keen to put some distance between the aircraft and the sea. And, sure enough, as they passed through 15,000 feet, the St Elmo's Fire was back on the windscreen, and number two engine

'Waddell's Wagon' – Boeing test pilot Frank Waddell had a truck built with a 747 flight deck above to allow the crew to prepare for taxiing the behemoth around airfields.

A rare photo of the original full double-decker design favoured by Juan Trippe, which was eventually shelved for the iconic design we all now recognize.

Developing the 747 nearly bankrupted Boeing, as this billboard outside the Everett factory suggests. Boeing is Seattle and Seattle is Boeing.

The roll-out of the first 747 in Seattle in 1968.

The 747 takes to the air for the first time, flown by Frank Waddell.

'The Boeing 747 is a pilot's dream' declared Waddell after landing.

Flight attendants representing the twenty-six airlines who had placed orders for the 747.

Boeing's Joe Sutter, who led the 747 design team.

Hired to fly on the 747, Sheila Nutt was Pan Am's first African-American Flight Attendant.

Pan Am's Juan Trippe drove demand for the 747. The second Jumbo was named after him.

The first-class cabin on the Jumbo's upper deck was the epitome of 1970s comfort and sophistication.

The 747 in its iconic Pan Am livery.

Operation Solomon. In 1991, an Israeli El Al Jumbo set a record for the most passengers ever carried when it evacuated 1,088 Ethiopian Jews.

Ed Force One. Iron Maiden's singer Bruce Dickinson piloted this specially painted 747 on the band's 2016/2017 world tour.

Air Force One overflies Mount Rushmore.

President Trump being interviewed whilst airborne for my National Geographic documentary *The New Air Force One: Flying Fortress*.

There are few who have had this view! Taking the flight-deck jump seat of the VC-25A during a training mission.

Rare access to the ramp and outside of the VC-25A fleet, where no detail is spared.

The exact layout of the VC-25A is classified, but this picture shows the 'Flying White House' elements of the aircraft – presidential corridor and seating area.

A 747 coming in to land at Hong Kong's Kai Tak Airport.

began vibrating violently. With some reluctance, Eric made the decision to shut the engine down again. As it seemed obvious now that there must be a relationship between the engine failure and the St Elmo's Fire, they all agreed that getting out of it again was probably a wise idea. Eric descended to 12,000 feet, now on a direct course for the airport.

Then came another oddity to contend with. It was a clear night in Jakarta, but despite this the crew were having significant difficulties picking out the airport or the runway. They asked for radar vectors to the instrument landing system, only to find that the glideslope, or vertical, element of this was not working. The localizer, or 'lateral element', was, however, enabling Roger to talk Eric down on a virtual glideslope, calling out altitudes against distance.

As they got closer to the runway, things became clearer. Or, rather, didn't. They hadn't been able to see because they couldn't see through the windscreen; for whatever reason, the glass was opaque. There was just one small sliver at the edge that allowed any visibility, and by looking through it, Eric was able to land the Jumbo safely.

Jakarta Tower asked them to vacate on to the taxiway, but as Eric turned towards the bright lights of the terminal building and apron that one small sliver clouded over. Enough, he decided, applying the parking brake. They should call it a night, and get towed to parking.

Conscious that the passengers had also experienced a somewhat stressful time, while they were waiting for the tug Eric headed downstairs to reassure them that all was now well.

'It's no big deal,' suggested a retired BOAC captain he came upon in First Class. Back in the day, he'd lost all four engines in a Lancastrian while flying over Bermuda, and that had apparently been no big deal either.

With no interest in a discussion with the customer on the subject, Eric quickly moved on down the cabin, and noticed that his shirt sleeves were covered in what seemed to be soot.

'We have it too,' one of the cabin crew members said. 'It's all over the cabin.'

Back on the flight deck, Eric showed it to Barry and Roger.

'I know what that is,' Barry said. 'It's volcanic ash.'

Having parked the aircraft, and once the passengers had all been disembarked into the terminal, the crew were finally able to disembark themselves, after what had been a somewhat eventful flight. And once at the bottom of the steps, Barry knelt down on the tarmac and kissed it.

'Why are you doing that?' Eric asked him.

'The Pope does it,' Barry replied as he stood up.

'Well, he would,' Eric replied. 'He flies Alitalia.'

So what exactly had happened to Flight 009? Unbeknown to the crew, to ATC, to anyone who could have diverted them, the crew had flown into a cloud of volcanic ash thrown up by the eruption of Mount Galunggung, which is about 110 miles south-east of Jakarta. This was what caused the failure of all four engines. It was a risk to aviation that had never been considered a threat to flight safety before. But that was all about to change.

As a pilot who trained after this incident occurred, I know that if I was to be asked to design a kryptonite for aircraft, I'd say volcanic ash would be about as good as it gets.

When a volcano erupts it can throw tons and tons of ash up into the atmosphere. And what we call 'volcanic ash' is actually a mineral dust, typically made up of small tephra – a mixture of pulverized rock and glassy particles formed from cooling magma droplets. Though the term 'tephra' refers to any kind of pyroclastic material, the ones found in ash clouds are typically less than 2 millimetres in diameter.

Easily carried thousands of miles on the wind (they can even circumnavigate the globe), these particles are so small they are undetectable by an aircraft's radar, which is optimized to detect water droplets in the atmosphere. This danger is therefore invisible to crews, making it easy to unwittingly fly into them, even in daylight.

Once an aircraft finds itself inside a volcanic ash cloud, things potentially can start to happen – to go wrong – very quickly. The fine dust easily enters all the engines, and all the other orifices of the aircraft, causing filters and vents to become blocked; in the case of fuel vents, it contaminates the fuel in the tanks.

As a result, various systems will quickly begin to fail, including pressurization, pitot–static systems (used for speed and altitude indications) and cooling. And it doesn't end there. The airframe, the windows and the engine blades will also take a beating, sandblasted as they are by this electrically charged cloud of dust – the cause of the St Elmo's Fire Eric and his crew had experienced.

This in itself can abrade the aircraft's structures and may eventually cause failures. But long before that happens there is a potentially lethal blow. With the combustion chambers of a jet engine running at around 1,400°C, they are more than hot enough to melt glass, which usually melts at 1,100°C. This now-molten glass adheres to any surface it meets, including those of the fuel inlets and the ignitors. Once they are blocked, not only can you not keep an engine running, you cannot restart it again . You are rendered powerless. The kryptonite has won.

So how did Eric manage to get his engines running again? Though not absolutely proven, and perhaps impossible *to* prove, the belief is that the engines were off for long enough that they cooled sufficiently for the glass to once again become solid and brittle, and that the movement of the engine components during the start sequence was enough to crack and dislodge it.

This would explain why engine number four, the first of them to fail, and therefore the coolest, was the first to restart. Through perseverance, experience and a welcome bit of luck, Eric and his crew managed to land the aeroplane safely in the face of what can easily be a plane killer.

With the potential danger caused by the eruption of Mount Galunggung now very real, the airspace that BA009 flew through was closed for nineteen days to give the bulk of the ash cloud time to disperse. The ash lingered, however, and three weeks later a Singapore Airlines 747 experienced the same problem as Eric and his crew and had to shut down and restart three of its engines.

The aviation industry is normally very reactive to learning from its errors and produces procedures to prevent reoccurrence of this type of potentially catastrophic incident. But these things take time and, in this case, it was a lot of time. In December 1989, after departing Anchorage, Alaska, KLM 687, a Boeing 747-400M (combi), suffered an almost identical incident to BA009. Despite it being daylight, the aircraft entered an area of contamination from the Redoubt volcano and all four engines flamed out. Though the crew managed to recover the aircraft at 14,000 feet and return to Anchorage safely, the disruption continued and further aircraft were compromised. It was clear the industry needed to act. They had been lucky so far, but at some point, that luck would run out and lives would be lost.

In 1991 the aviation industry decided to set up Volcanic Ash Advisory Centres (VAACs). Acting as a liaison between aviation meteorologists and vulcanologists, their job was to assess the threat to air transport from ash launched from erupting volcanoes. This worked up to a point. We could now predict where the ash was going to be and avoid it.

So the system worked, but when the Eyjafjallajökull volcano erupted in 2010, the ash cloud was on an unprecedented scale, and with a stiff breeze blowing it down over most of Europe, it blanketed the entire airspace, causing most of it to be completely closed for six days.

While the ability to predict the flow of the ash cloud and its concentrations had improved immeasurably, any concentration led to a total ban on aviation at this point. This is obviously the safest course of action but, like so many things in aviation, a balance needed to be found to allow the aircraft to safely fly while this dust was present, or lengthy bans would become the norm, something that was wholly impractical.

The International Air Transport Association (IATA) estimated that the losses to the industry for each day of disruption would be about $200 million, so there was considerable impetus to find a balanced solution. The engine manufacturers worked with scientists to swiftly develop a number for the concentration deemed safe, and set it at 2 milligrams of ash per cubic metre – anything below this would not have any implications for air safety if correct post-flight maintenance procedures are followed.

This study prompted further work, and regulators subsequently established a new category of a time-restricted zone, which allowed suitably authorized operators to fly in densities exceeding 2 milligrams up to those of 4 milligrams per cubic metre, any higher being prohibited. While it was difficult to calculate the concentration that Eric and his aircraft flew through, engineers recovered deposits of fused volcanic ash from the engine tailpipes that were, astoundingly, up to half an inch in diameter.

During the 2010 eruption many readings were taken of the ash cloud and, at similar distances away from the volcano, in 1982, when BA009 was affected by the Galunggung ash, and, in terms of milligrams per cubic metre the concentrations were into the high teens, showing just how conservative engine manufacturers and regulators were, and are, being with their limits.

As a direct result of what happened to BA009, aircrews are now trained in the simulator on how to avoid volcanic ash encounters, and, should they inadvertently find themselves in one – thanks to what we learned from Eric – how both to recognize it, and to get safely out of it before it takes a grip of the airframe. In true aviation industry style, there is also now a checklist for this on all airliners.

If anyone is interested in knowing the procedure, by the way, if you do recognize a volcanic ash encounter you do a one-eighty turn and get your ass outta there; descend, disconnect the auto-thrust, closing your thrust levers to make the engines as cool as possible, thus hopefully avoiding the knockout blow of the melting glass. Once clear of the cloud, resume normal operations and report the encounter.

The so-called Gallunggung Glider was repaired and after being renamed the *City of Elgin* it returned to service. It was retired in January 2002 and sold to European Aviation Air Charter. Its reprieve from the scrapyard was short-lived: having been taken out of service in 2004, it was cut up in 2009.

The acts of Eric and his team to get the aircraft safely on the ground were truly astounding and their skill was recognized by many organizations, with honours and awards for all involved. Eric was also awarded the Queen's Commendation for Valuable Service in the Air. A huge honour, and very well deserved.

Back in Iceland, Iain and I awake the next morning to hear that the Sundhnúkur volcano has erupted. Just a short distance from where we're having our breakfast, it's apparently not quite as ferocious as the one in 2010 but, in its own way, is doubtless no less lethal.

As we climb away from the airport we catch a glimpse of it in the darkness, our eyes drawn to the meandering scarlet ribbons of those impressive lava flows. But mostly I'm thinking about the part of it we *can't* see, that cloud of aircraft kryptonite winging its way up to the heavens. And how one captain's exemplary airmanship, plus Joe Sutter's fabled four engines, made us all so much safer today.

Captain Eric Moody flew west on 18 March 2024, aged eighty-two. He will always be remembered as a master of airmanship and, for that PA to his passengers in the midst of such a crisis, the master of understatement as well.

10. Air Force One

Victorville, CA, April 2019

It's 4.30 a.m. and I'm already half awake, because my body clock still thinks I'm in London. I am not here on a layover with the day job today, however, but with my side hustle as a documentary film producer, to bear witness to the commencement of an important project. It's been years in the planning, will be more in the execution, and my presence has required assent from not only the Department of Defense and the United States Air Force, but also the 45th (and 47th) President of the USA himself. I'm here to film the formal delivery of a single Boeing 747-8i to the United States Air Force (USAF), and even though the handover will largely go unnoticed, this is a momentous day for the nation. For this is no ordinary Boeing 747-8i. Today it will become designated VC-25B. Or, as most people know it, Air Force One.

Dedicated presidential air travel has been around in the USA since 1944, when a C-54 was put into service for Franklin D. Roosevelt. Harry Truman was subsequently carried around in a DC-6, and Eisenhower, who served as president from 1953 to 1961, was carried on the Columbine II and Columbine III aircraft – essentially modified Lockheed Constellations. It was during this period, after one of the presidential aircraft was confused with another with the same designation, that the radio callsign 'Air Force One' came about.

It was not long after this that the Constellations were replaced with purpose-built Boeing 707s and the metonym everyone knows became more widely known. The first of these, with the tail number 26000, was witness to many historic events; it carried John F. Kennedy to his final day in Dallas, and Lyndon B. Johnson, following his predecessor's assassination, was sworn in as US president on board.

It was Ronald Reagan, however, who really understood the benefits of having such a large, in-your-face symbol of the mighty USA. In 1985 he authorized a programme for its replacement, a bold venture to create an aircraft that would become the 'Flagship for the Nation'. And although the DC-10 was also considered for the role, there was really only one contender: the Boeing 747.

It would not be complete in time for Reagan to enjoy it. With his own tenure as POTUS over in 1989, it was the 41st President, George H. W. Bush, who had that honour, flying on a round trip to Kansas, Florida, and back to DC on 6 September 1990. And with the first (28000) being joined by a twin (29000) in December 1990, the Jumbo era of presidential travel had begun.

The next stage of its evolution starts today. It is a little after five by the time I meet my team in the foyer. Ben, who's directing, and Mark, who'll be filming, are similarly out of step with their circadian rhythms, but when we wander out into the parking lot to load our gear into our rented minivan, we are enveloped by the warmth of what promises to be a fine California morning.

Right now, though, the sun's yet to meet the horizon, so we're operating in the dark, and not just literally. All we have to go on is a set of coordinates which will apparently lead us to a secret rendezvous around half an hour's drive distant. With everything top secret, we can't just rock up at the gates; we're going to be met and then escorted to the scene of this historic handover by a team from the Department of Defense.

Ben gets his phone out to tap in the numbers. 'This is all a bit cloak and dagger,' he says. Mark and I agree he's right.

'And you're more Basildon Bond than James Bond,' Mark comments as he squints out into the endless blackness. 'Have we got an actual dagger? What if we get lost? I'm getting serious Jack Reacher vibes here.'

I do my best to reassure them that it's all perfectly legit, but as soon as we set off the drive quickly progresses in exactly the way cloak-and-dagger drives tend to. We go from tarmac highways to narrow side roads, to even narrower dirt tracks, and, since it's still very dark, we soon become spooked. Bar the faraway stars, there's not a light to be seen anywhere.

Six minutes away from our ETA and we are still surrounded by empty desert. I double-check the coordinates. Can they really be right? But just as we decide that we should perhaps make a U-turn, lights illuminate the track up ahead – the unmistakeable double flash of car headlights.

So they've been sitting there with their lights off? This is all now a bit *Breaking Bad*, and our anxieties are not stilled by Ben's mutterings about the price on the black market for kidneys. But crawling closer we see that the dark SUV up ahead, apparently parked in the middle of nowhere, is sporting government plates. Two women emerge from it, both dressed in dark clothing. Despite those plates, they still look pretty menacing. But as I climb out – well, someone has to – I recognize Develyn from our preparatory meetings. She's our Department of Defense liaison and is going to be our 'shadow' for the project.

'Welcome to the high desert!' she calls, waving an arm in greeting. 'Let's get you guys inside and get this show on the road, shall we?'

By 'inside', she doesn't mean her SUV, obviously. We're to follow them down the track for a mile or so to the gates of Southern California Logistics Airfield, one of the US's many enormous aviation graveyards. And it certainly feels like a graveyard. Having been admitted through a discreet side gate – one of many, apparently – our senses are immediately assaulted by the sight of hundreds, if not thousands, of dead aircraft. Or, rather, the ghosts of dead aircraft; with only the first vestiges of light taking the edge off the darkness, they are not fully visible. More like the tantalizing shadows of a colony of alien life forms. Mutant and deformed life forms; some lack tail fins, others wings, some entire nose cones or cabins. Come the sunshine, this will reveal itself as just the mother of all scrapyards, but for now, it's like walking on to the set of *Mad Max*.

Arresting though the defunct aircraft are, my eyes are soon drawn into the distance, where, adjacent to a hangar with the word 'Boeing' on it is a solitary 747-8i, its pristine white paint bathed in an orange glow from a couple of nearby mobile lighting trailers. It looks stunning, majestic, and we're all suitably awe-struck. And delighted, as well, that our obscenely early start has paid off – Ben's idea, so we can get a jaw-dropping time lapse in the can and reveal this fabulous creature in the best possible light – against the stunning reds, blues and oranges of a classic desert sunrise.

'Though no quips,' he makes me promise, 'about a new dawn of aviation.'

I'm not embarrassed to note that the butterflies in my

stomach are taking flight. I'm looking at one of the two aircraft future leaders of the free world are going to travel on. And I am going to step aboard it before any of them.

It is no secret that the procurement of these replacement aircraft for the ageing VC-25A Boeing 747-200 variants has been fraught with problems and political intrigue. The original order, placed by President Obama, was to build from scratch two new presidential aircraft that would meet the capability and connectivity needs of the modern world. When Donald Trump took office in 2017, however, this was one of the projects that was in his sights for 'recapitalization', on the basis that it was far too expensive. This threw all the plans into turmoil.

There were also rumours that Airbus was going to pitch an A380 variant, to be built in Melbourne, Florida, right in the President's backyard. This threat of competition prompted the teams at the USAF and Boeing to come up with a more economical alternative: the modification of two existing aircraft that, back in 2013, had been built for the Russian airline Transaero, which had folded before taking delivery. At just $9.8 billion for the pair, they could easily provide the savings the President wanted.

Politics and cost could not be further from my mind, however, as I'm introduced to some of the team who are here to take delivery, including Bob, an experienced engineer who is project-managing the new VC-25B programme, and Brett, one of the pilots from the Presidential Airlift Group (PAG), who will be flying with the aircraft from here to San Antonio.

Bob takes me on board, the better to show me what future presidents can expect when the refit is finished. We enter via steps at door two left and emerge into a galley, clearly designed by the previous owners. It's pretty weird to be standing on a future symbol of the USA and see all the signs are in Cyrillic.

Bob explains that most of what's in here is going to be stripped out. 'Except that,' he says, nodding towards what an estate agent would probably call a 'feature' staircase. The feature being that, unusually, it has a window at the top, something never normally seen on a 747. That aside, though, everything else is going to go. This aircraft is going to be taken back to its very bones.

As we head up the stairs, Bob delivers a warning. 'Don't use the toilets. This is a delivery-prepped aircraft, and they might not work as advertised.' He chuckles then, because 'might not' obviously means 'won't'.

The pre-handover inspection takes most of the morning, while our small film crew get our kit set up and start capturing what we can – establishing shots, plus some footage of the interior and exterior. Then, with the deal finally done, Bob invites me to board the aircraft again. 'So you'll be the first to step on board the USAF's VC-25B,' he says, grinning. This guy clearly understands my psyche all too well. So I climb the steps again, this time to the accompaniment of a drum roll in my head, to mark the significance of the moment. After all, there can only be one first.

I can hear other feet coming up the stairs behind me now. It is 'team aviator', the pilots from Boeing and the USAF who will be taking their new asset on a short flight to San Antonio in Texas, where, over a period of approximately three years, in theory, both it and its counterpart are to be transformed into identical flying White Houses.

I have already got to know these guys, having met with them in preparation for the documentary, and as a fellow pilot I know how big a day this is for them. They look as excited as I am to see this baby fly. However, this isn't going to happen quite as quickly as they had hoped. One of the pilots obviously didn't get Bob's memo; he's already used and flushed the upstairs loo. This has resulted in 'liquid' now coming through the roof of the business-class cabin.

As with anything in aviation, though, there is always an engineering solution and, having stemmed the flow, the engineers quickly jury-rig a machine normally used to blow conditioned air into aircraft. The dry desert atmosphere is now everyone's friend. Within an hour, you'd never know that the incident had even happened. Disaster averted.

With the USAF's newest purchase now ready to make its onward journey to San Antonio, our next task is to capture the moment. Well, two moments. In order to test the capability and, equally important, check that the brakes work, the aircraft first needs to execute a rejected take-off.

Mark, Ben and I set up shop at the edge of the taxiway, watching through the heat haze as the engines spool up. The aircraft, which had looked almost dormant until now, finally bursts into life. It begins taxiing straight towards us – the shot we were after – and watching this behemoth moving under its own power feels way more emotional than I expected. We're soon blasted by the hot jet efflux and bombarded with the smell of jet fuel and, strange to say, perhaps, when under such a sensory assault, my smile's probably visible from space.

As the aircraft nears the end of the runway, we jump into one of Boeing's SUVs (the one we came in obviously not being allowed on the airfield) in order to capture the moment. The brilliant white aircraft does not disappoint. Just as it approaches us, the roar of the engines abruptly abates and changes tone. Then the spoilers deploy, the nose immediately dips, and this super-sized aircraft, with all that momentum, decelerates and quickly comes to a graceful halt.

Now it's time for the actual take-off, the end point of this new beginning, and, once again, the desert heat is our friend. Though the lie of the land means we can't capture the moment when the wheels leave the ground, the next thing we see is straight out of Hollywood. First the lights, super bright, then the haze and the shimmer, then two vortices from the wing tips, producing perfect spiral patterns as it climbs, impossibly gracefully, into the sky.

As moments in aviation history go, it feels massive. The nation has just bought its new Air Force One. And only a handful of people know anything about it.

While April has seen us bearing witness to the ushering in of a new order, August is all about the present incumbent. We're now in Washington DC, which is reliably hot and humid, so as Ben, Mark and I cross the Potomac River into Maryland we are grateful for our car's cold, conditioned air.

Our destination this morning is a rather less photogenic hangar within Joint Base Andrews, the home of PAG, the Presidential Airlift Group. This is the team responsible for operating the current fleet of two VC-25A (747) aeroplanes. Since these aircraft provide transport exclusively for the serving president and his invited guests, it is one of the most secure military facilities on the planet.

Develyn is once again there to greet us, this time at the gate rather than in the middle of the desert, but the sense of what a big deal security still is becomes quickly apparent. Though I'm obviously not at liberty to divulge any part of it, the process is multi-layered and takes a good thirty minutes, much of it taking place outside, leaving us all gently broiling in the unrelenting humidity. And all this despite the fact that we have already been screened before reaching this point, both on paper and in person. The President is clearly very well protected.

We are at last admitted to the inner sanctum, where we're met by the boss, Alex, and Nathan, one of the senior engineers. We're not filming today. That will all start tomorrow. This visit is more of a pre-filming recce so we can familiarize ourselves with what's what. 'So the plan for the day,' Alex tells us, 'is the full guided tour, followed by lunch. Then we'll go up so you can follow the crew on a training mission, in the—'

I do not let him finish. Did he just say 'go *up*'?

'Sorry, *what*?' I splutter. 'You mean we're going *flying* today?'

'It's only a 747,' he says. 'You fly those all the time, don't you?'

'Yes, but not *this* 747,' I point out. 'And "we" as in *all* of us?' I knew Mark and Ben would be going up at some point in the process – they have to, lucky sods, to film and direct. But *me*? Course not. I'm just the producer.

But yes, he means me. And yes, he *does* mean today. It takes a moment for me to heave my jaw back into place. But Alex doesn't see this, as he's already off down the corridor, the guided tour apparently already underway.

Corridors, being functional, are often lacking in character, but this is one where I'd really like to linger. Running from Alex's office directly to the hangar, it's lined with lots of photographs, acting as a visual PAG history. But there are also many pictures that are more personal. Of the sort of famous families for whom family life tends to be lived mostly away from the public's gaze. They are snaps rather than portraits, unguarded and intimate, and it's an unexpected glimpse into a world few ever see. First families acting like any other families as they fly around the world in these amazing machines. I feel privileged to be able to look at them.

At the corridor's end there is yet more security. Then we emerge through a door into the '747 cathedral' which houses the two existing presidential aircraft. It is, fair to say, gob-smackingly enormous. The first thing that grabs my attention is the huge painted presidential seal on the floor; the noses of both the parked aircraft point at it at a precise ninety-degree angle. There is only one at home today, the other being in San Antonio for some maintenance, but it all looks so perfect, and so beautiful, that we're all lost for words.

'Yup,' Alex says, in response to my awed silence. 'You got it. That's the money shot right there.'

Yet it occurs to me that virtually no one ever sees it. This is not for show. Nor is it like a soldier's belt-buckle, being polished for inspection. It's just a manifestation of USAF's standards. Of their pride in their work. I find it unexpectedly moving.

Now we're in the belly of the beast, as it were, Alex introduces me to John, one of the aircrafts' crew chiefs, and Matthew, the chief steward, who are going to give me the tour of the hangar and the aircraft interior and introduce me to some of the other key staff. We begin our initial walk-around and John starts hitting me with some key facts. 'The jet is based on the airframe of the Boeing 747-200,' he tells me, 'although it is a hybrid of sorts, having the wing that was fitted to the -300, the engines of the -400, and the main landing gear that was used for the -400 freighter versions. The aircraft engines produce 56,700 pounds of thrust each,' he goes on, 'and propel the aircraft along at Mach 0.92, or 92 per cent of the speed of sound.'

I try to keep up with the stream of information. In fact, all 747s can reach that velocity, but they more often cruise at around Mach .86, because to go any faster would just guzzle fuel. They are optimized to fly at Mach 0.855, because at that speed they fly with the cabin almost flat – something much appreciated by cabin crews pushing laden trolleys. For presidents, however, speed might well be of the essence, so, Mach 0.92 it is. The robust gear also allows the aircraft to have a maximum take-off weight of 833,000 pounds (375 T), which allows sufficient fuel to be carried to give an unrefuelled range of 7,800 miles. The President can go far, and go fast.

With my military background, I notice and remark on some of the subtly added defensive countermeasures on the aircraft. But all Alex can say about them is that 'the President is well protected wherever he may wish to fly in this aircraft.' Point taken. Suffice to say the aircraft has passive infrared and active protective measures that would provide a broad spectrum of protection against radar and infrared guided projectiles.

We are now at the front of the aircraft, where the lower-lobe stairs have been extended. The aircraft is fitted with two sets of folding airstairs, allowing it to operate at airfields where they wouldn't necessarily have external stairs to reach the main deck doors. The front stair is normally used for the President and VIP guests, while the rear is used for staff and security personnel, as well as the travelling press corps.

I notice that the engineering team is polishing the entire aircraft by hand and that I can see my reflection everywhere – even in areas such as engines and landing gear.

'We treat the aircraft like it is our favourite classic car,' John tells me proudly. 'But then we take even better care of it.' Enough said.

I am now poised to go on board but, first, a quick brief from one of the 'Ravens', one of which is allocated to each visitor. The Ravens are an elite security force that protects the aircraft and its occupants both at home and overseas, and, almost inevitably, they begin with a warning.

'Don't take anything off of the aircraft as a souvenir,' mine tells me sternly. 'We have goodie bags with everything you could ever want, just please don't take it off the aircraft.'

It's a genuine problem – I mean, who doesn't love a cheeky souvenir? And though members of the public are not allowed to tour the aircraft, there's still substantial footfall; USAF personnel, PAG employees, their families, distinguished guests . . . And with the aircraft supposed to be good to go at thirty minutes' notice, taking anything from it could potentially impact that readiness. So, right down to the pens and cups and presidential M&Ms (red, white and blue, since you ask), absolutely no pilfering.

The Raven then clearly articulates that since the layout of the aircraft is classified, if we reveal it, we will be in very hot water. You may think this is ridiculous – many plans of Air Force One are already in the public domain, after all, and it's also appeared in many movies. But, actually, it turns out it's not. As I will soon find out, there is no plan or film (not that I've seen, at any rate) that accurately depicts the entire layout.

I can, though, at least give you a flavour. Unlike other 747s, Air Force One has three usable decks, all fully accessible during flight, and used regularly. There is the lower deck, normally split into baggage holds in a regular 747, which runs the entire length of the aircraft. As we start our tour, I can't resist asking the obvious question: 'So where is the escape pod?'

John laughs out loud. 'Ah, that is what everyone wants to

know.' Pregnant pause. 'Me included!' he finishes. (Just for clarity, if there is one, I didn't see it. Maybe Harrison Ford knows something I don't . . .)

On this real version, the lower deck houses some large freezer and refrigerated spaces, which we will come back to later, some space for the Ravens' equipment, and three main tyres for the aircraft. There is only a modest baggage rack, however. The rear cargo door is unusual, having an integrated baggage loader that folds out of the hold when the door is opened. Designed by USAF engineers, this is not only practical, but also a security measure, as it negates the need for third-party equipment to come near the aircraft.

Before we know it, we are at the back stairs, where there is a single jump seat.

'That's odd,' I remark, having never seen anything like it.

'It's where the last crew member aboard sits,' John tells me, 'should we have to depart while the air stairs are retracting' (i.e. in a hurry). He explains that if there's no time to make it to the mid-deck, they strap in here and ride for a period downstairs until safely airborne. Yet more amazing attention to detail.

We then go up the stairs on to the main deck, and I could not be more excited at the prospect of seeing the opulence of the most famous VIP transporter in the world. But what I've forgotten in all this excitement is that though this aircraft was delivered in 1990, it was designed in the mid-eighties, and it shows. Yes, it's refined, and it's classy, but it's a world away from the sort of high-end interior you'd see in a private jet or on an oligarch's superyacht. But perhaps that's as it should be. It's paid from people's taxes, after all.

Chief flight attendant Matthew now takes over. He starts by telling us that the aircraft has zones to separate the 102 people it can carry, including the twenty-six crew. And there are lots of them. As well as zones for the press and other visitors, there are ones for the ground crew, for security staff, for close staff and advisors, for White House Support Staff and personal guests of the President. There are functional spaces, communications areas, crew restrooms, meeting rooms and the inevitable office space. Add in private space for the first family, the galleys and the medical room, and there isn't an inch that's been wasted. Nor is there room left for 'creating impact' or 'observing the right feng shui' – but, again, this is a public-funded property, not some business titan's toy.

I sense Matthew can pick up that we're slightly underwhelmed. 'This aircraft has served the nation well,' he reminds us proudly, 'but the new aircraft will give us the ability to provide a service to the President beyond anything that the designers of this aircraft could have envisaged.'

He is not wrong. At over 250 feet long, as opposed to this one's 234 feet 4 inches, the new aircraft already holds the world record for the longest commercial airliner ever built. It's over double the distance of the first flight flown by Orville Wright in 1903, in fact – a true behemoth. It will give Bob, who we met at Victorville, the opportunity to use the 40 per cent more floor space to design something very twenty-first century.

As we move through the aircraft, John and Matthew share secrets that only those working on it would know. The carpets are different colours in each zone – darker ones for the utility and guest areas, and paler in the various White House zones. Those in the presidential zones are adorned with a pattern of subtle stars. Designed by First Lady Barbara Bush, they were specially made for the aircraft. It's no surprise to hear that runs of every carpet are stored in the hangar. If something is spilled, the entire carpet is replaced.

It is also meticulously maintained. It is the job of one of the engineering team to ensure that the carpet is flawless, and if any pulls are found they are shaved off at the earliest opportunity. 'And so precisely,' Matthew tells us, 'it's like they were never there. They're affectionately known as "Timmy's",' he adds, 'after a previous crew chief who had something of a carpet obsession.' (I guess certain people and certain jobs really are a match made in heaven.)

It's not just the carpets that are subject to such close scrutiny. The chair leather is also inspected after every mission and any repairs are a world away from make do and mend. 'To ensure continuity of colour,' Matthew explains, 'the unit bought a large supply of skins, which we had dyed at the same time, and these are stored in an environmentally controlled tannery within the facility.'

There appears to be no detail they haven't considered.

Matthew then takes us to one of the two on-board galleys. Having come from a commercial 747 background, I am surprised to see how small it is. It's also dated, though they do at least have a decent cooker; something we didn't have on 747s I used to fly – they had fan ovens that dried everything to a crisp.

Not that much cooking goes on here. An industrial kitchen is one of many facilities they have here at the PAG hangar, enabling not only the pre-cooking – using *sous vide* – of much of the menu, but also allowing the flight attendants, who are trained to both shop and cook for Air Force One, to source all their ingredients locally – a big security and food-safety plus. Needless to say, this is all done incognito, and I wonder what local retailers might have to say if they knew where their produce ends up.

By any standards, the scale of the catering operation is impressive. With the extensive climate-controlled storage on the lower deck, not only can every passenger have a steak cooked exactly to their liking, there is also enough capacity to take US-sourced and prepared meals for all the passengers for a period of two weeks overseas. The two galleys can also serve a hundred meals at any one sitting, and not airline food either – not as most of us know it, anyway. It is all plated and served as you would expect in any upscale restaurant.

John then takes us into the presidential private space and the first thing that strikes me is that there is no permanent bed here – just two couches that can be converted into singles for the President and First Lady. Other than those, there is just a small chair and desk, and a corridor that leads to their private bathroom. I peer into the latter, to be greeted by sanitary ware in full-on eighties icky pastel orange. John's obviously used to the expression this invokes. 'I believe it is called Sunrise Coral,' he supplies.

I'm also surprised at the lack of opulence, which I'd have at least expected here. Yes, there is a double sink, and perhaps the most bourgeois toilet I have ever seen on an aircraft – it looks so pristine you could eat your dinner off it. But the shower cubicle is so small that any normal person would struggle to even wash their hair in it – not without putting their back out. (And I know all about that.)

It's becoming clear why a replacement is so badly needed; most Gulfstream Business Jet facilities would eclipse this for luxury by some distance. The only thing that strikes me as feeling properly presidential is the stunning abstract tapestry on the back wall of the room. 'This wall hanging,' John tells me, 'was designed and commissioned by First Lady Nancy Reagan.'

It's beautiful. Reminiscent of a California sunset over the Pacific. Amid all the eighties naffness, it genuinely feels like a true piece of art.

Back in the President's office space, Matthew again points out the wooden desk that naturally dominates. Though hard to spot with the naked eye, the surface isn't quite horizontal but set to three degrees off, to mirror the angle of the aircraft when cruising, he explains.

He also shows us the storage that's built in behind. During his tenure, President Clinton would travel with an attaché case, which he would routinely place on the bureau behind the desk. During take-offs and landings it would shift and scratch the wood, so, since the grain meant the entire top needed constant replacement, someone came up with the idea of fashioning a purpose-built safety tray that would stop the briefcase moving around.

After his final flight as President, Clinton was presented with the tray by the crew, together with an explanation of how its existence had come about. He accepted it graciously, but rumour has it that he was mortified to have caused so much hassle. I rather like that little detail about him.

Next up on the tour is the medical room. One important qualification for running a country is that, for the most part, one is completely fit and well. US presidents, therefore, need to have a personal physician – someone who is available pretty much 24/7. In this case it's Sean, a naval commander, who as personal physician to the current incumbent of that office sees him daily and also travels with him every time he leaves the capital. This obviously includes any trips on Air Force One.

The room looks inadequate, both in terms of size and in modern medical capabilities. And apparently it is. 'It's fallen behind what you'd expect in any ER across the country,' Sean points out, 'never mind what should be available to a serving president.' Still, what they have achieved here is impressive. Though size and storage-space limitations both present challenges, this innocuous-looking room can still transform into a potentially life-saving operating theatre, albeit one without all the modern bells and whistles, which will have to wait for the new aircraft to be completed.

Sean is predictably tight-lipped about whether he's actually used it as such, though he does divulge that he's sewn up another head of state's ankle – the only, ahem, bone he's at liberty to throw us.

Our final visit is to the largest room on the aircraft, the conference room, where John introduces us to Cassie, one of the aircraft's three communication specialists. There is always a minimum of three of these specialists on board, jointly responsible for the eighty-five telephone lines, the internet and the secure communications that the flying White House needs.

'Back in 1985,' Cassie tells us, 'the world was very different. When they designed the architecture of this aircraft, they could never have imagined the capability of something as simple as an iPad, and how to connect it to the aircraft in a secure way.'

Could any of us? I think. Probably not. While the aircraft has been upgraded several times in terms of its communications capabilities, the vulnerabilities of this were really only exposed during the immediate aftermath of the 9/11 attacks, when, it having been assessed as the safest place for him, President George Bush boarded Air Force One in Florida with a plan for him to remain airborne till it was deemed safe to land. It was soon evident, however, that Bush could not lead his nation from thousands of feet up, so they were soon forced to land at a remote USAF air base.

It really does feel a world away from what's now planned for and needed – communications so sophisticated that the

President will have the capability to transmit live-streamed TV from the airborne Oval Office.

It is now time to get airborne ourselves, and we're invited to join the brief with the three main Air Force One pilots. Alex, Brett and Jason are accompanied by Mike the navigator, causing a bit of a double-take, since the 747 was the first airliner designed not to have one. In fact, no commercial airliner has since the early 1970s. But this is not a commercial Jumbo; it requires and has military-grade systems, which makes its operation a great deal more complex.

Not that we'll be needing those today. We're only off to a small airfield in Delaware, to practise RNAV approaches, for the pilots' own training and recency requirements.

Though, of course, with no president aboard the aircraft today, our callsign will be Venus 02, rather than Air Force One. And by 'president', I mean 'current president'. While former presidents retain their title for life, the associated callsign does not. It's why in 2018, when former President George Bush Jnr travelled on the aircraft to and from Washington with the coffin of his late father, former President George Bush Senior, the callsign prefix was not Air Force One but SAM, for Special Air Mission.

As is this mission, of course. But I'll settle for Venus. I feel lucky to be here at all.

After the briefing we process through yet more security, then it's back into the hangar, to see the vision of the VC-25A now out on the ramp, sparkling beguilingly in the late-afternoon sun. And as our Raven greets each of us in turn with a salute and a 'welcome aboard, sir!', I do, undeniably, feel a bit special.

Which is what, I reflect, this minute attention to detail is all about. With such an unwaveringly high standard comes a sense of security; whatever is going on in the world, this place represents safety, dependability, a sense that all will be well. And their immense pride in that ethos really shows. Air Force One is both a symbol of the nation and a visual reminder of the strength of the presidency, and everyone's pride to be a part of that is palpable.

While I settle into the presidential guests area with Develyn and we strap ourselves in, Alex and team head upstairs with Ben and Mark. Before take-off, they are going to practise their departure processes, including something that's unique to Air Force One and colloquially known as 'The Show'.

'The Show', which they practise regularly to keep it pin-sharp and polished, is a piece of political theatre designed by Ronald Reagan as a method of getting from Marine One to Air Force One. Marine One is a helicopter and, as it was normal for it not to be shut down during any transfer, the walk to Air Force One was a noisy and undignified business, with little opportunity for a photogenic 'presidential moment', due to the turbulence caused by the rotor blades. Perhaps in a case of 'once an actor always an actor', Reagan decided that a far better approach would be for him to remain on Marine One until it was fully shut down and only then make the short walk to the steps of the waiting aeroplane, climb them, turn around, wave and enter. This ensured that the focus would be at all times on the POTUS – a carefully timed and choreographed piece of theatre devised by someone who knew the value of onscreen focus.

It's only once we are moving that I notice another bit of subtle presidential branding. As the aircraft turns, sunlight on the wing reveals the lightest of artistic touches – the letters USAF in pale blue and its logo. Since no aircraft or drone would ever be allowed to fly above Air Force One, this really seems the ultimate expression of privilege – only the very few lucky enough to be on board will ever see it. One of whom is me, and I'm still having to pinch myself.

We're airborne, and when Matthew tells me I'm free to join the boss on the flight deck I'm unbuckled before he's even finished the sentence. Anyone who has flown 'the classic', as the Boeing 747-200 variant is known, would certainly recognize AF1's flight deck as being of that era, but this one has had a few upgrades. There are the two operating pilots' seats, with the flight engineer in the middle, and his array of dials and gauges off to the right. There is also a third pilot's seat, today occupied by Brett, and, behind him, an entirely standalone navigator station equipped with modern GPS equipment and radios that cannot easily be integrated into an ageing jet, plus some other military elements I'm not at liberty to talk about. As we cruise above the cloud layer, Alex points to where the primary flying displays have been upgraded to digital to allow them to fly in RVSM airspace and carry out GPS approaches.

Operating an aircraft that's largely out of service is challenging. When no one carries spares, you either need to have replacement parts manufactured as one-offs or haunt aircraft graveyards and do a bit of pilfering. It's one of several reasons why the cost per flight hour for this aircraft is in excess of $250,000, some $200,000 more than the $50,000 per flight hour you'd expect for a standard 747-8i. No wonder they are keen to get the new models up and running.

It's not just about cost, though. It's also about safety. The new capabilities – TCAS, GPWS, Autoland and GPS – will be game-changers. Indeed, the only capability that will be lost in the new aircraft is this one's ability to conduct air-to-air refuelling. Once again, though, we are living in a very different age; its extended range means it simply won't be needed.

I let Alex get back to flying the aircraft and as we carry out a few approaches at the airfield I wonder about the people on the ground looking up. Are they wondering who is up here too?

'How was that?' Alex asks as I follow him down the stairs.

'I have no words to describe how privileged I feel right now,' I answer truthfully.

He salutes the airman who is stationed at the bottom, then turns back to me.

He chuckles. 'We get that a lot.'

While I've been busy ticking off another item that wasn't even on my bucket list, back in San Antonio at the Boeing Defense facility known as 'Big Texas', work on the new aircraft has been gathering pace. By the time of our next trip in the autumn, to film work on the strip-down of the aircraft, they have already made remarkable progress. Engines have been removed. Internal niceties have gone. And one of them is already up suspended in a cradle, ready for the big event we've come to film: two enormous cuts in the fuselage for the placement of the fore and aft airstairs.

The two aircraft I saw in August were obviously manufactured from scratch, so built around two frames specifically positioned to support them, but not so here. The new aircraft were designed and built without these kinds of stairs in mind, and reconfiguring them now is a very big deal. In cutting such enormous holes, they could twist the entire aircraft, turning it into instant scrap metal. It doesn't even bear thinking about.

Bob, however, seems unperturbed. 'These supporting frames and jacks can detect even the smallest change in aspect of the aircraft,' he reassures me, 'and will compensate to prevent a catastrophe.'

They had better. As we watch the bigger of the holes being cut, it's hard to tell if any of the engineers are nervous. If they are, they're not showing it, but perhaps that's because I'm absorbing all their stress for them. The stakes are so high that, despite this being absolutely not my problem, I find that I'm holding my breath. On they go, cutting, then checking for stability, then, when they are satisfied, cutting again — till there is a hole in the fuselage you could drive an SUV through. I am in awe, not only of how calm they all are but at their confidence in their skill; they know that at no point will they fatally wound this nascent symbol of a nation.

Though rather less visually dramatic, the work inside is just as complex and challenging. I'm here part way through a complete electrical strip-down. 'The aircraft was built as a civilian airliner,' Bob explains. 'So we need to strip out the normal wiring and replace it with shielded military-spec stuff.' This is no small feat. There is a complex web of over a million feet of wire, all of which has to come out and be replaced. The sheer scale of the task is mind-blowing. At least for me: I speak as someone who is incapable of even rewiring a plug.

And that is just the start. Once the new wiring is in place, the task of installing the components of the internal design plans begins. There will be the updated galley spaces Matthew so needs, and a medical space for Sean that will rival any modern ER, complete with equipment that will ensure that even major surgical procedures can be undertaken on board. Cassie and her team will get the extra communications space they were hoping for, and John's team will get a modern and modular interior — one that is both easy to maintain and replace when it suffers the inevitable rigours of use. Bob and his team are building an icon, no less, that will serve US presidents for at least another thirty years.

Yet I am astounded that even with all this work it is still apparently cheaper to do it this way than to build from scratch. I know the $9.8 billion price tag was considered a bargain at the time, but we've since had a global pandemic to deal with and, with the inevitable delays and connected supply-chain issues, it no longer seems quite the deal it once was. It's way over budget now, too. But politics being politics, a refit it shall be; to have purpose-built new aircraft would have meant the President who ordered the jets taking some credit, and given the political tensions of the time, that was never going to happen, was it?

Perhaps the most controversial aspect of this project, however, is the paint job: the proposed new Air Force One livery. The current aircraft are adorned with a design by Raymond Loewy, from a vision imparted by First Lady Jackie Kennedy and completed in 1962. Though it originally included red and white along with her signature baby blue, tensions with the Communist East at that time meant the red was removed, leaving the white and blue everyone has long been used to seeing on the majority of the USAF's VIP aircraft.

As part of the launch of the new fleet, however, President Trump decided to change the livery again – taken from the palette of colours used in the United States flag, he ordered a much bolder red, white and blue. Though perhaps for some this was logical, it proved highly controversial, attracting a negative reception from a broad church of critics.

It was no surprise then, that after President Biden's inauguration one of the first questions put to his press secretary was 'will the President change the livery of Air Force One?'

The answer was a swift and simple: no.

For a while, therefore, the new aircraft were to be delivered with the familiar white and baby blue livery. As I write, though, it seems President Trump's choice of colour scheme might make a resurgence.

In any case, with its state-of-the-art avionics, Air Force One's future is assured, along with the safety of their high-profile passengers. And rightly so. However, first generation Jumbo avionics were far from sophisticated, and, in one case – difficult as it might be to believe – not only led to tragedy but also, potentially, a major conflict.

11. Getting Lost

How do aircraft crew know where they are? I'm not talking about the discombobulation of jetlag, by the way. It's a serious question. And though the obvious answer is 'by navigating, of course', how does navigation actually work in the twenty-first century?

In a much more sophisticated way than it used to. Due to what has been arguably one of the landmark advances in aviation safety, modern aircraft are able to accurately define their position to within metres.

It's May 2019, and I'm currently 38,000 feet over Nevada, just pulling myself out of the captain's seat. I've spent two and a half hours there, but the time has passed quickly. I'm flying today with one of my best pilot friends, Lyndsay, and while we've been monitoring the aircraft's progress across the continent, we've had time for a natter, as friends do.

I'm not the pilot flying today, though. I'm what's referred to as the 'heavy', and before quips come to mind about my chronic sausage-roll habit, the term 'heavy' is not about me.

On all long-range flights, such as this one to Los Angeles, we have a third pilot, 'the heavy', and this is my role today. The term's origin is from the callsign suffix that is given to aircraft weighing 136T (3 million pounds) or more, e.g. Speedbird 269 Heavy. It indicates that the aircraft is likely to cause significant wake turbulence due to its weight, but in our context these aircraft are also the ones that normally fly for longer, so need a relief pilot to allow the others to rest. This is where the nomenclature of 'heavy pilot' comes from; they are only found on 'heavy' aircraft.

As 'the heavy', my duties today are a little different than on a normal flight. Once the aircraft is safely airborne and heading towards the cruise, I will go to the bunk area for a rest. This rest period on most flights would be split equally into three, with the operating pilots heading back to their seats no less than sixty minutes before landing.

We're now at that point, so I relocate to the middle seat, slightly behind the two flying, and listen to their brief for the approach and landing into LAX.

Lyndsay is landing the aircraft today so will lead the brief for the STAR (Standard Terminal Arrival), i.e. how we get near the airport, and will also perform the final approach procedure. This afternoon, we will be following the ANJLL (Angel) 4, which is RNAV (random navigation) STAR, then on to the RNAV (GPS) approach for runway 24R (right) at LAX.

Confusing, I know. That's the nature of codes. But they're very important in aviation. All waypoints have five characters by convention, with some having an alphanumeric mix. They are constantly being added to, and having twenty-six letters, and the numbers from zero to nine, allows for many, many combinations and avoids repetition and confusion. ANJLL is a waypoint on this arrival, and themed for Los Angeles. Other waypoints created here have different themes, like Hollywood stars – HAKMN (Hackman), SHTNR (Shatner), BCALL (Bacall), LEMMN (Lemon), the cool IRNMN (Ironman) arrival, and classics such as MUPTT. They do this at other airports too. Austin, in Texas, has WINDU, SSOLO, GABOO, VADRR and JEDYI.

Any arrival, departure or approach with the RNAV prefix means that there is a required margin for error for lateral navigation on that procedure (Required NAV), for the ANJLL4 arrival that is less than one nautical mile.

On this initial approach the aircraft can use either GPS (Global Positioning System) or IRU (Inertial Reference Unit) navigation. I will come on to these clever bits of navigation magic in a moment, but for now let's just say we have a couple of ways of keeping the navigation error to less than a single nautical mile.

The final approach, the RNAV (GPS), requires even more precision. As we are getting closer to the ground and, therefore, to potential obstacles, this obviously requires less of a navigation error – normally less than 0.3 of a nautical mile, or in some cases, less than 0.1 of a nautical mile (185 feet), so it's very accurate indeed. The smaller the error of the navigation system, the lower you can descend on that final approach before you have to see the ground or go around.

All of this is done using on-board equipment to determine the aircraft's position, and has no reliance on ground beams or beacons to get on to the ground. So that covers the lateral deviation, but what about the vertical?

Each waypoint on the arrival has either an altitude at which you are required to cross or a bracket of altitudes you must fly between. On the ANJLL4 there are examples of both types, which can also be associated with speed control. In this case the aircraft should end the arrival at CRCUS, between 12,000 and 14,000 feet with a speed of 270 knots.

Prior to using GPS for these complex approaches, which often required visual manoeuvring to align with the runway, we would use VORs, or elements of the instrument landing system (ILS), like the approach at Kai Tak Airport in Hong Kong. (Plus, the 'Canarsie' approach at New York's JFK, which I'll come back to later.)

The 'chequerboard' approach at Hong Kong's Kai Tak

Airport is obviously now defunct, as the airport is no more, but it was used because of the proximity to the terrain. It was so named because of the large orange-and-white chequerboard painted on a small hill as a visual reference point for pilots to start their turn on the latter part of the approach. The hill still has this painting on it even now. The approach itself started over Lantau Island and utilized a traditional ILS that used two radio beams, a localizer for lateral guidance and a glideslope for vertical guidance, to guide the aircraft to what would in normal circumstances be a runway. However, in this case the guidance was there to place the aircraft at a particular point in space, where, if they were visual with the buildings and chequerboard, they would execute a visual, 47-degrees right turn to allow them to land on the runway. If they weren't visual by that point, they had to go around; continuing to follow the instrument guidance system would result in what the instrument chart refers to as 'a loss of terrain clearance', which I imagine is suboptimal.

The visual manoeuvre as they went abeam the chequerboard was done at less than 600 feet above the ground and would see passengers locking eyes with residents of the adjacent tower blocks as they flashed past. Seeing a 747 pulling itself around that turn at such low level has produced some amazing images from inside and outside the aircraft. Although my first Jumbo flight was to Hong Kong, it was after the closure of Kai Tak, and thus I never managed to fly this challenging approach.

Which is perhaps for the best . . .

As Lyndsay briefs for this arrival, she indicates that they will dial 12,000 into the autopilot if cleared by ATC to descend via the ANJLL4 procedure. This will allow the aircraft to use LNAV (Lateral Navigation) and VNAV

(Vertical Navigation) to manage the descent with the autopilot engaged.

When the crew is cleared for the final approach, they can dial up 4,000 feet, which takes them down to a point in space where a 3-degree approach from the runway meets their path and they descend as they would on any other approach, towards the touchdown zone.

I watch all of this from the middle seat as we pass through 25,000 feet. The flight deck is quiet now, Lyndsay and the captain only sharing information about the profile and calling out the differing descent modes as the aircraft copes with the ever-changing winds. Just like me, they are visualizing the descent in their heads and measuring what they are expecting versus what the aircraft is doing.

We are approaching the waypoint KOBEE at just over 2,000 feet above the ground when we break out of the low cloud in the LA basin; straight ahead are the airport and the runway. Lyndsay calls out that she has the airport visual, then at 1,000 feet above the airport checks the aircraft is correctly configured and on speed: 'Stable, Visual, I have control.'

The silence on the flight deck is broken when Lyndsay disconnects the autopilot and autothrottle, a siren shrieking out with both actions. Catching a glimpse of the famed In-N-Out burger restaurant as we approach finals I wonder if anyone is watching Lyndsay land this icon. Of course they are. It's a 747.

It is a wonder of modern technology that we have just flown for almost eleven hours, over some of the most remote parts of our planet, and during that time we haven't needed to use any ground-based systems to navigate. Instead, we have used GPS blended with our own inertial navigation systems. When blended with the crew's high situational awareness, they knew what they expected to see and ensured that happened. In short, they made it look effortless, which in some respects it is, GPS being something most of us now take for granted.

This wasn't always the case. With the invention of flying machines, the first method of aerial navigation was exactly the same as that used on the ground: look out, find a landmark and fly to it, using your Mk1 eyeball.

This was easy when aircraft had limited range, but as the range and capability of the aircraft developed there was a need to develop more sophisticated navigation systems, as visible landmarks weren't always available, when flying over the sea, for example, or at night.

The first step on this journey was the fitting of magnetic compasses, which, in conjunction with maps, could be used to aid air navigation. In the United States they went a little further and developed a transcontinental airways system that combined a 70-foot-long concrete arrow on the ground painted in yellow, co-located with a 50-foot-high metal tower with a rotating light atop it. These were placed at intervals along prescribed routes to aid visual navigation and can still be seen littered across the USA today.

Celestial navigation has been with us for centuries, and aviation has simply adapted many of its principles from the nautical sphere – though it's not easy to get a good star fix when you are bouncing around in an aircraft. Even if you're lucky, you could be in error by 50 miles or so. (As an aside, the C-130 Hercules was still fitted with a sextant well into the 2000s. Navigators had to use this periodically, to prove they still had the skill. On a good night, some could get their estimated position down to 10 miles or so.)

The era of radio navigation was born in 1927, a huge watershed, and started with something called 'A-N' beacons, generally sited on high hills, and used in chains. These emitted two radio signals along a particular course, direct to the beacon itself, a tone that pilots would listen to through their headsets. If they drifted left of the course the tone changed to the signal of 'A' in Morse (. –) and the pilot would have to adjust right to get back to the constant tone where the A and N radio lobes overlapped. The same applied if you drifted right and got the 'N' tone (– .) in the headset; it meant you needed to correct left.

This was agricultural, but it worked. It might also explain why, having to listen to that white noise for hours on end, some of those early aviators looked like they'd been participants in some cruel psychological experiment.

Perhaps partly in the interest of the mental health of pilots, this system was replaced by the NDB, or non-directional beacon. These beacons are in decline, but still in use in some parts of the world. They are dialled up on the aircraft's equipment and, as they are identified by their transmitted Morse code identifier, there is no need to constantly listen to them. The RMI (Radio Magnetic Indicator) in the aircraft displays where the beacon is. You can either fly to it or away from it on constant bearing or, if you have two, you can draw two lines on a chart to determine your position.

During the early 1940s this beacon was largely replaced for aviation navigation by the VOR (VHF Omnidirectional Range) beacon, which was a little more complex. It sent out two signals of differing amplitude and frequency, then through a process of alchemy the aircraft could determine where it was relative to the beacon. When combined with DME (Distance Measuring Equipment), it also allowed the aircraft to determine its distance from the beacon. This gave an accurate fix and was the staple navigation system for airways across the globe up until the early twenty-first century.

Other people, however, were still working on other things. After the Second World War, the rudimentary guidance systems that had been used in Nazi rockets were further developed. In the 1950s and early '60s, these became the guidance systems for the US ballistic missile programme and, latterly, the Apollo space missions.

These inertial guidance systems were first used in aircraft in the late 1960s, and the Boeing 747 was one of the first to embrace them, using a triple inertial navigation system called Carousel. This system contained three inertial measurement units (IMUs) made up of accelerometers and gyroscopes to measure angular and linear acceleration. The system knows where the aircraft starts from and, using a computer attached to these IMUs, knows which direction and speed it has travelled at, therefore a simple speed-distance-time calculation gives the current position.

The Carousel system allowed the crew to enter up to eight waypoints (remember those?) which they could fly between, but it was hugely unreliable and suffered from 'drift errors'. This is when the IMU, after a period, drifts away from the actual position of the aircraft as small errors build over distance and time. In these mechanical systems on the early 747s the drift could be measured in more than 1 mile of deviation for each hour of flight.

In the late 1990s the mechanical accelerometers and gyros were swapped out for a laser-ring gyro. These IMUs provide the same positional output but use a split beam of laser light and mirrors within a rotating gyro to detect and provide the precise movement of the aircraft. These are less prone to error and, on a flight of, say, ten hours, may only drift from the actual position by less than a mile.

The development of the INS meant that for the first time the aircraft had a navigation system that was truly autonomous of any ground-based beacon or transmission. This was a key moment in aviation history.

However, technology moves on. The Global Positioning System, or NavStar GPS as it was originally known, was launched in 1978. GPS, a complex way of achieving a speed-distance-time calculation, utilizes a network of satellites, and an extremely accurate atomic clock on board the space-based hardware allows users to determine their position on the earth. The satellite, which knows both where it is and what time it is, constantly emits that signal, at the speed of light, towards the Earth. A receiver grabs that data, compares it to the time it arrived at the unit and makes a speed-distance-time calculation for that satellite. But when four are used (an extra one is needed to give an altitude) this will give a three-dimensional position.

When this is done continuously, which it is, the GPS unit can start to predict what the next position is likely to be, and this allows it to identify and reject erroneous signals from GPS jamming or spoofing. This is important because erroneous signals sent with ill intent can result in incorrect positioning.

Jamming, the act of blocking GPS signals, is relatively easy; you just throw enough radio frequency noise into the air to block the signal from the satellite to the receivers.

Spoofing is a little more sinister. It sends an unreliable time signal to the satellite, which confuses its atomic clock, corrupting the data sent to the receiver. This produces an incorrect resolution in terms of that 3D position, and this can be either lateral or vertical.

All modern airliners use a blend of GPS and INS to navigate and can easily identify GPS jamming or spoofing and isolate those signals from the INS system, which remains independent, thus ensuring the flight stays on its intended flight path. This kind of jamming and spoofing is currently widespread across the area bounding the conflict zones in Ukraine and Gaza.

Back in 1983, however, GPS, which had been developed by the US, was still confined to military use. Commercial airliners still had to rely on the use of beacons, and the rudimentary INS systems, to help them navigate the globe.

This included a certain Korean Air Boeing 747-200 which had the ill-starred flight number of 007. And which was about to lose its way . . .

Anchorage Airport, 1 September 1983

It was a little before 2.30 a.m. and Captain Chung Byung-in was settling into the briefing for a night flight on his Boeing 747 back to Seoul, carrying 23 crew and 246 passengers. It was the last leg of what had been a five-day rotation, and the start in the small hours hadn't been the easiest; following a previous 747 cargo flight, from New York via Toronto, the layover had only been short.

Chung was flying tonight with his co-pilot, First Officer Sun Dong-hui, and Flight Engineer Kim Eui-dong. All were groggy with fatigue. But at least the weather was benign, and the flight plan familiar; a standard departure from Anchorage, flying over the Cairn Mountain NDB, then the Bethel VOR on the coast before pressing westwards into Anchorage oceanic airspace, where their INS would take them into Japanese Airspace then onwards to the coast of Korea. This route was designated 'Red Route 20' and was designed to skirt the eastern edges of Soviet airspace near the Kamchatka and Kuril Islands, then into Japanese territory and beyond.

With nothing amiss, the crew decided that evening's fuel load and proceeded to the aircraft to carry out their pre-flight checks. Running on time, the aircraft taxied for departure.

It is often said that it is rare that one mistake or error causes an accident or mishap in aviation. But one, a very important one, was about to happen.

A short time after they lifted off, the Anchorage departure controller called flight 007. 'Korean Air zero zero seven,' he transmitted. 'Anchorage departure, radar contact, climb and maintain flight level three one zero, turn left heading two two zero.'

'Roger, two two zero, climb and maintain three one zero, roger,' First Officer Son read back.

By giving them that particular heading, the air traffic controller was doing the crew a favour, trying to cut short some of the departure routing for them, allowing them to intercept their flight plan closer to the oceanic entry. This innocuous heading had set the stage for a catastrophe.

As the crew approached their cruising altitude of 31,000 feet, they were cleared to the Bethel VOR, their oceanic entry waypoint and, as per their SOP, they armed the INS mode for the autopilot. Chung then turned on to a 225-degrees magnetic heading in the belief that this would intercept his planned track in the INS.

A known vagary of the Carousel system was that if you engaged the INS mode and you weren't within 7.5 miles of the planned track, the mode would show as engaged, but the previous mode of heading would remain as the active lateral navigation mode, hidden in the background.

This led Chung to believe that the INS was navigating the aircraft with the autopilot.

But flight 007 was already outside 7.5 miles of the planned track and diverging further with every passing minute.

Without some intervention, it would never get within 7.5 miles of the plan, because the aircraft was using magnetic headings and the INS was using true north. The difference between the two in Anchorage is 24 degrees and at Bethel it is 20 degrees, and this difference would be constantly changing as the aircraft flew west. A magnetic heading of 245 would see the aircraft pass north of Bethel VOR by about 12 nautical miles. This wasn't spotted by the crew, nor the Anchorage controllers, before they wished the crew a good journey home, and lost radar contact.

The flight entered oceanic airspace and the crew passed their estimates of the upcoming waypoints to the oceanic control centre via the radio. They then settled in for a long, dark flight home over the ocean. The INS alert light activated normally as the aircraft passed abeam NABIE, their next reporting point. But for some reason the crew didn't notice their cross-track error was 60 miles and the distance to go never went below sixty either.

The pilot's Horizontal Situation Indicators, a crude moving map of sorts, would have also had flight 007 off track to the right, and by more than full deflection, but, for whatever reason, the crew ignored these conflicting indications.

For approximately the next hour the crew didn't make much noise on the flight deck or contact air traffic control. Some have speculated that the crew might well have been asleep, and I tend to agree. The probable outcome of the combination of the punishing schedule and early start, the short layover not allowing them to rest and recharge, meant they may have been blissfully unaware of their emerging plight.

Meanwhile, at Soviet Air Defence Command, Kamchatka Peninsula, Vladimir, a Soviet air defence radar operator, was monitoring the eastern skies towards Alaska. The Russian ballistic missile test planned for that night had been cancelled, but it appeared that nobody had informed the Americans. They had sent one of their intelligence-gathering RC-135 'Cobra Ball' aircraft, something they did almost daily, and it was currently doing never-ending doughnuts just outside Russian airspace to the east, patiently waiting to garner as much intelligence as possible. They would have a long wait, Vladimir thought.

It was at this point that Vladimir noticed a new radar track on his scope, coming west from Alaska towards the patrol area of the circling RC-135. Another tanker, he thought; perhaps a KC-135, bringing fuel. With the US constantly monitoring Soviet activity, both these aircraft, military derivatives of the popular Boeing 707 four-engine airliner, were commonplace in the area.

Making the reasonable assumption it was indeed a tanker, Vladimir allocated the new track the number 6065 and designated it as military.

The aircraft in question didn't alter its course. It passed the US RC-135, at that time circling about 75 miles to 007's north, causing Vladimir some confusion. So perhaps it wasn't a tanker but another RC-135 spy plane? Either way, it was heading straight for their airspace.

Vladimir wasn't too worried, however. This was another common tactic by the USA: trying to provoke a Russian fighter launch simply so they could monitor their communications and response times. But Vladimir wasn't falling for that one this evening. As soon as fighters launched, they would turn away from Russian territory and a game of cat and mouse would ensue as they both raced towards international airspace. Instead he continued to watch track 6065 as it proceeded south-westward. As it wasn't turning away as normal, however, he decided maybe it was time to wake up his boss, Air Force Commander of the Far Eastern Military District, General Valeri Kamenski.

He was glad he'd done so. Because track 6065 had now breached Soviet territory and was continuing over the peninsula. They needed to intercept it.

'*Zapustit samolet opoveshcheniya!* – launch alert aircraft!' Vladimir's voice bellowed out from the speakers in the hangar at the Russian air force base. Pilots duly ran to their Su-15 interceptors.

Launching into the night sky, their afterburners lit, the fighter pilots thought they knew what to expect once vectored to intercept the rogue aircraft. Having done this many times before, they knew track 6065 would, having seen them, already have turned tail.

But there was no change of heading. Not only did the aircraft not attempt to make a dash for international airspace, it seemed not to react to the fighter jets at all; it simply continued on its south-westerly course.

This was very perplexing. And with the target not having followed the usual pattern, the controllers now vectored the fighters to chase it. This was less than ideal. They'd been caught out and, in trying to predict the actions of the target aircraft, had wasted precious time and fuel.

The Jumbo was flying at over 500 knots, and though the fighters were supersonic, they carried a limited fuel load and their available time at high speeds was restricted, limiting their ability to protect the homeland. (The fuel load was limited to prevent fighter pilots from getting it into their heads that it would be easy to slip into international airspace and defect, landing in nearby-ish Alaska or Japan.)

Despite their best efforts, by the time track 6065 entered international airspace, the two fighter aircraft were still more than 5 miles away. The chase was clearly over. The 'Americans' had beaten them. Their fuel exhausted, they had no choice but to turn back. The aircraft was now in international airspace anyway.

Track 6065, meanwhile, now over the Sea of Okhotsk, was indeed flying over international waters. But if it carried on its present track, it would once again cross Soviet airspace – over Sakhalin Island and the Kuril Island chain, home to the 40th Fighter Aviation Division and the 41st Fighter Regiment. What was going on here?

The 40th was immediately put on alert status and its commander, General Anatoly Kornukov, woken from his slumber by a telephone call from his operations officer, Major Kostenko.

'Comrade General,' Kostenko said, 'excuse me for waking you. We have a zero zero [code for an air defence alert] that there has been a border violation in the Elizovo area, an RC-135, now tracking 240 over the Sea of Okhotsk, moving towards us. That's all for the moment. Distance is somewhere around 500 kilometres. I have sent a car for you.'

'Okay, I am getting dressed. That's all,' said Kornukov and hung up. Shortly after this call Kostenko brought all his alert aircraft to high readiness, and travelled to the base to intercept track 6065. If the aircraft didn't change course, it wouldn't evade his fighters this time.

A little under fifteen minutes later, a MiG 23, callsign 163, took off from Smirnykh airbase and began climbing towards the Bay of Terpeniye (Bay of Patience). Just as this was happening a single Su-15, callsign 805, was climbing through 8,000 metres and was on course to intercept the target if it again entered Soviet airspace. But the fighter controller on the ground, Captain Solodkov, was thinking this target was acting unusually and expressed his concerns to his superiors.

'Somehow this all looks very suspicious to me,' he said. 'I don't think the enemy is stupid, so . . . could it be one of ours?' he suggested. His concerns were immediately dismissed.

General Kornukov entered the command centre three minutes later and issued an order for the target to be destroyed. 'Upon violation of state borders. Destroy the target.'

With the order then given for a second Su-15 to launch, the trap was set; if the target aircraft violated Soviet airspace, it would be destroyed.

Once again, Captain Solodkov expressed his concerns. But when one of his staff phoned the civilian controllers to double-check, they were told they had no traffic in the area. However, civilian radars didn't reach that part of the planet and relied on the aircraft radioing the position to the controllers, and then manually plotting it.

The crew of Korean Air flight 007 had been passing these position reports but had no idea where they actually were.

Fighters 805 and 163 were now shadowing the target some 8 kilometres behind and for the first time in this game of cat and mouse, they could see target 6065.

With the target in sight, Kornukov was keen for clarification.

'How many jet trails are coming from it?' he asked. 'If there are four, then it's an RC-135.' He was expecting it to be a spy plane, and the entire command was falling into the same confirmation bias.

'Unclear,' replied the pilot, adding, 'it is flying with flashing lights,' almost as an afterthought. This was missed by the controller; only the fact that the type was unidentified was passed on to the general. However, Captain Solodkov was uneasy. It was unusual for a spy aircraft to fly with its lights flashing. He asked his staff to contact the civil controllers again. Something didn't feel right about this. Not right at all.

General Kornukov was now also growing uneasy. The target had been identified by the pilot, Osipovich, still at a range of 8 kilometres, and he wanted him to close up to 4 kilometres to visually identify the target.

The target was now only 100 kilometres from Soviet airspace and still making no attempt to change course. Surely, thought Solodkov, they must be aware of the presence of the fighters trailing them? Why weren't they turning away?

Kornukov, meanwhile, had come up with another theory. Perhaps it was a 'friendly' – another Soviet aircraft being used to test his procedures. This sort of thing wasn't uncommon, and he wouldn't necessarily know about it in advance or during the test. He decided to interrogate the IFF (Identification Friend or Foe) of the aircraft's transponder. If it was friendly, there would be a reply.

But the target, Korean Airline's flight 007, was a civilian aircraft. So it didn't have military IFF on its transponder, and could not respond to any request for an electronic handshake. By default, they were unfriendly.

General Kornukov, however, did not factor this in.

'805, interrogate the target,' he ordered. And when the pilot informed him there had been no response, he mulled this information over for a few seconds. 'No response?' he said finally. 'No response, roger. Be ready to fire.'

The 747 was now 45 kilometres from the state border.

Kornukov lifted the phone beside him and was put through to his superior, General Kamenski, at the regional command post.

'Target 6065 is over Terpeniye Bay tracking 240, 30 kilometres from the state border; the fighter from Sokol is 6 kilometres away. Locked on. Orders have been given to arm weapons. The target is not responding to identify [*sic*], he cannot identify it visually because it is dark, but he is locked on,' reported Kornukov.

Kamenski said they needed to identify the aircraft. It could be civilian, and this seeded doubt into the thoughts of Kornukov, though he didn't show it in his tone. In fact, he rebuffed the idea that it could be a civilian aircraft and stated that if it crossed the border, he would give the order to shoot it down. With what appeared to be some reluctance, Kamenski agreed.

Kornukov's doubt remained. He asked the controller to confirm with 805 whether the enemy's navigation lights were on. As he tried to get the information from an unhelpful controller, Korean Airlines flight 007 unwittingly crossed into Soviet airspace and one of the Su-15s, callsign 805, was positioning itself to engage the aircraft with missiles.

'There are nav lights, Comrade General,' came the reply from the controller. This was curious, thought Kornukov. He hurriedly ordered 805 to make some more confirmatory checks. He wanted the fighter to close within 2 kilometres and flash its own navigation lights to attract attention.

This garnered no response from the target.

The general then ordered 805 to fire a burst of machine-gun fire across the path of the aircraft. This was done but, again, there was no response from the aircraft.

This wasn't surprising. The Su-15's guns weren't fitted with tracer rounds so the stream of bullets would have been invisible.

Kornukov was perplexed when 805 reported, 'The target is reducing speed and has pitched up.' What on earth was this aircraft doing?

*

Meanwhile, on the 747, First Officer Son transmitted, 'Tokyo, this is Korean Air 007, requesting climb to Flight Level 350.'

'Clear to climb to Flight Level 350, report maintaining,' replied the controller in Japan.

The aircraft was now light enough to climb to its final cruising level and, clearance now given, Captain Chung selected the new altitude on the autopilot controls and pressed the button to climb. The Boeing 747 increased the thrust and pitched up to start the climb, slowing a little as it waited for the four engines to spool up from cruise power to full climb thrust. The crew, meanwhile, were talking about what they were going to have for breakfast before arriving in Seoul.

Nothing seemed out of the ordinary.

Aboard Soviet Interceptor 805, Osipovich had been surprised by the sudden change of speed and pitch after the target had been so stable for so long, but he was now recovering and slipping back and under the enemy aircraft to prosecute an attack if ordered.

The order came. General Kornukov's voice was loud in his helmet. 'Carry out the task,' he said. 'Destroy it!'

If there had been any doubt previously about the target's intentions, the apparently evasive manoeuvres by the aircraft had clearly sealed the deal. His job now was to obey his orders and down it. He took great care to position himself in the optimum area for his missiles and despite the continuous 'noise' from the command post demanding updates he remained silent, so focused was he on his task of prosecuting the Jumbo with extreme prejudice. And with a roar, two missiles left his fighter and streaked towards the target, now just some 5 kilometres distant.

Far above the coast of Sakhalin Island, Korean Air 007 had just levelled off when a bright ball of light shattered the pre-dawn darkness.

'The target is destroyed,' Osipovich confirmed.

It had not been. One of the two missiles had missed the aircraft completely, but the other had slammed into the 747's fuselage, close to the vertical stabilizer, causing catastrophic damage to the aircraft's flight controls and the hydraulic systems. The massive hole in the pressure hull had also caused a rapid decompression.

'What happened?' one of the pilots on the flight deck shouted.

'Engines normal!' came the call from the flight engineer – an entirely unexpected call, as most would have thought this was some sort of uncontained engine failure, especially after the stress of a cruise climb.

The aircraft pitched up and began to climb again. In an attempt to lower the nose, the captain retarded the thrust, but with only one working hydraulic system this was already doomed to failure and, peaking at 38,250 feet, the aircraft slid into a left bank and began to descend. It then rolled further and established itself in a rapid left-hand spiral descent, sealing the fate of all on board.

Keying his microphone, First Officer Son transmitted the aircraft's last message: 'Tokyo Radio, Korean Air zero zero seven, ah, we, are experiencing . . . rapid compressions. Descend to one zero thousand . . .'

Tokyo Radio couldn't make out the transmission and, 104 seconds after the explosion, both the cockpit voice and the flight data recorders stopped working.

On the Sea of Japan just west of Sakhalin, some Japanese fisherman heard the sound of what they thought must be a low-flying aircraft, closely followed by a loud boom and a flash on the horizon.

Flight 007's journey was over.

As with any tragedy that is mired in political controversy, the truth behind the downing of Korean Airlines flight 007 took decades to emerge.

We now know that as soon as a few hours after the shootdown, it became apparent to the Russians they had shot down a civilian aircraft and, keen to hide their mistake, they launched a rescue effort to recover the black boxes from the aircraft.

The rest of the world did not know any of this. For a few days there was widespread consternation and confusion, until the US leaked having transmissions from Soviet fighters which claimed to have downed a large four-engined target over its territory.

These transmissions were played at a session of the United Nations as evidence that Osipovich, the pilot, could clearly see the plane but, equally clearly, didn't care that it was a civilian airliner.

It was a cleverly worded piece of statecraft on behalf of the USA. The Russian story was slowly unravelling, and the Soviets needed to take control of the narrative, hence the scramble to recover those black boxes before the Americans did, and stop the West having an opportunity to investigate.

The International Civil Aviation Organization (ICAO) was appointed to investigate the crash. With the Russians refusing to cooperate in any way, the ICAO team needed the black boxes; they would be crucial in establishing the cause of the accident. The Russians also refused to cooperate in the Sea of Japan and conducted their own recovery operation, at the same time hampering the efforts of Japan and the USA to recover the black boxes. Most will know that these black boxes are designed to emit a 'ping' when submerged, to make them more easily detectable. Only the Russians could accurately pinpoint the location of the aircraft, and to put the Western forces off the scent they dropped similar devices that emitted an identical ping in areas far from the site of the crash. Soviet divers recovered both black boxes two weeks after the crash and left the area, without any other nation identifying the location. No bodies were ever recovered, although some weeks later some remains washed up on the shores of Hokkaido Island, where a memorial to the victims now stands.

The Cold War ensured that the facts surrounding the shoot-down of this flight were unlikely to come to light, so that void was inevitably filled with wild conspiracy theories. The Soviets fuelled some of these wild theories themselves, suggesting that flight 007 was a spy plane sent there to test their defences, and a number of people – both from the press and conspiracy theorists – openly supported that theory because aboard the flight, it transpired, was Congressman Larry Howard, and, staunchly anti-Soviet, he was a 'legitimate target'.

Other specious theories abounded. One blamed the USA for accidentally shooting down the aircraft while engaging in an air war with the Russians over the Sea of Japan, and another posited that the aircraft was forced to land in Russia and that the entire crew and passenger load had been sent to secret labour camps.

It was only in 1991, when the USSR collapsed and various people wanted to cash in by selling secrets that these theories were proven to be untrue. It was during this flurry of repositioning that Marshal of Aviation Pytor Kirsanov revealed that the USSR had both found the wreckage and recovered the two black boxes two weeks after the tragedy.

While many had always believed this to be the case, this first official acknowledgement led to a search for Osipovich, who confirmed that this was indeed true. In a new period of détente between Russian and the West, President Yeltsin cooperated fully with the US, handing over the boxes and all the Soviet data, including the military communication transcripts. The ICAO, almost a decade after the tragedy, could finally complete its investigation.

The ICAO report came to many conclusions, but one statement particularly stands out for me. Referring to the downed Korean aircraft, it reported that:

> During the period of the interception, the statements and actions on the CVR [cockpit voice recorder] were inconsistent with a crew that knew it was in hostile airspace. There was no evidence that any of the pilots knew they were being intercepted. The FDR recorded a constant magnetic heading of 245.4 degrees from three minutes after take-off until the time of the shootdown, conclusively proving that the INS was never engaged.

As I have already mentioned, it is rare that one thing alone leads to the direct loss of an aircraft. More often it comes following a series of related events that in tandem or in sequence lead to catastrophe. The airline industry has always been brutally honest and open about our mistakes, so that others can learn and avoid repeating those missteps, and in this case the ICAO report highlighted the lack of rigour in mode checking and navigation – something that's since been addressed, as you'll recall from our LAX landing at the start of this chapter.

But the tragedy had an even greater positive impact on aviation safety than most would imagine, extending even into our everyday lives. Just months after the crash President Ronald Reagan authorized the military Global Positioning System (GPS) for civilian use, which promised to make transoceanic and other navigation more accurate, and therefore much safer.

While GPS alone may not have saved flight 007 from its navigational error, the moving map displays that accompany this system would have undoubtably made it easier to spot errors. The system became commonplace in airliners from the 1990s, so one important legacy of this tragedy has been the proliferation of GPS, which is now in everything from our cars to our smart devices.

It is everywhere. In fact, I cannot imagine the world functioning without it.

One last observation. Technology and pilot training have come a long way since 1983 and it's reasonable to assume this type of incident has now been consigned to the history books. Sadly, it hasn't been. As recently as 2014, a Russian Buk missile downed a Malaysian Boeing 777 over Ukraine, and in 2020 Iranian Air Defence Forces misidentified a Russian 737 as a cruise missile and shot it down as it climbed away from Tehran International, with the loss of all on board.

There is no panacea to solve this. As long as there are political tensions and humans willing to launch weapons against others, we will have to do our best to avoid getting into those situations in the first place. Though the legacy of Korean Air Flight 007 has, to some extent, been mired in conspiracy theories (and, I dare say, in some quarters, still is), in reality, whether on the ground or in the air, this was nothing more than the outcome of a number of mistakes made by humans while doing their jobs.

These human errors are the biggest threat to aviation

safety. It is why airlines invest significant time and effort in not only improving pilots' technical skills but also developing those non-technical ones that are key to eliminating human errors in the aircraft, as well as those from external, state and non-state actors.

As a consequence, aviation has never been safer. Indeed, in 2024, Willie Walsh, IATA's director general, commented that:

> Aviation places its highest priority on safety and that shows in the 2023 performance. Jet operations saw no hull losses or fatalities. 2023 also saw the lowest fatality risk and 'all accident' rate on record. A single fatal turboprop accident with 72 fatalities, however, reminds us that we can never take safety for granted. And two high-profile accidents in the first month of 2024 show that, even if flying is among the safest activities a person can do, there is always room to improve. This is what we have done throughout our history. And we will continue to make flying ever safer.

12. Learning through Failure

On 9 February 1969 the Jumbo took the aviation industry on a journey which, as we know, would change air travel for ever. Fifty-five years later, it is still going strong, and, with its iconic silhouette and that signature hump in place, it still bears a striking resemblance to the first one. However, as Willie Walsh noted at the end of the last chapter, there is always room for improvement in aviation and the 747 these days is a very different beast to the one that left the factory all those decades ago. The latest 747s are several generations from that first aircraft and encompass the sort of ultra-modern engines and avionics that are expected by airlines across the globe. But how did it evolve over those decades? Did Sutter continue to innovate? Did his 'four of everything' mantra win through? As with many kinds of progress in the world of aviation, lessons had to be learned, and these often came about through failures.

Boeing delivered 167 of the core -100 variants – the one that launched the Jumbo – and the aircraft was in service with almost every major carrier in the world. In general, this variant of the 747 was famed for a small upper deck with three windows and an internal spiral staircase which led to a lounge where passengers could mingle while on their journey. In later variants the lounge was scrapped and seats placed instead on the upper deck to maximize the number of passengers, and the three windows upped to seven. Several special derivatives of the -100 series were also designed to meet the demands of specific markets. The -100 SR (Short

Range), for example, was developed for the Japanese. As they were after a high-density aircraft for domestic flights, it carried less fuel but had 550 seats, all in economy configuration.

This potential for capacity increase eventually led to a request for high-density long-range planes, the -100B being the result. This variant had the ability to carry 486 passengers over a distance of 5,800 miles. The -100SR (Short Range), of which twenty were made, evolved from this and was, again, an aircraft made specifically for the Japanese domestic market. The aircraft was designed with high numbers of short flights in mind, rather than the long routes that were the stock in trade for most other 747s, and, because of the punishing nature of frequent short flights, they beefed up the gear, and the airframe, due to the higher number of pressurization cycles.

This variant was also the first aircraft to have the stretched upper deck that is now so familiar (every other variant since has had it too), and the first two of these were made in 1986. Thirty-four were made in all and, of those, two had a stretched upper deck, which allowed them to squeeze in even more passengers – those two aircraft could hold 586.

JAL operated these aircraft on domestic routes until late 2006, when they were retired. One of these short-range high-density aircraft operated by JAL suffered a catastrophic failure – one that even Sutter could not have envisaged.

Haneda Airport, 12 August 1985

It was a warm summer's evening at Tokyo's Haneda Airport when Captain Masami Takahama and his First Officer, Yutaka Sasaki, reported for their short flight to Osaka. It was the holiday period of Obon and, like many around

Thanksgiving weekend in the USA, thousands of travellers were making their way home for the holiday period.

This flight was also special for another reason. It was an upgrade for Sasaki, who was tonight acting as captain, under the watchful eye of Takahama; if he did well, he'd soon be a captain too. They were joined on the flight deck by flight engineer, Hiroshi Fukuda, who had already completed three short sectors on this aircraft today.

At 18:12 the Boeing 747-100BSR lifted off from runway 15 left and started its climb over Tokyo Bay, turning north towards its destination of Osaka. Some twelve minutes later, however, just as they were approaching their cruising level of 24,000 feet, there was an almighty bang and the aircraft depressurized.

In the passenger cabin it was pandemonium. Anything that wasn't secured had been sucked towards the rear of the cabin and had disappeared out of view. There was no time to think about that, however, because the oxygen masks had dropped from their stowage and passengers were scrambling to get them in place.

On the flight deck, Takahama, realizing this situation wasn't good, had changed the 747's transponder to the emergency code and asked Tokyo control if they could turn back to Haneda. The request was quickly granted, and Sasaki started the right turn, but when he tried to level the wings again it became quickly apparent that he couldn't. He had no control.

It was at this point the flight engineer announced that they had 'lost' all four hydraulic systems, meaning they had no way of controlling the aircraft.

Tokyo control transmitted, 'Japan Air 123 heading 090,' but all Takahama could reply was 'Uncontrol'.

None of the crew could have known that, as they launched

on that flight, a cancer had been growing unseen at the back of their aircraft.

It had stemmed from a repair done by a Boeing engineering team seven years previously after the pressure hull at the back of the aircraft was cracked in a hard landing. The repair had not been done correctly; something that had gone unnoticed by JAL engineering staff. The repair had been covered by a patch, a perfectly normal thing to happen, but its presence meant that the repair, which had been unsuccessful, was hidden. The hull would flex every time the aircraft pressurized and, with the pressure inside the aircraft being more than on the outside, the repair was, due to the high cycles of the aircraft, regularly put under extreme stresses.

The aircraft's cabin is essentially a pressure vessel, not dissimilar in appearance to the inside of a Thermos flask, with the rear of the cabin in a 747 very similar in shape to the bottom of the flask. As the aircraft climbs, air from the engines is pumped into the cabin, and as the rate at which it is expelled is less than its rate coming in, the pressure naturally builds and the air remains breathable.

As Takahama and his crew climbed out over Tokyo Bay the 747 had just started its 12,319th cycle of pressurization, and it was at this point that the repair to the rear of the pressure hull finally gave way, blowing outwards and ripping away the rudder, tail and APU – the small jet engine in the tail – from the aircraft.

The result was an immediate depressurization and a total loss of all four hydraulic systems. Takahama was yet to realize his plight, however – much less the grave danger they were in. Indeed, oddly, he seemed to be taking it all very calmly.

Sasaki had got the aircraft wings level using some differential power, as it seemed the controls were entirely useless. But the aircraft was oscillating back and forth in a sickening way, caught in an aerodynamic phenomenon called Dutch Roll. Sasaki and Takahama were struggling to counter this with their actions on the thrust, and it was becoming harder to think with each moment. Was this the stress getting to them, or was it perhaps something else?

The normal actions for any airline crew in a depressurization scenario are largely common to all aircraft types: protect yourself by taking on oxygen, attempt to fix the pressurization problem, then, if you can't, initiate an emergency descent.

The flight deck crew of Japan Air 123 had done none of these. With the aircraft still at over 20,000 feet, they were becoming hypoxic, and as the moments slipped away their decision-making and motor skills were suffering, although – a cruel twist in an already terrible situation – the lack of oxygen meant they were oblivious to the impending disaster.

The flight engineer called down to the cabin to see what was happening and, although the messages were unclear, he believed that the rear right passenger door had parted company with the aircraft. This triggered an automated response in the engineer's brain, and, despite his hypoxic state, he suggested to the captain that they don their oxygen masks and make an emergency descent. The captain agreed. Yet, again, they did neither.

The two pilots were struggling to keep the aircraft under any semblance of control, and the flight engineer suggested dropping the gear. Although they had no hydraulics, it could be extended using a gravity-drop method, perhaps allowing them enough aerodynamic drag to start a controlled descent.

During this period the aircraft had been pitching and dipping in a phugoid state between 20,000 and 22,000 feet. The captain agreed and the gear was dropped using the manual system. This immediately helped with the pitch control and a slow descent was started, but the rolling continued unabated and appeared to be getting more pronounced. It seemed hopeless, but they did not give up, even if it did seem like they were attempting brain surgery wearing oven gloves. In their attempt to lose altitude the aircraft had slowly slipped into a terrifying dive towards the ground. Nothing but mountains filled the windscreens.

'Power! Power!' yelled the captain as the peaks loomed near his window. Yutaka applied full power and the four engines spooled up to give every ounce they had. The nose reared up and they started to climb, but they couldn't stop the pitching. The aircraft was now nearing 40 degrees nose up, a ridiculous attitude. The high nose meant that they ran out of energy quickly and, despite full power, the speed washed off and the aircraft entered an aerodynamic stall. As the nose dropped, once again the speed began to increase, and the first officer suggested lowering some flaps to assist with the stability.

'Do it,' instructed the captain. The flight engineer selected the emergency flap extension system, which uses small electric motors to extend the flaps. It is slow in doing so, which is important, as the emergency extension is also a simple on/off switch; as a crew, you decide when to start and stop the flap, and it's good practice to do that in short bursts.

The flap was coming out now, and this at least seemed to be stabilizing everything. Perhaps they could get out of this after all.

But they were not out of the woods. It was now 18:48, and with all their energy and focus having been on not crashing, neither pilot now had any situational awareness. 'Where are we?' asked the captain.

The flight engineer asked Tokyo control. Focused on the

basics of aviate, navigate, communicate ingrained in pilots' brains from those first days of flight training, it was the first communication they'd had with ATC for some time.

The controller replied that they were 55 miles north-west of Haneda. Takahama and Sasaki regrouped: they now had to focus on getting the aircraft back to Haneda.

At this point the pilots noticed the aircraft was beginning to roll to the right. The flaps had been extending and were continuing to extend, the left side far faster than the right.

One of the vagaries of the emergency extension of the flap is that the asymmetric brake protection is lost, which means the flap can come down unevenly – which is why it should be done in those short, on/off bursts. The effect of more flap on the left will be a greater lift on that side, meaning that wing will rise, causing the aircraft to turn right. This is not normally a problem, because you can counter this with aileron control input. Unless, that is, you have no flight controls.

The pilots belatedly noticed, and tried instinctively to recover the roll with power, but the first officer mistakenly added more on the left side, which compounded rather than reduced the increasing roll rate. The aircraft rolled violently and entered a steep dive; within seconds they were descending at 18,000 feet a minute. Full power once again abated the rate of descent, but not in time to prevent the right wing impacting a ridgeline. It was now 18:56. Their fight for control had failed.

An American military C-130 aircraft happened to be nearby and, after twenty minutes of searching, sighted the smoke from the crash site. It immediately offered its help, plus the service of the USAF search-and-rescue teams. The Japanese authorities turned them down, however: they would launch their own rescue.

A JSDF helicopter arrived at the crash site just after nightfall. Darkness and poor visibility prevented them from landing, but the pilot reported that they could see no signs of life. Given this information, rescue teams did not set off for the site until the next morning. On arrival, the medical staff found just four survivors, and lots of dead people with what had been potentially survivable injuries.

'If the discovery had come ten hours earlier,' one doctor commented, 'we could have found more survivors.'

The four people who did survive recounted hearing screams during the night, which had faded as the hours ticked by. It was, by any measure, a disgraceful accident response and, for Japan, a national embarrassment.

So, what good came from this tragedy?

Firstly, it was agreed internationally that a rescue response to an air accident would never be delayed again. JAL also took responsibility for not spotting the ineffective repair, and, to prevent this type of unseen spectre lurking unseen until it is too late, maintenance procedures for this type of work were universally changed so that patches, such as the one that had been applied to the repair, were routinely removed and the integrity of the repair itself inspected.

As a part of this, Human Factors Training for engineers was also suggested and is now mandated across the globe.

The airline was also criticized for poor crew communications. Throughout the entire emergency the actual damage to the aircraft was never fully ascertained by the flight crew, despite the cabin crew having information that may have aided the pilots. Although I think it is unlikely to have changed the outcome in this circumstance, as a result of what happened flight crews are now trained to go through a list of questions, and require detailed and descriptive answers from their cabin crew counterparts, to help build a 'mental model' of what the other is seeing, since, in a time-critical emergency such as a fire, small details may mean the difference between life and death.

The last changes were to the design of the 747 itself. Since it's generally agreed that pressure vessels do not break, even in the wildest of scenarios, this type of failure had never been anticipated. However, Boeing agreed to make design changes to the 747 to prevent this type of explosive decompression causing significant damage to the tail. There was also a redesign of the hydraulic systems, introducing 'circuit breakers' that would prevent a total loss of hydraulics – all vulnerabilities that 509 passengers and 15 crew had to sacrifice their lives to expose.

The Jumbo was evolving all the time. That's how engineering, design and manufacturing work. And though, as we've seen, design changes were sometimes triggered by tragedy, much of the evolution of the 747 came about through the needs of the customers. As with the modern mobile – which, in the case of the iPhone, is already at its sixteenth iteration – nothing stood still for very long.

Shortly after the maiden commercial flight of the -100 series, the first of the 747-200 series were delivered to KLM. Made to KLM's spec, these brought extended range and a larger number of options for customers.

There were four core variants of the -200 series, including the passenger version (-200B), the dedicated freighter version (-200F), the 'combi' (-200M), which we met a few chapters ago, and the convertible (-200C).

The convertible -200C aircraft could be transformed from a passenger plane to a cargo variant by using specially designed removable seats. It was claimed that it took only three hours to convert the plane from one role to the other.

The -200C was also the only passenger version of the 747 that had a cargo 'lifting' nose fitted.

Airlines loved the extended range (6,905 miles) of the -200 but wanted more power and the ability to carry more weight over those distances. This led Boeing to sign agreements with General Electric and Rolls-Royce to provide engine options for the 747-200B. The first order for these planes came from British Airways, which bought twenty-five of the first Rolls-Royce-powered 747s with the venerable RB211-524B engines.

For those readers who love a stat or two – and I know there are a few of you – here are some numbers for you to chew on. Between 1971 and 1991 Boeing built a total of 393 747-200 aircraft. In addition to the combis and convertibles, they built 225 passenger aircraft and 73 freighters, in the 'classic' variant, as it is known. The first 747-300 variant was delivered to Swissair in March 1983 and last to Sabena in November 1990. Boeing built only 81 of this variant, and they were predominantly for passenger use (56), as were the combi version, the -300M (21).

The 747-300 was the first 747 where the extended upper deck was not an option but a standard fit. It was also the first variant to have the easily recognized upper-deck escape doors and slides. The -300 also boasted several performance improvements that allowed a Mach 0.85 cruise speed, which was slightly faster than the Mach 0.84 of previous variants.

In February 1989, twenty years after the first 747 rolled out, Boeing introduced the first -400, which was delivered to Northwest Airlines, which operated it on its Minneapolis to Phoenix route.

Although Boeing called its new aircraft a 747, this variant was actually a clean-sheet design; Boeing had started from scratch and improved almost everything about it, while retaining the iconic 747 profile.

This was by far the most popular 747, with a total of 694 delivered, in six derivatives: the -400 passenger model, the -400F freighter model, the -400M combi model, the -400D domestic model – developed for short-range operations and with seating for 624 passengers; and, finally, the extended-range -400ER, made especially for Qantas, and the -400FER (freighter) model, which is the subject of our next catastrophic failure.

There are nine classes of dangerous cargo that are carried by air, sub-divided into two main types. The classes are globally recognized, using an international system of numbers. Class 1 is explosives. Normally, you wouldn't think that you could carry explosives in a passenger aircraft. There are instances, however, in which they can be carried in a passenger aircraft as the risk from them is very low, due to the way they are packed. An example of this might be sporting ammunition for a target rifle, or similar (which would be classified as 1.4G). This would be what is described as a 'Restricted' dangerous good.

On cargo aircraft the rules are slightly different and those limitations that are rightly put on passenger aircraft are somewhat relaxed in terms of types and quantities that can be carried. These dangerous goods are described as 'Controlled' dangerous goods and can only be carried on dedicated cargo aircraft.

All captains, before departing, are delivered, by the ground staff, a piece of paper called a NOTOC (notification to captain), which details the proper shipping name of all dangerous goods carried, plus their UN ID number, and the class and division, plus their location aboard the aircraft. The loader will have already signed this to confirm the items have been packed in accordance with the rules and that the dangerous items are not damaged. The captain must sign this to accept and acknowledge the items on board.

But what if the captain didn't know he had dangerous goods on board?

Aboard UPS Flight 06, Dubai International Airport, 3 September 2010

Captain Doug Lamp and First Officer Matthew Bell, both pilots with UPS, were looking forward to their seven-hour trip to Cologne. After a 24-hour layover in Dubai, it would take them one step closer to home and being back with their families.

Doug and Matthew were driving a dedicated freighter version of the Boeing 747-400 series, one with an opening nose, that had recently arrived from Hong Kong. As the pilots prepared the aircraft for departure, the ground staff were busy unloading some of the freight and filling the newly available space with some more, bound for Europe.

There was only one technical issue of note. The 747 has three air-conditioning packs to pressurize the aircraft, each of which takes bleed air from the engines and cleans and cools it before it is pumped into the cabin to allow crew (or passengers) to breathe. Pack 1 normally feeds the flight deck and upper-deck area, and the incoming crew had had a Pack 1 failure. It had subsequently been reset by the previous flight crew and the engineers couldn't find the fault that caused it. It wasn't deemed too much of a problem, however, because if it, or any other pack, should be faulty, the flow from the other two was still sufficient to pressurize the cabin.

As they approached departure time, with everything looking rosy, they pushed back from their stand on time, at ten minutes before eight in the evening. There was a short taxi out to runway 30R and they depart into a setting sun, which only got brighter as they climbed, prolonging the day, as they leave Dubai behind and climbed towards their cruising altitude of 32,000 feet, navigating westwards down the centre of the Gulf.

It was such a lovely evening that Matthew, who was flying, decided to manually fly the aircraft for a period. He'd only been doing so for ten minutes before the warning horn went off. It was the Pack 1 fault again.

Having engaged the autopilot, Matthew and Doug ran through the checklist to reset the pack. Though that worked, there was obviously something not right, so they made a note that it would need further investigation in Cologne.

The autopilot levelled the aircraft at 32,000 feet and at 20:10 the UAE controller in Dubai asked flight UPS 06 to change to Bahrain ATC on their radio. Doug made the change on the radio and checked in with the Bahraini controller and, with the pack 1 problem now largely forgotten, chat on the flight deck shifted to what they were going to do in Cologne. At 20:13, however, their conversation was rudely interrupted. And by a noise, loud and unmistakeable, that shoots fear into any pilot: the fire bell.

Both looked down to the centre console and saw the red warning: FIRE MAIN DK FWD. This signified that the smoke detection system had activated on the main deck, alerting them to the possibility of a cargo fire. Doug took control of the aircraft, asking Matthew to run the checklist for a fire on the main deck. Declaring an emergency to Bahrain ATC, Doug was offered the airport of Doha, just 100 miles away, but he turned this down, electing to instead do a one-eighty turn and return to Dubai, some 180 miles away.

Doug started the turn and a descent to 25,000 feet in

anticipation of needing that altitude in the upcoming checklist, the first item being to don their oxygen masks and smoke goggles, which both did.

What Doug and Matthew were not able to determine was what was happening on the mid cargo deck. The 747 freighter's smoke detection system doesn't detect heat, and the fire they'd been warned about, having been active for some time, was by now an inferno.

Just aft and below the flight deck, on the main deck, was a pallet of 81,000 lithium batteries. The pilots were reportedly unaware they had these on board; they had been incorrectly labelled and manifested, so were not included in the NOTOC. We will, of course, never know, but had they been privy to that information, it may have changed their decision-making.

Shortly after the departure form Dubai, one of the lithium batteries contained within the pallet had suffered a thermal runaway. This had been the catalyst for a cascading failure; within a couple of minutes there would have been tons of these batteries on fire. With the heat at which the batteries were burning so immense, the fire was quickly spreading and belching acrid black smoke into the cabin.

Back on the flight deck, unaware of what was happening beneath them, Doug and Matthew were working through the checklist. The aim of the list of actions was simple: to put out the fire. This consisted of turning off air-conditioning Packs 2 and 3, stopping air from being pumped in, opening the outflow valves at the rear of the aircraft to slowly depressurize the cabin, then, finally, descending to 25,000 feet, the altitude deemed optimum to achieve low enough levels of oxygen within the cabin to snuff out the fire.

Pack 1 would be giving the flight deck a slight overpressure compared to the remainder of the aircraft, so the smoke would be pulled to the back of the aircraft and any fire would eventually be starved of oxygen and snuffed out.

This doesn't work for a lithium battery fire, however, as they are very quickly self-sustaining and notoriously difficult to extinguish unless totally immersed in water.

Doug now took the autopilot out and started hand-flying the aircraft. In the confusion, and with the high and intense workload, both pilots missed that Pack 1 had now failed again, placing them in even greater danger.

Doug decided to descend to 10,000 feet so they could come off the oxygen, and started this almost immediately. At about the same time dark, acrid, smoke started to billow on to the flight deck. This wasn't good. It meant the fire had breached the fire liner, the blanket of fire-resistant material that enveloped the mid-deck.

'I have no control,' Doug shouted.

'What?' Matthew shouted back. 'No control at all?'

This was a pivotal moment. It meant the fire must now be so hot it was impacting the control wires, or 'elevators', that controlled the pitch. They were possibly stretching due to the heat, and, with even large adjustments, Doug could not control it.

The situation on the flight deck was now dire and, with acrid black smoke enveloping everything, the visibility was almost nil – it was like being in the darkest box imaginable, with a cacophony of wind and jet engine noise overwhelming their remaining senses.

With things now desperate, Doug asked Matthew to pull the smoke evacuation handle, a manual lever in the middle of the overhead panel. This would open a hole to the outside, at the back of the flight deck, which would act as an escape for the overpressure; as the pressurized air escaped, so the smoke would go too.

With this open, things improved very slightly, and at 20:18 Matthew was able to set up the flight management computer for a straight-in ILS approach on runway 12L, the runway they had departed from just over twenty minutes before. Things were now looking up for the beleaguered UPS crew: they now had the ability to autoland the aircraft using the ILS – they didn't need to see for that.

The slight lessening in the smoke was short-lived, however, as they still hadn't noticed that Pack 1 had failed. In reality, the hole in the roof was acting as a venturi and was now pulling the smoke from the cabin up into the flight deck, and it wasn't going overboard in any meaningful way. And just when Doug thought things couldn't get any worse, he started having difficulty breathing – his oxygen supply was failing. This necessitated handing control to Matthew, who seemed to be unaffected, and getting out of his seat to go to the back of the flight deck to get the P3 oxygen mask, which, of course, involved removing his own mask. 'Can't see,' he told Matthew.

Taking control, Matthew put the autopilot back on, which, because it didn't rely on the cables, being connected directly to the control servos, seemed to bring back the controllability.

With Doug absent, both Matthew's workload and his stress levels had gone through the roof. To compound things, he was no longer able to hear Bahrain ATC and, despite his best efforts, could not change the frequency to Dubai ATC as he could not see the radio controls.

He was now reliant on what we call a relay, which was complicating things. He was flying blind, literally, and needed regular updates on his height, distance and speed from Dubai. Because Matthew couldn't see to change the radio frequency, he was now stuck talking on a Bahrain frequency, but as he was now out of range of their ground transmitters, he required a relay. His requests were relayed through another aircraft, a Fly Dubai flight, on to Bahrain ATC, who then contacted Dubai ATC via telephone. The answer then came back the other way, wasting precious time that UPS 06 did not have.

Matthew was now in some weird game of whispers. At 20:36 the aircraft passed through the regular glideslope for runaway 12L but didn't capture it; a few seconds later he started his own descent to 4,000 feet. Dubai ATC relayed down the chain that UPS 06 was too high and fast, and, to lose the height and speed could they execute a 360-degree turn?

For Matthew, the message came too late. Even if he could, he knew he had little time to do so. He dropped the gear and selected full-speed brake, while, in a last-ditch attempt to get down, also dropping all the flaps. He was now at 7,000 feet and descending fast – just passing 9 miles to go to the field. For comparison, a normal approach would have had him at 3,000 feet at that point. He dialled 1,500 feet into the autopilot and armed the approach button in the hope it would latch on to the ILS beam, but was too far away from it for that to occur properly. Then, having slowed, the flaps extended to their landing configuration, which brought on another warning; he had selected landing gear down, but it had malfunctioned, and you can't select land flaps without the gear being down,

'Where am I?' Matthew asked the aircraft relaying for him. The reply was not the news he hoped for. He was overflying the runway at 4,000 feet and had no chance of making Dubai. All was not lost, however. Sharjah Airport was on a heading of 095, at a distance of 10 miles – and he was perfectly positioned for a straight-in approach.

This was the last throw of the dice for UPS 06. Matthew

reached up to the autopilot controls and accidentally dialled in the heading of 195, rather than the needed 095. The aircraft turned right, away from Sharjah, and as it did so the bank angle warning started to shout, warning of an overbanking situation.

Matthew instinctively disconnected the autopilot, and that action unexpectedly threw the aircraft into a 14 degrees nose down attitude. The aircraft was now pointing at the suburb of Silicon Oasis and, realizing, Matthew pulled back with all his might. Due to the reduced effectiveness of the elevators because of the cable damage, however, this meant little change. As the speed increased, that little amount of elevator deflection had a greater effect, resulting in a slight dive recovery, sufficient to mean he cleared the housing estate.

The decaying speed reduced the effectiveness of the elevators again, and the nose dropped. At 20:41 UPS 06 impacted the ground and both men on board sadly perished. That there were no fatalities on the ground was due to the tenacity of Matthew, who fought with the aircraft all the way to the end.

Having read this account, I am sure that many of you will be wondering why the captain elected to return to Dubai and not take the closer option of Doha. It is easy for us armchair pilots (some professional ones, too) to look at this decision from the comfort of our homes and conclude it was the act that doomed the aircraft.

The reality was that it almost certainly was not. This was a fire so intense, and so severe, that in every scenario the investigators ran – to Doha, Bahrain and Dubai – the outcome was likely to be the same. The controls and oxygen would have been compromised at the same time, and the fire would have reached its peak well before a safe approach to any of them could have been carried out.

But there were things to learn from this tragedy for both pilots and passengers, and the obvious place to start is the cause of that out-of-control fire. Almost everyone is aware of the term 'lithium battery' because, these days, they are in almost every electronic device we own, whether it be a laptop, a mobile phone, or even hair straighteners. Every electronic item with a lithium battery presents the same risk to the safety of an aircraft as we tragically saw here with this UPS crew.

This is the reason none of these items should ever go in your hold baggage and why the limits and restrictions airlines place on them should always be complied with. Not all lithium-ion batteries can be carried on passenger aircraft and you really do need to check if yours is permitted, especially if it is an unusual device – for example, certain drone batteries are prohibited, but that's far from all. Neither you nor I can predict how or when a battery will combust, although those dropped or damaged are more likely to.

The second thing learned was perhaps the most obvious in hindsight: to add thermal detection into these vast cargo spaces so that fires, no longer reliant upon the build-up of smoke to trigger an alert, can be detected much faster.

The third was making the containers freight is shipped in more fire-resistant. And the final change was the invention of something called the Emergency Vision Assurance System (EVAS). This is a simple solution that counters the problem of not being able to see either instruments or the outside when the flight deck is full of smoke.

EVAS is a square-shaped, transparent, large inflatable balloon – a clear air void that can be placed on instruments or windows which, when a pilot presses their goggles or facemask against it, allows them to see through. An EVAS can even be shaped to inflate in the entire window space of specific aircraft, so that when inflated it is held in place by its own volume. A genius idea that directly resulted from this tragedy.

As an industry, aviation is working hard to have less of an impact on our fragile planet and is investing billions in innovative schemes to support that. Many are aware of this, but what might be less widely known is that the impact of climate change is already being felt by airlines.

Paul Williams, Professor of Atmospheric Science in the Department of Meteorology at the University of Reading, has been studying atmospheric turbulence for some time, and has discovered that climate change could as much as treble the amount of severe turbulence in the atmosphere. This has led him to develop an award-winning new aviation turbulence forecasting algorithm that has already helped thousands to enjoy smoother journeys.

But it's not just passengers who feel the effects of our increasingly turbulent weather. It impacts hugely on that bit of flying that feels, to many, the most fraught: getting those many tons of aircraft back safely on the ground – a job done by pilots, and very often under scrutiny . . .

Like trainspotting, plane-spotting is a harmless pursuit that brings pleasure to thousands, if not millions. Storm watching, similarly, has its devotees, and though, unlike my co-writer, I think the latter is like watching paint dry, but how about a form of entertainment which combines both?

When it comes to entertainment, everyone loves a bit of drama, but I don't think, if we went back, say, some twenty-five years, that extreme weather at airports and planes coming in to land would combine to provide a form of entertainment for the masses; especially in the form of *live* entertainment. Yet that's exactly what has happened.

As with many unlikely concepts that find success in the digital world, live-streaming aircraft battling terrible weather is, these days, pretty big business. It is streamed to viewers from major airports right across the world.

At London's Heathrow during 2022's Storm Eunice, for example, the quirky commentary of BigJet TV's Jerry Dyer as he streamed landing attempts by crews literally weathering the storm, quickly became a global sensation. At some points over 200,000 people were tuning in to watch pilots demonstrating skill and good judgement by either being able to land or go-around to try again.

While watching crews landing in adverse weather conditions has become a titillating TV fix for many, Jerry, whose dad was an airline pilot himself, is acutely aware of the work being put in by those crews to get their passengers down safely.

It takes raw flying skill, obviously, but it demands something else besides – some of the most critical decision-making a pilot can make. When to park your precious pride and to go around for another attempt. And, sometimes, that's exactly what you must do, because once you're down on the ground and those reversers are selected, you are all out of options. And the landing you committed to out of a misplaced sense of hubris may not always be the safest place to be.

What price reputation?

Aboard Qantas Flight 01, Approaching Bangkok Airport, 23 September 1999

The prestigious flight number of '01' was, and still is, allocated to the prime route between the United Kingdom and Australia. With origins dating as far back as 1935, when

Imperial Airways and Qantas operated a series of short 'kangaroo' hops between cities, Flight 01 had also gained the name 'the Kangaroo Route'. Though originally the flight was from London to Brisbane, today it is still used on the Sydney to London flight.

On that September day back in 1999, Flight 01 was captained by Qantas Senior Check Captain Jack Fried, flying a 747-400. As the aircraft was approaching Bangkok the weather there was significantly worse than had been forecast. As they set up for the final approach, the first officer was flying the aircraft, with no idea that just ahead of them another Qantas 747 had just executed a go-around as, due to driving, heavy rain obscuring their vision, they could not see the runway at their decision altitude.

The first officer of Flight 01 turned the 747 on to the ILS and descended towards the runway. Though a little fast and a little high when approaching the runway, they were still well within the stability limits mandated by the company, so they continued the approach. The rain was so heavy now that the runway lights were only visible during each wiper stroke across the windscreen, before being completely obscured again.

The first officer disconnected the auto-thrust and autopilot and attempted a landing. The aircraft, however, had other ideas, and that little extra speed and height meant that it was floating down the runway, now leaving over 3,000 feet of asphalt behind them.

Being unable to see the end of the runway due to the appalling weather, the captain announced, 'Go around.' The first officer advanced the thrust levers, but for some reason did not press the TOGA button which would have cycled the aircraft from the approach mode to the go-around mode. As this happened the aircraft at last settled down on the runway, but it was now accelerating towards the end. Almost immediately visibility improved, and the captain grabbed the thrust levers and retarded them to idle.

Well, almost.

He retarded three of them, the other remaining at full power. The first officer, totally startled by the captain's actions, was now essentially out of the loop. Fried noticed his mistake with the thrust levers, but this had, unbeknown to him, knocked out the automatic braking, and by the time this was noticed the braking did not start until 5,200 feet, almost halfway down the runway. It also meant that he didn't select reverse thrust.

(It's possibly worth noting that, had this happened in 2022, it would have been a great scoop for Jerry . . .)

As the captain stomped on the brakes the aircraft aquaplaned and skidded its way down the runway. Having quickly left the paved surface at the end, it was now continuing across the boggy grass, slowing as it collided with a radio antenna, which caused the nose and right-wing gear to collapse. The Jumbo finally came to rest with its nose on the airfield perimeter road.

Thankfully, it turned out that there were only minor injuries, and the passengers and crew left the aircraft about twenty minutes after they came to rest. History does not record how the passengers eventually made it to the terminal.

Let me take you back to Jerry now, and his filming of those numerous go-arounds, why these are likely to have happened, and the safest thing to do in the circumstances. Every airline has its own safe landing criteria and, although the limits may be different, based on the risk appetite of the airline, they all encompass the same elements. The first is landing performance calculations. As we do with take-off performance planning, we also ensure that it is safe to land

and stop on the chosen runway in the actual environmental conditions, with the planned configuration.

The 747 has different landing flap settings, different braking options and, of course, either idle or full reverse thrust on the engines. Before these settings are decided the weather and runway conditions are taken into account. Is it wet? Is there snow? Are there ice patches on it? All of these affect the deceleration rate. If we know we can make it, then we are good.

It is important to note that all of these calculations assume you land in the designated touchdown zone on the runway — those big white boxes you often see painted on the tarmac. If you are beyond those, you have no guarantee that you can stop before the end, and, where I work, that is a mandated go-around. We don't do guessing. The next element comprises something that is known as the stability criteria. These are essentially to ensure you are correctly configured, on the planned approach path, on the correct speed, and with the landing checks complete, all at a fixed altitude above the landing field.

The threshold for this is normally 1,000 feet but there is some latitude with speed down to 500 feet to allow you to fit in with other landing traffic. If you don't meet these criteria, you cannot land and must, at a suitable and safe point, carry out a go-around.

The last part, and I have partially touched on this already, is that the aircraft must touch down in the marked zone. If you don't, then it is safer to go around and have another go than persist with something you haven't planned for. You can always go around, even if you have already touched the ground, and pilots regularly practise this in the simulator.

What I am trying to highlight in this short incident description is that we don't just pitch up at an airport and 'give a landing a go'. Indeed, this crash, which was totally avoidable, is now used as an example of what can potentially happen when you start guessing, going off piste and 'giving it a go'.

What happened to Flight 01 has become a learning tool for the industry. These days, every landing is carefully planned, briefed and then executed. There is always a plan B, and if we do have to go-around, so be it. We execute the plan indicated by the conditions. It's our *job*. So, despite how it might appear on the big telly in your living room, the only ones getting excited are Jerry and his viewers. In the flight deck it is all calm and businesslike.

The Qantas 747 story has a weird twist to it, though. The aircraft was written off by the insurers and they naturally suggested scrapping it. But Qantas wanted to retain its record of having no 'hull loss' accidents (ones involving the writing off of an aircraft) since the advent of the jet age. So what did they do? They paid a whopping *one hundred million* Australian dollars to repair the aircraft and return it to service.

Again, what price reputation?

Finally, why these stories in particular? As I write, there have been sixty-four hull losses of 747s, any of which I could have chosen to illustrate how our industry learns from failure. All would have been interesting to analyse, and for you to read, I am sure. However, none will have allowed me to convey how we work to safely operate any aircraft, or how they have improved flight safety in a significant way, as well as I think these stories do.

I'm now going to focus on another that does that, one I doubt will need any further introduction . . .

13. Lockerbie

On 21 December 1988 at a little after seven in the evening, Paul Malner, a paramedic in the Scottish Ambulance Service, was out with his girlfriend delivering Christmas cards. They were driving towards Sherwood Crescent, on the edge of the town – the street on which Paul had been brought up, and still home to Jean Murray, a neighbour and long-time family friend.

They were just coming down Main Street when something in the air seemed to change; there was a strange, ominous silence, then a sense of vibration, a low-pitched rumble that in just a matter of seconds grew into an almighty roar overhead. Then a flare of white light as all the house roofs and chimneys lit up and the sky started raining flames and metal.

Paul's first thought was that a military jet had crashed; they'd been doing a lot of training there recently. And though he wasn't on duty – his cousin George, a fellow ambulance man, was on call that evening – he dropped his girlfriend safely home then hurried back to see if he could help.

He had no idea that a bomb aboard a commercial Jumbo Jet was about to see his home town forever linked with one of the most appalling acts of terrorism ever seen in the United Kingdom.

If not in the military or in the middle of a war zone it is almost impossible to imagine the scale of the carnage on the ground when an aircraft weighing over 330 tons explodes many thousands of feet overhead.

I am a military man, or at least a former one, so let me see if I can give you at least some kind of a sense of just how apocalyptic would have been the resulting scene when Pan Am flight 103 *Clipper Maid of the Sea* exploded in mid-air and fell to earth.

Back in the Second World War a new kind of bomb was created, based on a concept invented by Barnes Wallis, the famous aeronautical engineer. Called the 'earthquake' or 'seismic' bomb, it was designed to cause maximum damage to large areas and structures, as a consequence of being dropped from extremely high altitudes, allowing it to gather great speed as it fell. It would then penetrate deep underground before exploding, causing huge craters and doing much of its damage by creating seismic shockwaves – ones large enough to register 2 on the Richter scale.

When the wings and fuel tanks of Pan Am flight 103 landed on Sherwood Crescent, the British Geological Survey at Eskdalemuir, 23 kilometres away, recorded a seismic event registering 1.6 on the Moment Magnitude (Mv) scale – a more accurate extension to the Richter. It created an impact crater some 550 cubic metres in volume, flattening three houses and instantly killing everyone inside them, including three members of the Flanagan family, who lived in Paul Malner's former childhood home. Some 90 tons of aviation fuel ignited and the resulting fire raged through and destroyed several neighbouring homes, including that of his close family friend Jean Murray, where he'd been heading to deliver her Christmas card.

Paul himself, full of adrenaline and anxious to help, found himself, alongside many other locals who'd rushed to offer their assistance, unable to do anything useful. They had no equipment and as one of the aircraft's engines had landed on the main water pipe they were struggling to get water as well.

With the press now converging en masse on the area, fleets of ambulances, some forty-five of them, were struggling to get there. It was, in short, chaos.

Another of the first responders called to the town of Lockerbie that night was Mike Cassidy, then a senior paramedic, and head training officer in the Scottish Ambulance Service. The first he knew something had happened was when while running a training course in Glasgow he was informed via pager that an aircraft had disappeared over Lockerbie, a small town around 70 miles to the south-east, near Dumfries. On standby, and with his young paramedic colleague Jimmy White, Mike set off down the A74 at top speed. They were to get their first taste of the reality about five miles north of the town, when the smell of aviation fuel became so strong it was beginning to catch in their throats, forcing them to close all the car's vents. Not long after that they were ordered by the police to leave the motorway. The devastation at Sherwood Crescent also pushed the edge of the motorway up approximately a metre as well as creating a fireball which set several cars alight.

As the senior paramedic on site Mike's first task was to help set up search teams. There would be several, in part due to the 100-knot winds that had been reported at altitude, the crash site was vast. Substantial parts of the aircraft had come down in six different locations, so they were dealing simultaneously with six critical incidents spread over an area of many, many square kilometres. And though many in the emergency services had begun rushing to the central holding point outside the town hall, the scene Mike found there was one of mayhem. There was so much aviation fuel in the air that radio communication was impossible; with all the chemicals in the atmosphere, the RV frequency would spark. They could only use cell phones. But with limited capacity, and no means to prioritize the emergency services, once the media had descended the chaos only deepened as their communications began blocking the channels.

By now there had been reports that the nose section of the aircraft had landed in Tundergarth Field over to the east, and at least the possibility that someone up there might be alive still. Mike teamed up with Dr Tony Redmond, a consultant in disaster and emergency medicine, and with a local man to guide them they travelled to the site.

The bodies of the flight crew and several passengers were strapped into their seats, and the men quickly established that nobody was still alive. There were the cruellest, most visceral signs of mass death. A very experienced A&E consultant, Dr Redmond had obviously seen a lot, but for Mike, even with his long experience as a paramedic, it felt like he had entered a kind of hell. They spent the next thirteen hours or so in the bitter cold and wet, trampling bleakly in the dark through mud strewn with bits of anatomy, people so recently living reduced to body parts. Everywhere Mike looked his torch was illuminating shattered limbs, chunks of muscle and internal organs. And all around them was the stuff of the futures they'd never have – Christmas cards, letters, gaily wrapped gifts. It was probably a blessing they had so little light.

Having established that no one was alive and with no means to tag anything they found, there was little to be done until it was fully light.

Mike returned to Lockerbie. The chaos had, if anything, intensified. They could only wait and, to help them process the atrocities they'd witnessed, share their terrible stories. Of the woman strapped into her aircraft seat, now lodged in the roof of a house; the toilet door with a man's dismembered hand attached to it. The blonde-haired baby, apparently uninjured but dead, found by a farmer and his son in the middle of a field.

A makeshift mortuary had by now been set up in the town hall, and the fire brigade was running a mobile catering unit, handing out cups of tea and bacon butties to the exhausted searchers. Paul Malner had been deployed with another paramedic to take traumatized residents to nursing homes and local hotels. With little else they were able to do, however, they were sent home at midnight.

Too full of adrenaline to even think of trying to sleep, Paul could only lie on his bed listening to the *whomp whomp* of Chinook helicopters overhead. At 4 a.m., he drove back to the ambulance station. His cousin George, who'd remained out since the time of the explosion, was already there. On arrival, he had made an awful discovery – the body of a young woman had fallen to earth on the grassed area outside the door of the ambulance station. He had covered her body with a blanket, and a police officer had been sent to stand by her until her body could be taken to the makeshift mortuary.

For the first responders and the residents of Lockerbie it was a night of similar heartbreaking discoveries, images they would struggle to forget. And when dawn finally broke over another dark December morning and the extent of the carnage was fully revealed, it felt like the aftermath of a war zone.

And it was. The terrorists who planted that bomb on Pan Am flight 103 had, in pursuit of their political ends, slaughtered 270 people.

The destruction of Pan Am 103 over Lockerbie remains etched in our collective memory and continues to have a profound effect on those who experienced the aftermath and in the broken hearts of everyone whose loved ones were lost.

However, many will be shocked to learn that in 1985 a very similar terrorist event took place – something I only discovered myself while researching this book.

This forgotten tragedy involved the downing of an Air India Boeing 747. It was en route from Toronto to London, and a bomb smuggled aboard detonated in mid-air; the aircraft exploded and broke up approximately 120 miles off the coast of Ireland. It remains the single largest loss of life to terrorists in Canadian history.

The inquiry following that tragedy lasted almost twenty years, and concluded that several intelligence and security failures by the Canadians facilitated the opportunity for these criminals to kill the 329 on board.

The parallels between this and the Lockerbie tragedy are striking. The only key difference is that one happened over the ocean and the other over land. Had Pan Am Flight 103 departed Heathrow on time, it would have suffered the same watery fate – and how much less might we have learned as a result of it?

As it was, a great deal was learned. Just as the crash at Tenerife led to improvements in the safety card and briefing, what happened at Lockerbie has profoundly changed the way airlines mitigate risk when we travel. As you approach the security checkpoint at any airport now it is difficult to imagine air travel being anything other than the tightly controlled security operation we are all so familiar with. 'Did you pack this yourself?' 'Are you carrying anything for anyone else?' 'Do you have any liquids over 100 mills?'

Are we a little blasé? Perhaps. Are we irritable? Often. Was it always this tedious? No.

In fact, as recently as the 1960s you could walk through an airport and on to a waiting plane without being subjected to any more than the most cursory screening. Things only changed after a coordinated terrorism event that took place in September 1970. Known as the Dawson's Field Hijackings, it involved five commercial aircraft, boarded at Frankfurt, Zurich, Bahrain and Amsterdam. It also included a Pan Am 747, *Clipper Fortune*, which the hijackers in Amsterdam had managed to board *after* having been denied boarding on their original target aircraft.

The hijackers, all part of the Popular Front for the Liberation of Palestine, or PFLP, had boarded the aircraft carrying both guns and hand grenades. And while only three aircraft were successfully landed at Dawson's Field, and one hijacking attempted was thwarted, the Pan Am Jumbo, which ended up landing in Cairo, was also full of explosives; all secreted in the terrorists' baggage in the hold. It was blown up only seconds after the passengers were safely evacuated, the first ever hull loss of a 747.

This was the first catalyst for change towards the security restrictions we all love to hate today and saw the introduction of manual metal detectors for passenger searches. It was a start, but progress was slow. The technology, then still in its infancy, was lacking and perhaps unbelievably to our twenty-first-century ears, progress was further stalled by an unwillingness to inconvenience passengers further.

As well as baggage, over 80 per cent of the freight carried by air is in the holds of passenger aircraft, and prior to 1988 it was rarely screened prior to carriage. For freight there were already a couple of mitigations in place. As most explosive devices at the time used analogue timers, having freight stay on the ground for twenty-four hours prior to travel was one useful measure, as an explosion would happen during that period. They would also, from time to time, use sniffer dogs.

But for passenger-hold baggage, there was no such mitigation. Who would want to travel by air knowing that their holiday clothes wouldn't be arriving until the following day? And so it was that, as recently as 1988, it was still possible to smuggle a bomb aboard a commercial aircraft.

Anyone who has ever seen the aftermath of a bomb being detonated will understand the ferocity and indiscriminate nature of the blast, as the shockwaves and shrapnel billow outwards with such a destructive force. Although I have never witnessed this first hand, I have spoken with those that have. Even decades after the event, one of them could still recall the gruesome sights, the level of destruction, and the smells of the aftermath.

When an improvized explosive device (IED) explodes it is often the blast, or pressure, wave caused by the detonation that causes the critical damage. This wave expands out quickly from the detonation point with massive amounts of energy, embedded with high-velocity fragments. We know from forensic recoveries that in the case of Pan Am 103, the bomb, a small amount of Semtex, was located within a Toshiba radio cassette recorder placed in a Samsonite suitcase in the baggage bin (unit load device (ULD)) on the left side of the aircraft, just forward of the wing. Once it detonated the pressure ruptured the hull adjacent to the bin, and the remainder of the explosive wave expanded outwards. This wave met resistance as it encountered the other bins and baggage and reflected towards the hole in the aircraft skin. Assisted by the pressure differential of the cabin, this reflective wave opened the skin of the aircraft like a zip and, a mere three seconds after the initial explosion, the forward part of the aircraft separated, swung to the right and fell away. It's this incredible force that saw the nose cone come to earth so far away from the fuselage and wings.

After Lockerbie, two solutions were looked at to ensure nothing like it could ever happen again. The first was to have

100 per cent screening to avoid anything harmful getting aboard an aircraft in the first place. The second – a more pragmatic view – was to assume something might, and to design baggage containers that would withstand the force of a similar-sized bomb being detonated.

The UK government tasked the Defence Research Agency with the role of providing a bomb-proof solution for the airline industry that would effectively negate the effects of a small explosive device in a piece of baggage. The solution wasn't as easy as many may have expected, however, as building a heavy bomb-proof box was never going to work for the airlines. They needed something that was robust and light, and allowed them the utility the current ULDs provided.

Further research led the scientists to two viable solutions: a composite ULD; and one made of aluminium, which was sectional. When the hard use around airports and costs were both assessed, the practicality of the composite solution was dismissed, leaving only the newly designed aluminium ULD, which performed well in tests. On the final explosive test, with a device the same size as the Lockerbie one, the outcome was not only that the integrity of the ULD wasn't breached, it also showed that the pressure wave surrounding the ULD would not have been catastrophic for the aircraft's hull.

This bomb-proof baggage bin was one that the industry could have adopted immediately. But in aviation, as in many other sectors and professions, rather than just rely on mitigation after a problem occurs, we try to avoid the problem in the first place. The industry therefore decided that, rather than use a costly new version of the ubiquitous ULD they would focus on ensuring 100 per cent baggage screening instead.

But what happened at Lockerbie proved without doubt

that much more sophisticated screening methods needed to be deployed than were currently in use, such as X-ray machines and magnetometers. To give you some idea of the scale of the task to make flying as safe as possible, over any single Thanksgiving weekend in the USA, the Transportation and Security Administration (TSA) screens almost 8 million passengers, plus their hand luggage, and over three times that number of items of hold baggage and freight.

This tradition of screening passengers, however, stayed largely unchanged until 2006, when a new kind of terrorist threat emerged. Following a months-long surveillance operation by the British Metropolitan Police, twenty-four people were arrested and taken in for questioning during an overnight operation in a number of locations involving the terrorist group al-Qaeda. They had been plotting to detonate liquid explosives, smuggled aboard aircraft disguised as soft drinks. Thankfully, the plot was thwarted before it could be executed, but once again security needed to be tightened. It's why, as anyone who travels by air already knows, we can no longer carry bottles of liquid larger than 100 millilitres in our carry-ons.

In 2009 passenger screening evolved yet again, when a man travelling from Amsterdam to Detroit on a Christmas Day Northwest Airlines flight attempted to set off a plastic explosive device sewn into his underwear. The attack ultimately failed (instead causing burns to the would-be terrorist's genitalia and hands), but since he'd managed to board an aircraft with explosives on his person, screening had to evolve once more, in the form of the now familiar random full-body scanning.

By random, by the way, I do mean properly random. Where it would be uneconomic to completely scan every single passenger on every single flight, the arbitrary nature of who ends up getting a full-body scan means that no potential terrorist will ever be able to identify a pattern, making every day a potential day-you-get-caught day.

The investigation into what happened at Lockerbie spanned many years. But one thing that emerged within a day of the disaster was that, just a few weeks before Flight 103 was blasted from the skies there had been a warning of a bomb plot, considered credible. The US Federal Aviation Administration took the threat seriously and cabled a security bulletin to dozens of embassies, as well as disseminating it across all US airlines and associated airports, leading to enhanced security measures on all affected routes. Indeed, Pan Am took the bulletin so seriously they demanded passengers pay a five-dollar surcharge to cover the cost of an enhanced, and very thorough, security programme.

In the sort of coincidence that happens only rarely, it turns out that my co-author, Lynne, can confirm this in person, as, along with her husband and their 22-month-old son, she travelled from London Heathrow to Los Angeles with Pan Am just the day before the tragedy. Just like every other passenger who boarded that flight, she had no idea why it took three hours to clear security, much less why they were asked to stand in line for much of that time, queuing to put all their hold luggage through scanners themselves. The first she knew of the bomb that had exploded over Lockerbie was on waking in San Diego the following morning. It wasn't long before they realized it could have been them; also originating in Frankfurt, theirs had been one of the flights the terrorists had threatened.

So why, given the robust response to the warning, did the plot succeed?

Because where Heathrow had taken the threat seriously and ramped up their security, Frankfurt, where the Lockerbie bomb had been smuggled aboard a feeder flight in a suitcase, had not. The following day it emerged that the security team there had adopted no such extra measures. The bulletin that could have saved those 259 lives aboard the aircraft, and of eleven Lockerbie residents, was found buried beneath a pile of paperwork.

The consequences of the explosion at Lockerbie would reverberate for years. And though the human cost with all that loss of life is incalculable, there was also a financial cost to Pan Am. Following the disaster, public confidence in the airline fell off dramatically. With two horrendous disasters on its record, both involving unprecedented loss of life, the company was perceived, rightly or wrongly, as being unable to guarantee the safety and security of its passengers. Ticket sales, already falling due to a global recession, quickly declined even further, leading to a marked drop in revenue.

While the downing of flight 103 wasn't the sole reason for the dip in Pan Am's fortunes, it was a big contributory factor to the company's decline. Just three years after Lockerbie, in December 1991 this giant of the aviation revolution ceased trading.

Meanwhile, increment by increment, the town of Lockerbie managed to put itself back together. In the days following the disaster local people tried to do everything they could, tirelessly searching for personal items among the debris, cataloguing them and wherever possible identifying their late owners, to send anything salvageable to grieving relatives. Even tiny shreds of clothing, once no longer needed for forensics, were gathered up and carefully laundered; small individual acts of humanity that helped everyone heal.

There were also important changes made within the emergency services as a direct result of what had happened that night. First responders, who'd had to search for hours in the cold and wet without appropriate footwear or clothing, would henceforth be issued with much more practical jumpsuits, as well as waterproof boots. And communications, so badly hampered by having to use open channels, would have a dedicated radio frequency so incidents could be managed without the complicating factor of normal business. It was also put in place that specific phones used by the emergency services would have priority access to the mobile phone network in times of crisis which required a swift response.

For some of those who helped in the aftermath of the disaster the mental scars from what they witnessed will never truly heal. Though offered counselling, Mike Cassidy felt he'd be better off dealing with it in his own way — through conversation and mutual support among friends. But then he started getting nightmares, which were grim and recurrent and, on visiting the GP for a health check two years later was stunned to find out his blood pressure was a shockingly high 210/160. He was just thirty years old.

Decades on, Paul Malner still bears mental scars. He feels that not only were his cherished friends lost that night but that his entire childhood was obliterated. He still suffers from survivor guilt and PTSD today.

There was, though, a small chink of light that emerged from the darkness. Once the damage to the ambulance station and surrounds had been cleared up Paul and his cousin George decided to plant a rosebush in the small patch of garden in memory of Suzanne Miazga, the young woman whose body had fallen there, adding a plaque to mark the place where she died. As with many of the victims' families, Suzanne's mother, Anne Marie, flew to Scotland from the US shortly afterwards and was naturally deeply moved by what she found. And with Paul's cousin George having been the one to look after her, they formed a close bond, and remained in touch.

In 2002 George's wife, Elma, sadly passed away. And in 2005, after conquering his fear of flying, George and his son went over to the US to visit Anne Marie. Both would go on to emigrate to a new life with her in America. And when the ambulance station at Lockerbie relocated in 2012, the rose bush went with it. It is still there, and still blooming in Suzanne's memory.

Most collective memories, however powerful, tend to fade with time. But it's worth remembering that those small inconveniences you face at airport security are the direct result of those who made that same journey to the airport but never made it to their destination. So next time you roll your eyes when you are selected for a search, or when your handbag or backpack is chosen for extra screening, remind yourself that the hard-working security professionals you meet are trying to ensure that you and your family *do* arrive safely. They are there to disrupt criminals that see no value in your life other than as a means of increasing publicity for their cause.

Think about that. Take a breath.

And maybe even thank them for doing their job so robustly.

14. The Human Factor

I open my eyes to find the Boeing 747-400 I'm piloting pointing straight up into space, more like a rocket than an aircraft, and rolled over to almost 70 degrees of bank. The thrust levers are closed, the life-saving speed is washing off and the captain is apparently asleep. What the hell is going on?

'And . . . recover,' says a voice from behind me.

There are some things that are engraved upon every pilot's mind; life-saving techniques that are drilled so thoroughly into muscle memory that they become almost automatic. In my case, right now, it brings these words to mind. They are 'nose-up recovery'.

Feeling the heavy buffet of the impending aerodynamic stall – akin to driving your car at 70mph on a stony road – I push forward on the column to unload the forces on the wings and at the same time apply full power on the four Rolls-Royce RB-211 engines. Once the rumbling stops, I roll the wings level and continue to push forward until the aircraft is once again flying straight and level, and the speed, thankfully, is increasing. As we near 250 knots, I can ease back on the power. Imminent disaster is averted.

A few minutes later, and I open my eyes once again. This time it's to see that the entire windscreen is filled with green. Green, as in the lush grass of the Cotswolds. With the nose pointing to the ground (not a normal view), I now concentrate on first rolling the wings level and cutting the power, before pulling back on the column just enough to allow me to recover in time, without entering a deadly aerodynamic stall.

I navigate the recovery, nibbling at the bumpiness of the stall intermittently as I pull extra G-force to bring the nose up. As it comes above the horizon and the speed begins to decay, I feed in the power to ensure I don't end up back where I started. A second disaster is averted.

Either of the above scenarios can kill you, of course, but for me and many other pilots nose down is the harder of the two to recover from, because you have the secondary danger of aerodynamically stalling the wing if you try to recover too quickly, adding those extra G-forces. Plus, as you have no idea *when* it might stall, it feels a bit like walking a tight rope with a blindfold on – not a great situation to be in. It will also result in the largest loss of altitude, as a stall recovery will inevitably necessitate a further drop in altitude.

Upset Prevention and Recovery Training (UPRT) is now part of initial commercial pilot training, and where we learn how to recover the aircraft from unusual attitudes both in light aircraft and in the reassuring safety of the simulator.

Training pilots for these recovery scenarios is essential. As a passenger, you'd expect nothing less. Far better, however, is for them never to happen, which is why airlines place great emphasis on training their pilots to operate their aircraft in such a manner that they avoid being in these situations in the first place. But, as we've already seen, even with the best training in the world, unfortunately, sometimes they do.

The Boeing 747, as I've already outlined, took the aviation industry on quite a long journey. And, for the most part, that's down to the fact that Joe Sutter and his engineering team never rested on their laurels. Once their baby was out in the real world doing all the things it had been designed to do, they kept on refining and refining. And as you'll also recall from a couple of chapters ago, this process reached its zenith with the launch of the Boeing 747-400.

The -400 propelled the aircraft into a completely new era, with an all-glass flight deck and, new, longer wings featuring this variant's signature winglets. Performance improvements included a new range of more reliable, efficient and powerful engines which when combined with new tail fuel tanks gave the plane unparalleled extended range.

Another big change for the flight crew was the reduction of dials, switches and knobs – from a whopping 971 to a modest 365. Together, these changes removed the requirement for a flight engineer, reducing the crew complement. For the first time, the aircraft could be operated by two pilots. Performance enhancements improved fuel efficiency against previous models by 4 per cent. While this may not sound significant, on a trip from London to Singapore it would equal about 5 tons of fuel. But, even more important, they delivered much more powerful and responsive engines.

The -400 was, by some margin, the aircraft you'd want to be on, should you be unlucky enough to encounter something you could never have foreseen while in the air. Sometimes, however, as with so many incidents, there is often a chain of events, including the human factor, which cannot prevent a tragedy even so.

Camp Bastion, Afghanistan, 29 April 2013

Camp Bastion is a desolate place. A citadel for soldiers erected in a relatively remote desert area, it lies north-west of the town of Lashkargah in Afghanistan. Built by the British army in 2005, it's a sprawling mix of tented and semi-permanent accommodation (for upwards of 20,000 troops from allied countries) and has an enormous airfield, dominated by a 3,500-metre runway. At the height of the Afghanistan conflict Camp Bastion was a hive of activity, with over 700 helicopter movements alone each and every day, but by 2013 it was a shadow of its former self, with only a few operational movements taking place, as the allied troops finalized their planned withdrawal. The once busy ramp was now dominated by large cargo aircraft as they swallowed the military equipment from a thirty-year war and took it back home.

On one such day, the ramp was filled with the shape of a striking blue-and-white-liveried Boeing 747 freighter aircraft, with the word 'National' in 10-foot-high blue letters adorned on the side. This aircraft, having earlier arrived directly from Châteauroux in France, was flown in by 34-year-old Captain Brad Hasler and his crew. They comprised four pilots, two engineers and a loadmaster, who was preparing to accept a load of outsized vehicles for the long journey back to Dubai, via nearby Bagram Airbase, to top up some fuel. The load they were scheduled to carry was a first for everyone on board, comprising five MRAP (Mine Resistant Ambush Protected) vehicles, three Cougar variants, each weighing 18T, and two M-ATV variants, which weighed in at a slightly lighter 12T each. These vehicles were enormous and as such required special loading and handling on all aircraft, including the Boeing 747.

I have a bit of experience with loading and restraining outsized loads. Back in 1990 I joined the RAF as an air-loadmaster and spent the first seven years before becoming a pilot, being responsible for the safe loading, weight and balance, and carriage of danger goods on C-130s. While the C-130 is not on the scale of this Boeing 747 freighter, the principles of safe loading are the same, regardless of the platform; you need to ensure the load is suitable to be carried and doesn't exceed the weight and balance limitations of the aircraft. This isn't just about weight of the item and what the aircraft can lift; it is more complex, because the floor structures all have limitations on them and, beyond that, you need to ensure you can get enough restraint on the item to ensure it doesn't move at any phase of flight, or even in a crash. Putting the parking brake on and hoping for the best just isn't going to cut it.

The Boeing 747 freighter Brad was flying that day didn't come out of the factory entirely in its cargo configuration. It was originally delivered to Air France in 1993 as a combi aircraft, one of those that carried freight and passengers together on the main deck. Having been retired by Air France mainline services in 2007 it was then converted to a dedicated freighter and subsequently sold to National Airlines in 2010.

This freighter conversion was designed to have the main deck filled with Unit Load Devices (ULDs), which are similar to the aluminium containers that you will see at airports all across the world, used for carrying baggage in aircraft holds. These ULDs are designed to have freight placed within them, after which they are restrained to the aircraft floor by a system of locks. It's the combination of the container's structure and the floor locking system that ensures the items are securely restrained throughout the flight. This system will restrain the load to withstand acceleration forces of 9G forwards, 2G vertical, and 1.5G aft and lateral. This means that during even the most violent of take-offs, or crashes, the load will stay in place and not become an additional hazard by flying around.

As an aside, the UK military use 3G, 2G and 1.5G as minimums for restraint of military cargo in their aircraft but try to exceed this wherever possible. For loads that don't fit within ULDs, such as those vehicles that were being loaded into Brad's aircraft, these are described as special loads and need to be planned carefully to ensure the correct restraint is applied and that aircraft limitations are not exceeded. The main things to consider are whether the aircraft floor is strong enough to carry the items. With ULDs the weight of the freight is distributed across the base of the container; with vehicles this is concentrated through the tyres, and this may exceed the floor loading capability. The second element to consider is the restraint required to adequately secure the item. When the senior loadmaster at National Airlines assessed this load, some weeks before Brad arrived at Camp Bastion, it was determined that the vehicles would have to be loaded on freight pallets to spread the vehicles tyre load on the floor. The Cougar, due to its exceptional weight, would have to be loaded on to a double-stacked pallet to further spread the load and protect the floor. These vehicles would then be attached to the pallets and loaded on the centreline of the 747's freight bay. The senior loadmaster then used a rule of thumb to determine the additional restraint required to secure the vehicle to the floor. These would be straps attached to the vehicle and then attached directly to the floor to provide the required restraint, to meet the regulations. Essentially the rule of thumb is to take the weight of the item, multiply it by the G-factor it is to be restrained against, then take the restraint value of the strap or chain and divide it by two. Then take these two numbers and divide the restraint value into the weight number. So, let's say we are restraining a Cougar at 18T, that would produce a first figure of 162T if we are to restrain to 9G. We use straps that are rated to 5,000 kilograms, let's say, so 2,500 is the number from this. That would mean a total number of just more than sixty straps to ensure that the item was restrained to 9G. Some of these would already be in place, as they will be used to secure the vehicle to the pallet, but you'd definitely need more.

The last element of the loading plan is to ensure the aircraft is in balance longitudinally, and the plan for this saw the two lighter vehicles fore and aft, with the heavier Cougars in the centre. There is also a little vagary of the 747 in that it has an unusual height restriction on special loads which are taller than 96 inches, which both of these vehicle types are. This details how far forward this type of cargo can be positioned in the 747 main deck to protect the upper deck and the crew, should the load become detached in a greater than 9G event. This latter element, for whatever reason, was never considered by the National Airlines senior loadmaster.

Just after lunchtime, with the loading complete, Brad and his co-pilot, Jamie-Lee Brokaw, climbed into their seats and started the 747 for their short transit to Bagram Airbase. The 747 lifted away from the runway at Camp Bastion without incident and started climbing to the north-east, towards Kabul and their fuel stop. The crew arrived for their fuel stop at Bagram in what had seemed to be a completely uneventful sector, but this proved wrong when Jamie-Lee sat on the flight deck and informed Brad what he had learned from Michael, the loadmaster. 'One of those straps is busted,' he said, which started a conversation about the load among the pilots. There are 'a bunch' of straps to keep the cargo from moving forwards and 'a bunch' to keep it from moving backwards, Jamie explained. 'All the ones that were keeping 'em from moving backwards were loose,' Jamie-Lee informed them.

Brad was obviously concerned. 'I hope . . . rather than just replacing that strap, I hope that he's beefing the straps up more,' he said.

'He's clinching them all down,' Jamie-Lee assured him, so the pilots went back to preparing for their departure to Dubai. About fifteen minutes later, Michael, the loadmaster, came on to the flight deck, and Brad asked him, 'How far did it move?'

'They just moved a couple of inches,' replied Michael.

Brad commented, 'That's scary,' and 'Without a lock man, I don't like that,' finishing with 'I have never heard of such a thing.' A short conversation ensued about the load and the restraint, during which Brad stated, 'Those things are so ... heavy, you'd think, though, that they probably wouldn't hardly move no matter what.' The loadmaster replied, 'They always move ... Everything moves. If it's not strapped.' The conversation about the load was then over and the crew continued its departure preparations.

Jamie-Lee was flying the departure, and they got the aircraft started and asked for taxi clearance a little after 15:15 local time in Bagram. The air traffic controller cleared them to taxi to runway 03 for departure, and with that their journey to Dubai continued. The crew taxied to the runway, and a little over ten minutes later the same controller cleared the 747 to take off from runway 03. Jamie-Lee acknowledged the take-off clearance and advanced the thrust levers. The engines spooled up and the aircraft accelerated down the runway at Bagram. A little under a minute from the start of the take-off roll, Brad announced 'rotate' and Jamie-Lee pulled back on the column to get the aircraft into the sky. A few seconds passed and Brad stated, 'Positive climb'; in reply, Jamie-Lee commanded, 'Gear up.' Brad then said, 'Keep an eye on that, wait!' – the last words that were recorded on the aircraft's cockpit voice recorder (CVR).

Military journalist Steven Hartov was on Bagram Airfield's perimeter road at that time, returning from a day of taking photographs for a magazine. With it looking so shiny and new in the sunlight, he noticed the 747 straight away. But just after it rotated to take off, Steven noticed that something wasn't right; he'd seen many 747 take-offs from this runway and this one looked really steep. Indeed, too steep.

The 747 continued to pitch up. Steven got out of his car and saw that the aircraft appeared to have stopped in mid-air; then the right wing dipped and the aircraft began to slide sideways back towards the ground, creating an explosion so enormous that it rocked the ground Steven was standing on. Less than thirty seconds from leaving the runway, Flight 102 and all on board were lost. The final moments of this event were captured on the dash camera of another nearby vehicle and within minutes beamed across the world for all to see. But what went wrong, and how did this accident change the world?

Accident investigation in modern aircraft is very often assisted by the data contained on the 'black boxes'. These recorders capture millions of data points continually and the voice recorder gives insight into what the pilots are saying and how they are reacting to the event, all of which are key parts of the puzzle. Investigators always keep an open mind as to the cause, though, and always look to explore all of the possibilities. As this was a departure in a war zone, some of those possibilities would be different to those, say, at a civilian airport in Europe. However, when the investigators recovered the black boxes from the crash site, it was apparent that both the cockpit voice recorder and flight data recorder stopped working some two seconds after take-off, which was perplexing. Without that crucial evidence, they return to the crash site to see what story the wreckage tells them. The majority of the aircraft was consumed in the fire, but the rear portion, including a single vehicle, was recognizable and relatively untouched by fire. They had also recovered some debris from the runway, just around the area that the aircraft lifted off from. At that point there was some debris that included two small pieces of aircraft skin, parts of an electronic rack assembly thought to be those that housed the black boxes, a piece of hydraulic line pipe and, weirdly, part of a M-ATV MRAP antenna assembly. This latter element was evidence that perhaps the load had shifted and that it was in a part of the aircraft it wouldn't normally be. But how could this have happened? Was it the result of some enemy action, a bomb, say, blowing it outwards? Chemical analysis of the crash site quickly ruled this out, and the team focused on a simpler cause. The vehicle must have somehow broken free.

Over the next few weeks the evidence led the team towards a hypothesis that the load had indeed shifted, but in every scenario they simulated, the shifting aft of the entire load alone wouldn't have caused such a catastrophic crash. There had to have been something else.

The evidence came from the spare tyre, and on pieces of debris inside the aft vehicle. This indicated that the aft vehicle had come loose at rotate, rammed through the aft pressure bulkhead, ripping out the black boxes, damaging hydraulic systems one and two, and stopping abruptly when it rammed into the solid jackscrew that controls the stabilator trim setting. But how had the load managed to move and what impact did these subsequent failures have on the outcome of the flight? The simple answer was very quickly determined by the team when they consulted the senior loadmaster at National Airlines and then compared this with the data from Boeing. The senior loadmaster's planning had the pallets placed on the centreline of the aircraft, where the floor locks could not be used, so the pallets were not attached to the floor but free-floating. The only restraint for the load were the bands used to attach these vehicles to the floor. He had reportedly used a factor of 1.5G to provide the total restraint figures. Boeing estimated that they would need a minimum of sixty bands to meet the 9G requirement but, according to eyewitness reports, the team at National had only used twenty-six. Boeing also determined that only a single of the smaller vehicles could be carried, due to the lack of suitable tie-down points for the straps. The cargo-restraint manufacturing company was consulted and it went further, saying it could not see a way to carry any of these vehicles on floating pallets and still meet the regulatory requirements. It was now clear that the vehicles were not restrained correctly, but more importantly they couldn't, and therefore shouldn't, have been carried at all.

I started this chapter with an exercise that largely simulated the situation these pilots found themselves in. As pilots, we are trained to instinctively recover from this scenario in the same way, by pushing forward on the column and applying full power. I have no doubt that these pilots did exactly that. However, the rear vehicle impacting the stabilator screw jack had consequences they could never have imagined. The investigators hypothesized, based on evidence, that the damage either pushed the stabilator downwards and fixed it in a position that could not be countered by pushing the column forwards, or the stabilator had become free-flowing and tipped forward because of its balanced weight. In this latter scenario, recovery actions that are drilled into us all would have resulted in the nose coming further up and being irrecoverable. Tragically, once that vehicle had moved, the outcome was inevitable.

It is broadly accepted that the aviation industry has a 'no-blame culture', an openness and honesty that allows it to learn from its mistakes so these are avoided in the future.

This accident is no different. The honest and open statements from the team at National Airlines highlighted several deficiencies in its training of loadmasters and in their oversight of these unusual loads. It also highlighted deficiencies in the FAA's oversight of these specialist carriers working in support of the military, moving special cargoes across the globe. Through a voluntary collaboration of freight carriers and the FAA, these training deficiencies and oversight challenges have now been addressed in way that ensures the tragedy of Flight 102 cannot occur again.

You will no doubt be thinking that this chapter is ending on a bit of a low, and I am sorry this is the case. But I do think it is important to realize that aviation is a business that is full of complex risks. These risks are mitigated every day by professionals, using their training and knowledge to ensure a safe outcome for all. In the case of Flight 102, the crew did what they believed to be the right thing but, due to major issues around the load they had been tasked to transport, sadly wasn't. Thankfully these scenarios are extremely rare and, due to that culture of always learning and improving, we will not see a similar tragedy again.

Cosmic Girl, the Virgin Orbit 747 that successfully launched satellites using an air-launch rocket system, with *Launcher One* attached to the wing on a pylon that was originally designed for ferrying a fifth engine, and (below) released during the 747's high-energy launch manoeuvre.

NASA's SOFIA was rarely seen at low altitude with its telescope door open, let alone doing a flypast. But this rare airshow image from Palmdale shows the size of the opening.

SOFIA may be retired but its legacy has fuelled scientific research that has paved the way for new lunar exploration and a better understanding of our own planet.

The massive mirror for the radio telescope being removed from SOFIA prior to it being retired from service.

Loading the Space Shuttle Orbiter on to the Jumbo required the shuttle to be hoisted up and the 747 taxi beneath it.

The Shuttle Carrier Aircraft 'launching' the Orbiter during flying and landing tests of the Shuttle *Enterprise*.

The Doomsday Plane – the E-4B airborne command-and-control post – positions itself to take on some fuel from a KC-135.

Not unlike the VC-25 fleet, the E-4B has a situation room where the Secretary of War can manage the mission with his military commanders.

The experimental Boeing 747 Airborne Laser aircraft, YAL-01.

The Dreamlifter, a heavily modified 747, can transport whole fuselage sections of smaller airliners.

The 747's high cockpit meant the whole nose could be opened up to load freight.

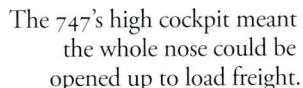

More recently, modified 747s have been used to fight wildfires.

Flying a 747-400 in my early Jumbo career.

With my co-author, Lynne, on the flight deck of a Boeing 747 simulator in Cheshire.

747 designer Joe Sutter on his ninetieth birthday being honoured by friends and former colleagues.

The last 747. The final body join brings together the three main parts of the fuselage and mates them for the first time.

The end of the line. With the last ever 747 as it enters final assembly, bringing to an end over half a century in production.

Forever incredible. The Queen of the Skies flies into the sunset.

15. The 40-Year-Old Virgin

The twenty-second of June 1984 saw me blowing out the candles on my thirteenth-birthday cake. It was an important milestone. I was now old enough to join the RAF Air Cadets and was so aviation obsessed that I was watching and reading everything I could about the industry.

Earlier that day, I had been glued to the television because news of the launch of a brand-new airline was being reported, one set up by a young entrepreneur called Richard Branson.

The airline seemed very exciting. It promised all the glamour of transatlantic air travel but, incredibly, the cost of just £99 ($120) for a one-way ticket to New York in economy – or, as the airline itself called it, 'Riff Raff Class'. (Though if you wanted to spend a little more, you could also upgrade to 'Mid Class', or even 'Upper Class'.)

Richard Branson, already well known as a titan of the record industry, was standing in a pilot's uniform at London Gatwick Airport, alongside his newly leased aircraft. Aptly named *Maiden Voyager*, it was of course a Jumbo Jet – a 747-200.

The reporter was hailing this as a revolution in air travel, something that would directly challenge the established carriers, the likes of which had not been seen since Sir Freddie Laker launched his Skytrain service to the US in 1977, offering single fares to New York in the region of £35 ($46). Laker made a profit on the routes, and though his airline didn't make it through the recession of the early eighties, he was a key advisor to Branson on his own bold aviation project.

I watched in awe as celebrities and press climbed aboard this red-and-white whale, seeing it depart in clear skies from Gatwick with its striking red tail with 'Virgin' adorned across it. 'Viva la revolution!' the reporter declared. Virgin Atlantic was born.

Richard has told the story of his first 'airline' many times, and the fact that it involved a much smaller aircraft, significant disappointment and a beautiful lady – all the great elements for a Virgin adventure.

He was returning to the Virgin Islands (not part of the Virgin Group – yet!); he hadn't seen a certain beautiful lady for a while and was on a mission to get there, but American Airlines bumped him off the flight in Puerto Rico, along with a fair few other passengers.

Now on a mission, Richard rented a small aircraft on his credit card, and after writing 'Virgin Air: $39 to the Virgin Islands' on a board he managed to find soon filled up the flight with all the bumped passengers.

As they landed, one of them told him, 'Virgin Airways isn't too bad – smarten up the service and you could be in business.'

That was all it took to spark the idea in Richard's head. Why not start his own airline?

As luck would have it, there was already an airline out there that was looking for a new beginning. This established venture was a joint one between a US-based lawyer and the chief pilot of the recently gone-bust Laker Airways, whose management had had a mad idea to start a scheduled service to the Falkland Islands, a British Overseas Territory, in the wake of Britain's war with Argentina.

Due to the limitations on the runway at Port Stanley, this was technically impossible so, naturally, they pivoted to a not dissimilar route, the one from London Gatwick to New York's JFK Airport. But that would need more investment. *Much* more investment. In a chance meeting with Richard Branson they found their new partner, and the Virgin brand was going to make the airline a success.

Like Juan Trippe, Branson could see the economic sense of using the 747 to launch his new airline; indeed, the aircraft that had democratized air travel would be the key to Virgin Atlantic's success. So Branson rang up Boeing and said he wanted to lease a 747 for a year and, if things didn't work out, he would like to be able to give it back. Boeing naturally almost laughed him out of the door. But seeing he was deadly serious (and presumably liking the cut of his jib), they reconsidered. They did have an ex-Aerolineas Argentina 747-200 that might fit the bill.

Boeing were being shrewd here. When you lease or buy a 747 you are not just buying a collection of rivets or aluminium – you are buying a thirty-year relationship with the manufacturer. Someone at Boeing could see the value in this upstart airline being led by this famous entrepreneur. So they made him an offer and, without hesitation, he took it, epitomizing his mantra of 'Screw it, let's do it.'

Using money from his record store empire and its stores to sell air tickets, the promised 'party in the sky' was proving a popular and affordable travel option for many. Only a few regulatory barriers needed to be overcome before they could launch their sole aircraft on its first flight on 22 June.

On 18 June the aircraft was presented to the global media and, with his charismatic style, Branson made this new airline feel fresh and exciting, removing the stuffiness he felt other airlines excelled in, in a way only a cool record label mogul could.

A day later all the airline's staff in character as pretend

passengers climbed aboard the 747, alongside the Civil Aviation Authority inspectors for the final proving flight to gain its operator's certificate for the 747. All went to plan. The aircraft lifted smoothly off the runway at Gatwick, then BANG! Flames, followed by thick, dark smoke emanating from one of the engines.

The *Maiden Voyager* declared an emergency and returned to Gatwick – not to a sea of party lights but to the blue ones atop all the fire engines and emergency vehicles that had now gathered there. Not quite the reception party they were hoping for, obviously, but the engine was replaced quickly and the proving flight went ahead on the 21st without further drama.

The inaugural commercial service had all the trappings that we now associate with the Virgin Atlantic brand. The flight was filled with celebrities and had a real party feel as everyone, including Branson, in that dapper pilot's uniform, climbed the steps for their journey to New York's Newark Airport and made a big show of going to the flight deck for those that could see him. For this first commercial departure, he was going to be near the helm.

The crew then announced that, for this special departure, the passengers would be able to view a live camera on the flight deck – something that was unheard of then. (And, indeed, even now.) Eagerly watching, the passengers were afforded an exciting bird's-eye view of Richard sitting down in the flight engineer's seat and hearing everyone in there having a high old time.

Strangely, this seemed to still be happening at take-off, the pilots seeming to be more interested in chatting than flying, to the slight concern of many who were viewing. Surely they should be taking all this *slightly* more seriously?

Nevertheless, the Jumbo did manage to get airborne, and moments later, as it made its way over Hampshire, the pilots took off their headsets and turned to face the camera. It turned out it wasn't a live feed at all – and the pilots weren't pilots; they were cricketing legends Ian Botham and Viv Richards, and it had been filmed days before in the 747 simulator at Gatwick.

Everyone laughed, probably partly with relief.

They were on their way to the US, and it was time to get the party started. The ensuing eight hours was a continuous celebration, with perhaps predictably Madonna's 'Like a Virgin' being played. There was dancing in the aisles, and the seventy cases of premium champagne that had been provided were all consumed before they'd even reached the halfway mark.

On arrival in New York, the party was set to continue, with invited guests hosted by the mayor of New York. But for the budding young airline entrepreneur, that was not to be. In all the excitement of launching his first airline he had forgotten to pack his passport, and millionaire or not, Customs and Border Patrol sent him back on his own aircraft to the UK, ending his party somewhat prematurely.

From that point on Virgin Atlantic didn't look back. They hit their first milestone of turning a profit within that self-imposed twelve-month limit, largely due to the fact that other parts of the group funded the lease of a second 747 to take advantage of the 1985 summer rush.

To persuade people to fly in his Jumbos, rather than the emerging twin-engine aircraft like the 777, Branson famously coined the mantra of 'Four Engines for Long Haul'. To his mind, that there was something about the 747 that captured the world's imagination, in just the same way as it had captured his heart – that magical sprinkling of seventies chic and glamour that was lacking in the more modern aircraft.

I reckon he was right.

*

Without the 747, I think it's reasonable to suggest that Virgin Atlantic might not even exist. As it turned out, it thrived. And over the next thirty-six years the airline had the relationship with Boeing that their canny salesman had foreseen back in 1984.

Virgin flew thirty 747s in total over that time and, for the bulk of it, they were the mainstay of its fleet. They've flown fourteen 747-200 classics and thirteen 747-400s, with just one 747-100 making it to the line-up. Like many other passenger airlines, they had already planned to retire them at some point during the 2020s, but the emergence of the Covid-19 pandemic accelerated that. In the spring of 2020 they all but disappeared overnight.

But one Virgin Jumbo flew on. A rather special one, a Boeing 747-400 (G-VWOW). The launch aircraft for Virgin Orbit, *Cosmic Girl*.

As part of the research for *The Last 747*, my Smithsonian documentary, I was keen to include the Virgin Orbit operation, and came into the orbit of (sorry) two guys I refer to as the 'two Dans'; Digital Dan, head of digital media, and Dan Hart, CEO. This led to another of those pinch-myself moments I'm always banging on about, when I was invited to the Virgin Orbit facility at Long Beach Airport while I was there on a layover, in the hopes of seeing Virgin's last 747.

As with accessing Air Force One, and particularly as a non-US citizen, I first had to jump through lots of security compliance hoops, but by 4 April 2022, I was driving alongside the airfield and got my first sighting of this very special aircraft. *Cosmic Girl*, resplendent in her new Virgin Orbit livery, was parked away from all the buildings, so before going to the VO facility further down the road I pulled over and took a few pictures.

She looked very much like a stock 747, but there was an obvious addition, inboard of the number two engine on the left wing. It looked like an enormous cradle, like those you'd see on a fighter aircraft for a missile, but this was colossal.

I drove a little further around the perimeter to a large warehouse-type facility. It looked pretty anonymous; you'd never have guessed it housed a cutting-edge space business. But I assumed that was the point.

I called Digital Dan, who came out to meet me, and when I entered the building the first thing I saw was a cardboard cutout of Sir Richard wearing a Virgin Galactic space suit next to another dude with a cut-out to stick your head through. And, yes, I am that child and, yes, I do have the photo to prove it.

Important social media work done, you've got to get those Insta shots. Dan took me inside, to their state-of-the-art rocket-manufacturing facility. I am not sure what I expected a state-of-the-art rocket-manufacturing facility to look like, but it wasn't this. I had visions of having to wear those white coveralls you see police wearing when called to the scene of a murder, long white corridors and 'clean rooms' with scientists in white coats hunched over microscopes. What I viewed as we came into the large, 16,500 square metres of open space, was a socializing space that had a real collegiate feel to it, filled with people in T-shirts and jeans, all working on laptops and poring over drawings of 'rocket stuff', while Run DMC blasted out over the speakers.

Dan could see I was taken aback, and I explained why. He told me that they did have some areas that better fitted my vision, but that much of the factory was focused on the development and building of the rocket and its engines, and that at the early stages of these processes they didn't need to be 'surgically clean'. 'It's not rocket science,' he told me, with a smile.

The vision for VO, Dan explained, was based on a pioneering idea called 'rapid responsive launch'. It meant they could launch a payload such as a government satellite or one for communications from anywhere in the world within a matter of days or hours of the flight being called up. Virgin Orbit would launch a two-stage liquid-fuelled rocket called *Launcher One* from under the wing of *Cosmic Girl*, a combination that meant they could operate from almost any commercial runway in the world.

In an increasingly competitive commercial space sector, it would be a novel and affordable launch system that would make Virgin Orbit stand out from the crowd.

The facility we were touring was geared towards building the Newton rocket engines that powered the first and second stages of the rocket as well as the composite rocket, which was 21 metres long and weighed 25,000 kilograms. The jewels in the crown in this process were a 3D printing machine the size of a bus that could take a pile of metal powder and transform it into a fully formed machined rocket-engine part, plus an enormous autoclave to bake the composites for the rocket structure.

The scale of the operation was mind-blowing, and the ambition was huge; a typical Branson-envisioned project, to disrupt the norm in an industry and to offer the same outcome in a very different way.

Matthew, an RAF test pilot who had been seconded to Virgin Orbit to train on the Boeing 747, was slated to be the commander for a planned launch in the UK in the coming twelve months and was very clear on why he was so keen to do it. 'Rocket science is cool,' he quipped, 'but launching a rocket from a 747 is much cooler.'

Matthew was also clear on why it had to be a 747: it was the only aircraft that would be capable of air-launching a huge rocket in this way. And the air launch, of course, was key to the project. It wasn't just about portability but also the fact that taking a rocket up into the atmosphere, up to around the 35,000 feet mark, means thinner air – thus resistance for the rocket to accelerate is much less.

The Jumbo would also be travelling at about Mach 0.86, or 86 per cent of the speed of sound, when they started the manoeuvre to launch it, so they could give it a significant head start in terms of altitude and speed, which in turn meant a rocket with less fuel and more payload.

The 747 has always had the capability to carry a fifth engine on the left wing as cargo, but Matthew explained that this would be where Launcher One was attached, the weight counterbalanced by putting the fuel in the other wing.

Taking off with the rocket under its wing is no different to flying any other 747-400, and climbing to altitude is just like in any airliner. Then the countdown to launch begins. This is where the test pilots put a 747 deliberately into an unusual position that all other Jumbo pilots try their best to avoid.

They accelerate level and then initiate a 2G pull up until the nose of the aircraft is pointing skywards at 35 degrees nose up, and with the speed decaying, the rocket is released, and it ignites and continues skywards, as the aircraft is rolled to 60 degrees of bank and falls away from the accelerating rocket.

It all sounds so simple, but the complex framework of elements that must all align to get to the launch point are enormous. Dan Hart, the CEO, explained to me that the system was designed to allow the rocket to fall away from the aircraft for four to five seconds before it fired the rocket engine. This was to protect the crew of *Cosmic Girl* if there were some unforeseen consequences of this methodology.

The first time they launched it, in 2020, during the height

of the Covid-19 pandemic, the rocket released and fell away, becoming slightly nose down in the ensuing seconds, as expected, before the engine fired. The rocket fired and began very quickly to right itself, but some four seconds later it shut down and started to tumble to earth. The cause was a failure of the main propellant line to the engine, due to some aero loads on the rocket that had not been fully appreciated by the team.

This was not only a new technology they were developing but an entirely new method of air-launch delivery. Not everything can be predicted. The learning from this mission meant that the next four launches in a row went without a hitch and delivered their over thirty payloads to space for commercial companies, NASA and the Department of Defense. The next step was for Virgin Orbit to take the show on the road to Cornwall in the UK to prove the system's portability.

Cornwall Spaceport, October 2022

The former coastal military airfield of RAF St Mawgan has since 2008 been known as Newquay Airport, and it was here where Virgin Orbit was going to transform it into Cornwall's Spaceport. Looking out over the sea that night, a small group of officials had gathered to await the arrival of one of the largest military transports ever built, the Boeing C-17 Globemaster. The landing lights of the aircraft appeared out of the low cloud, and then the form of this giant aircraft, which appeared, due to its size, to be almost standing still. It touched down on the runway with a small puff of smoke from its tyres and then an increase in sound as the reverse thrust was applied.

Despite its size, the aircraft stopped in less than two thirds of the 9,000 feet of asphalt available. While a British-military-operated C-17 at this airport is not unusual, the cargo this one contained was a first for the UK. It was *Launcher One*, the Virgin Orbit rocket, and the newly designed modular support equipment to facilitate launches away from Mojave.

Hart and his team had planned carefully and well, and, as such, thought the time between arriving and launching would be a matter of weeks. They were wrong. As soon as they arrived a number of CAA regulatory processes put the brakes on progress, compliance with which created a phenomenal amount of bureaucracy for the small team to deal with. In space terms, Virgin Orbit was a cottage-industry provider – not a Lockheed Martin or Boeing capable of whistling up thousands of people to a project to overcome such challenges. Busy as they were, though, they duly waded through it all.

Hart's team were, he told me, incredible. And as they worked through what was needed, a good relationship developed between the engineers and the CAA regulators. And not only did they learn a lot about deployed operations, the CAA was also brought into the world of regulating space launch system development. Almost three months later, on 9 January 2023, the regulatory piece was completed, the Virgin Orbit Team had worked through technical issues found during the launch campaign, and the system had a green light for launch.

'On launch day your focus shifts,' Hart tells me. 'It goes from thinking about what is yet to be done, looking under every rock for problems, back-processing what activity could go wrong and taking action to mitigate or avoid that. But on launch day, that all becomes irrelevant; you cannot go back.

It is all about the here and now. If the system is green, we are going forward from here on in.'

Dan's confidence in his launch team was extremely high as they worked through some launch-day issues. They were going to send this rocket today and make history. It was a crummy, wintry, windy and rainy night in Cornwall (Dan's words) and for most conventional rocket-launch systems the teams would have packed up and gone home hours ago, planning to come back in the summer. But one of the significant advantages of this launch method is that it is not impacted by the weather at the airfield in the ways that rockets at launch pads are, other than for the fuelling of the rocket, which wouldn't mix well with lightning. So they could spool up the 747 and take off in the worst of weather, climb above it and take the best path to the launch point.

No other system can do this. It is truly groundbreaking, and obviously cost effective, as you don't scrub lots of launches due to environmental factors you cannot control. That doesn't mean that the launch is easy. It is anything but.

The pilot brief started with the challenges of strong winds aloft. The storm front that was battering the airfield was driven by high-level winds that the team had never experienced before. The pilots used the adaptability of their 747 to plan a flight path that was out of the core of these winds.

There was then a solar flare to contend with. These giant explosions on the sun and the associated coronal mass ejections they throw out are essentially solar magnetic storms that can interfere with a rocket's avionics or even critically damage them with their high levels of radiation.

The team worked out the problem with some quickly called help from the US Space Force and their satellites and decided that, although a huge event, this time, the flare was heading in a direction that wouldn't have a direct impact.

One of the restrictions put on the launch window was that VO couldn't start fuelling the rocket until the last commercial aircraft of the evening had landed and the passengers had collected their baggage. They then had to have completed the launch and returned the 747 to a 'safe' condition by the time the first flight departed in the morning – one of the unforeseen regulatory challenges of operating at a commercial airfield. It was going to be an all-nighter.

As part of the safety measures taken, a sterile area, or maritime exclusion zone, had been established offshore in the case of a launch failure. A boat now strayed into it, just as the aircraft was taxiing. You couldn't make this up; the sailors were completely oblivious to the impact they were now having on a moment in history.

However, the team pinpointed the boat exactly and plotted its course, which was on the edge of the area, and with some very fast help from the Royal Navy the boat started to turn and leave it. All systems were now, finally, 'go for launch', so, a little after 2200 hours local time, *Cosmic Girl* launched into a miserable dark evening with *Launcher One* under its left wing, primed for its own launch. Thousands had braved the weather to watch in the pouring rain as the Jumbo lifted off the runway, to be quickly enveloped by the low cloud and disappear.

The fly out to the launch point was not without its problems either, as an air-conditioning fault on the rocket threatened to stop the countdown. The team worked on the problem and resolved it without any need to delay. The entire Virgin Orbit crew had lived in the Cornwall community for months by now and were very conscious of the importance of this launch for the community and the country. They were going to do their darndest to make it work.

'Everything looked solid,' Hart remarks. 'The rocket, the

flight crew, the telemetry.' Then all voice comms with the aircraft failed. It was ten minutes to launch, and they had nothing. Very quickly the ground team established comms with the aircraft using their mobile phone, and they were back in business.

'Accelerating,' came the call from the aircraft, causing everyone in the mission control to fall silent. 'Pulling,' was the next call, as the aircraft pitched up into that 2G climb that Matthew explained.

'Release, release, release' saw the rocket fall away from the aircraft, then, 'Good light,' as the rocket engine ignited and started *Launcher One*'s journey to space.

Matthew rolled the 747 on its side but managed to glimpse the rocket in his periphery as it lit up the sky with its first-stage engine. His job done, he focused on the 747's safe return to Newquay.

In mission control, Dan watched the rocket climbing on his guidance screens, 40 . . . 50 . . . 80 . . . 100,000 feet and accelerating . . . The rocket was really moving now. It was in space, and the second-stage engine fired up right on time . . . 350,000 feet . . . 400,000 feet, when the vehicle suddenly started to lose altitude. This wasn't a good sign. They'd had a failure of the second-stage engine. The disappointment in the launch control room was palpable. You could hear a pin drop as Dan and his team watched the vehicle fall off the coast of Africa and their chance of mission success ebb away.

As the dawn broke over Cornwall *Cosmic Girl* slid out of a rainstorm to touch down safely back at Newquay. Dan had already apologized to the dignitaries at the event and to the customers whose satellites they didn't manage to deploy. But there was also an upbeat spirit. They had launched on the first attempt and very nearly achieved orbit. They were determined that one day they would go again. The national news media, however, described the event as a failure.

Hart has taken part in over 140 launches of all types of space vehicles, and he described it as 'the hardest countdown I have ever done.' He was 'over the moon proud of the broader Virgin Orbit–UK Space team for getting this launch off.' To have it described as a 'failure' was difficult to take.

Although it was reported widely as such, I have deliberately not called what happened with the Virgin Orbit launch a failure, because, in so many respects, it wasn't. Okay, they didn't deliver the payload to its destination, but there was so much more to celebrate about that evening. This was the first ever rocket launch from UK soil into space, the first from Western Europe, and the system had not only proven that it was viable, it had already been a success, even in low-rate initial production. It was also unique in the way it delivered the responsive launch using the Boeing 747 as its launch platform. It is now a proven system that can launch from any airport. No system has ever had that flexibility before, or since.

I could not sum it up better than by using the words of Dan Hart: 'A narrow MBA would say this was a failure as we couldn't raise enough investor money, but an engineer, or technology leader, like myself, would take a very different view. They would say that we crushed it. We were a risk-managed programme that achieved so much as a private company. We made it work through the innovation and the skills of an amazing team. In the history of space launch, this was a first and, despite it not being an easy thing to do, with time, resources and grit someone will get there again in the future.'

I'd go a little further. Orbit might have had two launch failure missions, but it also had four successful missions – delivering both commercial and government satellites into orbit. A pretty good success rate for a start-up launch company. Shortly after this mission, however, the financial viability of Virgin Orbit was reassessed and it filed for Chapter 11 protection so it could restructure its debts, and shortly thereafter ceased operations, selling its assets to its competitors, including *Cosmic Girl*.

But this is a book about Jumbos, not rockets, so what part did Hart believe the 747 played in this historic endeavour? '*Cosmic Girl* was in many ways more complicated than the rocket,' he told me, 'but the engineering design underpinning the aircraft was so strong that it brought the project a level of confidence that no other aircraft could bring.'

I think that about covers it.

Cosmic Girl might have been the last 747 to proudly bear the Virgin logo, but the airline itself is still going strong, an achievement built on the foundations of the young airline's 747s.

Like so many other airlines, Virgin has now changed from the 'four engines for long haul' to the more efficient and environmentally friendly twin-engine airliners. And, together, Virgin and British Airways have called for a radical collaboration between government, airlines and aviation fuel providers to work towards a net zero target year of 2050.

But Virgin is rightly still very proud of its 747 roots, and Branson, in a way that only he could, describes the airline as one of his children. And he is as doting as any other dad about his babies. 'Bullied as a child by other airlines, I fought to protect them, and now I am the proud father of a 40-year-old Virgin.'

16. A Force for Good

For almost five decades, the 747 was the mainstay of operations for many airlines, allowing them to change the economic model of air travel across the globe, as well as impacting commerce in a way never seen before. But it also offered those companies the opportunity to use the aircraft's reliability and utility as a force for good in the world, whether that be delivering much-needed relief or medical supplies or evacuating the persecuted and vulnerable from the horrors of genocide or war.

Several airlines have used their 747s in this way, including British Airways, Virgin Atlantic, El Al and Pan Am, and during my time flying the Jumbo, I've been privileged to 'do my bit' in this regard too.

The first trip took place in March 2011, after the devastating impact of the Tohoku earthquake and tsunami in Japan, where we staged through Seoul in South Korea. I was co-pilot on a humanitarian trip which delivered medical supplies, specialist search dogs and around seventy emergency and rescue workers; a straightforward operation that got help where it was needed, and fast.

The second, later that year, was a rather different animal, in that I was piloting a 747 ultimately bound for Nairobi, to deliver aid to help with the crisis then unfolding in Africa following the lengthy East African drought. My leg, however, was to take the aircraft to Copenhagen, where it would be stuffed to the gunwales with aid provided by the United

Nations Children's Emergency Fund (UNICEF), which is headquartered there.

Proud as I am of my modest contribution, however, some humanitarian efforts involving the Queen of the Skies have the power, almost literally, to take one's breath away.

In 1975, after some twenty years of ugly conflict, the war in Vietnam was reaching its final days. The North Vietnamese troops had already taken the city of Da Nang, and the capital, Saigon, was being shelled daily. It was feared that, if and when Saigon fell, as surely it must, thousands of lives would be at risk, including those of many orphaned children. These children were particularly vulnerable, being predominantly mixed race – the product of fleeting relationships between largely black GIs and Vietnamese women – and to whom the North Vietnamese regime had previously shown little mercy.

With pressure mounting on the US government to act to help the refugees, on 3 April, President Gerald Ford, in San Diego to give a talk to the US navy, gave an unexpected press conference.

'We are seeing a great human tragedy . . .' Ford began, and then went on to outline that he had directed some $2 million to be used to fly 2,000 orphaned refugees to the USA as soon as possible. There would be thirty flights in all and, due to the danger, these would be on C-5 and C-141 military transport aircraft. The children would be flown to Travis AFB on the west coast of the United States and, through Holt International, an adoption agency which still exists today, and a number of other agencies, then placed them with their adoptive families in the US, Canada, Europe and Australia. 'This is the least we can do,' the president finished. 'And we will do much, much, more.'

Operation Babylift was in motion.

On 4 April the first aircraft, an enormous C-5A transporter, was watched by the press as it departed Saigon containing 300 souls, including military personnel, medical staff and, of course, lots of children.

But in this already tragic situation, tragedy struck again. Having successfully negotiated the danger of small-arms fire, the aircraft was climbing through 25,000 feet when, for some reason – we'll never know – the locks on the ramp at the rear of the aircraft failed, causing the large door to separate completely from the aircraft and a rapid decompression of the cabin. The damage to the aircraft as the door detached was critical – it severed control cables and rendered two hydraulic systems useless. The crew wrestled hard with their badly injured bird and, using a combination of power and the limited controls they still had, managed to line up for landing on the runway they had only minutes ago departed.

In making the final turn for that runway, however, the rate of descent increased uncontrollably. In a last-ditch attempt to save the aircraft the crew added full power to bring the nose up. It touched down briefly in a rice paddy and skidded for a quarter of a mile, and though it did manage to get briefly airborne again, it hit a dyke and split into four parts.

I cannot comprehend what this appalling accident might have looked like, though the words of a CBS reporter who'd witnessed its departure, probably said it all. 'A hand here, a head there,' he reported, as only an eyewitness could. 'It is too grotesque to describe. When will the misery in this country ever stop?'

Though, miraculously, 175 people survived the crash, sadly 138 perished, including 78 children.

Juan Trippe had already been taking a keen interest in the emerging situation in Saigon and had been in regular contact with Al Topping, the company's in-country director for Saigon and Cambodia. At that time, Pan Am was the only American airline still flying into southern Vietnam, and had been flying orphans back to the US in small numbers for a period of a year or more.

After seeing the horrors of the C-5 accident, however, they realized that to bring the misery to an end and prevent an even greater tragedy they needed to send a Jumbo and get them all out.

Not far from Trippe's office, Robert Macauley, another wealthy businessman, was also watching the events unfold in Saigon. Macauley, a philanthropist who would go on to found the charity Americares, had been using his private wealth to quietly support orphans in Saigon since the early 1970s. He too understood the urgency and called Pan Am World Airways to ask if he could charter a 747, mortgaging his own house to do so. Though the two men had acted independently of one another, together they had provided the beleaguered government and military with a speedy, albeit dangerous, solution.

With time of the essence, the news was conveyed to Al Topping within hours, with a message from Pan Am's control centre being transmitted, simply saying: 'The Jumbos are coming.'

Having witnessed the departure of the C-5 that morning and the subsequent crash, Al, over in Saigon, had had a sleepless night. This was a warzone, and he was about to bring to the airport, in broad daylight, two of the biggest targets the North Vietnamese would ever have. Would they get enough volunteer crews? This was a hugely perilous endeavour, after all, and how they'd mitigate the threat – both from the air and on the ground – had to be thought through and resolved.

Al's first thought was to not have both aircraft on the ground at once. The war was already causing chaos at the airport and adding 747s to that would conceivably tip it over the edge – having two Jumbos there felt almost like provocation. Sending one at a time was obviously the way forward, so it was relayed to the team in New York that their arrival and departure times would be staggered by ninety minutes.

Within hours, the crews, medical staff and escorts were all on board the Jumbos and on their way to Saigon. Al had done as much preparation as he could, and the outcome was now in God's hands.

Less than twenty-four hours after the tragedy of the C-5 crash, the first Pan Am Boeing 747 made its final approach to Tan Son Nhut Airport. Once they were down, the priority for the first aircraft was to evacuate not only the orphans but also those who had survived the crash the previous day so they could receive expert medical care in the US. The crash was in everyone's mind, especially as the cause was still uncertain.

As it was a war zone, following Al Topping's lead, extra vigilance was shown, everyone and everything that went on to the aircraft being searched. Such was the paranoia about hostile acts that Al himself had to search babies' nappies for potential explosives. This act and the thought that someone would use a child in this way sickened him.

The babies and survivors were loaded on to the aircraft and, just before closing the door, Al walked the aisles to take one last look. There were babies in Pan Am bassinets, in cardboard boxes, on seats and on the floor, and the noise levels were as deafening as would be expected – a cacophony of crying, screaming and shouting.

Al exited and assisted the crew to close the door. He wished them well and God speed but privately wondered quite how they were going to survive all the noise on the flight, which was to San Francisco, via Guam, Manila and Hawaii.

No sooner had Al watched the first flight disappear into the heat haze than the lights of the second aircraft came into sight. Though fearful that some kind of assault might yet come, the loading of refugees went once again without a hitch and, within hours of the first aircraft having left Vietnam, the second was airborne as well.

In the late hours of 5 April, that first 747 touched down in San Francisco, to be met by President Ford and the First Lady. The aircraft carried 300 children, and the first family allowed the most seriously injured to be deplaned and transported to specialist care before approaching the aircraft themselves.

President Ford and the First Lady then carried two of the babies to the awaiting transport, both manifestly moved by the enormity of what they were seeing. They would have been all too aware, also, of those prospective adoptive parents who were anxiously waiting to find out if their child was alive or dead, it not being yet clear who had perished in the C-5 crash the previous day.

But Operation Babylift had also saved lives – it would go on to save 3,000, many of which, with Saigon falling to the North Vietnamese just days later, would almost certainly have been lost.

Sadly, the lift would later become mired in controversy, it being discovered that some of the babies who'd been rescued were not orphans at all – they'd been placed in orphanages temporarily by desperate parents to spare them from the chaos and dangers of war.

I don't doubt that the controversy will continue, and perhaps rightly. As President Ford commented in his memoir, 'Everyone suffers in a war, but no one suffers more than the children,' and the pain of displacement cannot be underestimated.

But as a humanitarian act, whatever the complexities involved, Operation Babylift was made possible by two amazing philanthropists and two iconic aircraft.

Marginalized groups have been a feature of human society for as long as people have been on the move and have gathered around cultural and religious beliefs. And perhaps nowhere, certainly during the last millennium, has been more beleaguered by warring cultures than Africa.

The Ethiopian Jews, the Beta Israel, are a religious community that, though distinct from Rabbinic Judaism, share many of the same theological elements. They have suffered marginalization and persecution since Christianity began to spread across the African continent, becoming increasingly isolated but always remaining independent. This state of affairs persisted until the seventeenth century, when they were defeated by Emperor Susenyos and had their lands confiscated. This earned them the egregious name Falasha, which means 'without land'.

As a result, the Falasha, the Beta Israel men, became ironsmiths and weavers and the women potters, making themselves indispensable to the country. Through the centuries the community dwindled, however, and with the establishment of the Israeli state in 1948 many emigrated to that haven through Sudan, which had assisted getting them on to aircraft. By the early 1990s there were as few as 15,000 Falasha remaining.

Ethiopia had essentially been at war with itself since the early 1950s – albeit not necessarily a shooting one. In the 1950s Ethiopia had its own empire, and under its emperor, Haile Selassie, it was a powerful state, and had been so since the establishment of the Solomonic dynasty back in the late 1200s.

As he tried to reform Ethiopia through the 1950s and 60s, Selassie was seen externally as an internationalist, joining the United Nations as a charter member in 1963 and presiding over the establishment of the first iteration of the African Union. He even attempted to rival the concept of a federal Europe with a United States of Africa.

One could be forgiven for thinking this forward-leaning leader would have been just as progressive within his own country. Sadly, he was not. Described by human rights groups as autocratic and illiberal, his oppression of his people led to a popular uprising in 1974, in which Selassie was overthrown by the very army that had been his pillar of strength for decades.

This group, which would become known as the Derg, assassinated Selassie in August 1975, causing the fall of the empire of Ethiopia. The ensuing two decades saw the persecution of ethnic minorities within the country, the imposition of socialist ideals and the fighting of both internal rebels and those from neighbouring Eritrea.

Keeping a long and complex story short, by the start of 1991 they too were losing their grip on Ethiopia and, combined with an acute famine, the country was about to fall under rebel control. In the confusion of war, Israel saw an opportunity to offer the Ethiopian Jews who were stuck in this mire safe passage to Israel. Previously prohibited from leaving Ethiopia, these people now had a chance to escape, as the Derg, who treated them as subhuman slaves, saw an opportunity to profit from their removal.

In early May 1991, in a secret office in the centre of Tel Aviv, the Jewish Agency was working to enact an audacious plan to transport all 15,000 Beta Israel to the homeland, saving thousands of lives. Leaving them in Ethiopia was no longer an option because if the famine didn't kill them, the rebels were sure to do so.

The negotiations were tortuous as the Ethiopian regime balanced its greed with the inevitable fact that its days were now numbered, as the capital was becoming encircled by the rebels. Eventually an agreement was reached. In order for the airlift to Israel to go ahead, a payment of $35 million was made to the Derg by the Israeli government. On 24 May, the deal done, Operation Solomon was enacted. They had thirty-six hours to get everyone out.

Meanwhile, in Addis Ababa, in the Beta Israel community, word had been spreading of the efforts being made to rescue them. Slowly, the space outside the Israeli embassy had been taken over by the Beta Israel people; they were literally setting up home and, for a period in early May, thousands of children were being taught there, making it the location of the largest Jewish school in the world.

During this period, the embassy had been screening the assembled masses and, in anticipation of the lift happening, also providing documentation. Then, without warning, early on 25 May, Israeli soldiers wearing civilian clothing started to appear in the encampment, ushering people towards dozens of buses in an effort to get them to the airport, telling them to leave everything they couldn't carry in their hands and get on board.

Many thought they were being moved to another site and

were naturally cautious around, if not wary of, the armed soldiers. Frustrated, one of the soldiers, who was of obvious Ethiopian descent, stood in the centre of the amassed crowd. 'We are going to Jerusalem,' he shouted. 'Get on the buses!'

While this military operation had begun in Ethiopia, it had been apparent that the military alone could not airlift potentially 15,000 people in the time window demanded by the Ethiopian regime, so the El Al fleet was called upon to bolster the efforts. This included their Boeing 707s and, of course, their enormous Boeing 747s.

Before leaving Tel Aviv, however, it was already apparent that using the airliners in a conventional way, sitting one passenger in one seat, wasn't going to give the capacity they needed to achieve in the mission within the time constraints. Another methodology needed to be deployed. It was agreed that the airliners would have all the passenger seats removed and that for the short four-hour trip to Tel Aviv the 'customers' would be sitting on the floor of the cabin. Not the most comfortable of journeys, but the only practical way to achieve the aim.

The thirty-four aircraft involved flew around the clock, pausing only for an hour in Tel Aviv to refuel and, on occasion, swap crews. Nearing the end of the operation, a single 747 was on the ground in Addis, dominating the ramp space and the airport with its immediately recognizable lines. This was going to be the last civilian aircraft to leave, with the troops following along in their Israeli Air Force C-130 once the Jumbo had departed.

The El Al captain was determined not to leave one single person behind, and the crew and Israeli troops managed to squeeze every last person into that Jumbo. People were standing and sitting on the floor, they were on the stairs, the upper deck, in the toilets, and, reportedly, there were even twenty-five on the small flight deck. They taxied and departed Addis not knowing that they had just made history of a different kind: with a staggering 1,086 persons on board, they had set a world record for the number of passengers on an aircraft, ever.

And promptly broke it. Because between taking off in Ethiopia and landing in Israel, two small bundles of joy had been added to that number, making the official total now 1,088. Please do find some photos of the inside of this aircraft on the internet – I have no idea how anyone managed to give birth in what was a sea of people inside an aluminium tube, but two women did just that.

Although the official Guinness World Record stands at 1,088, they do acknowledge that it may have been as high as 1,122, such was the confusion on the day. To give some context to this number, let's use the Airbus A380, the world's largest airliner, as an example of comparable passenger numbers. Where I work, this double-decker monster is configured for 469 passengers, but most users will manage to fit in about 525. The maximum certified capacity of the aircraft is 853. This is around 235 fewer than they squeezed on to this Jumbo if we go with the official number, and some 269 if we opt for the anecdotal one. This equates to the passenger load of an entire Boeing 787 on top of the A380's maximum certified passenger capacity, all squeezed into a single Boeing 747. A tremendous feat of humanity, airmanship and engineering.

All told, Operation Solomon airlifted 14,200 immigrants to Israel, in forty-one round trips. This would not have been possible in the time frame had they not used the Boeing 747s from the El Al fleet. The record-breaking final flight has gone down in the history books, as it should. Two days after the completion of the operation, Addis Ababa fell to the rebels.

There have been all sorts of humanitarian heroes in the commercial airline industry, and many, many lives have been saved as a consequence of their actions. Some we know about, obviously, but others we don't, and what follows is notable not just for the aid it delivered but for its architect's sheer audacity and personal bravery. It was a bold act by a benevolent billionaire who wanted to make a tangible difference to those who were living at the end of the road that had become notorious as the Highway of Death. And he didn't just do it once. He did it twice.

The spring of 2003 was not a great time to be in Iraq. It was hostile, and very much a shooting war. Basra was targeted by the coalition at the start of the conflict, as it was deemed a city that would fall quickly and 'would yield immediate photogenic results' in what was very much a PR war.

The battle for the city was not the pushover that was predicted, however, and British forces met stiff resistance along the way, having to resort to a significant targeted bombing campaign and the use of psychological warfare to achieve their aim of taking the city and controlling it. They entered Basra on 6 April 2003 and with their overwhelming numbers secured the city in twenty-four hours.

But that simple victory had come at a huge humanitarian cost. Water was undrinkable and electricity largely unusable. The International Red Cross announced that 60 per cent of Basra's population did not have access to drinking water and warned of a 'coming humanitarian crisis'. UNICEF said there were 100,000 children in Basra at risk of severe fever and death because one water treatment plant had stopped functioning.

The coalition denied bombing Basra or its key infrastructure and blamed the Iraqi army for the damage, but that didn't help those in dire need. Pictures were being beamed across the world of the appalling conditions faced by those Iraqis, especially those in the city's main hospital.

These images were obviously horrifying, and Sir Richard Branson, who had significant history in the region, decided to act, but not for the first time. This was potentially Branson's third intervention in Iraq, and I am sure many of you will be totally unaware of the others.

Let me take you back to 1990 and the invasion of Kuwait. Sir Richard was friends with the King and Queen of Jordan, a friendship that had come about after they'd flown across Amman in one of his hot-air balloons. The royals mentioned to Richard that 150,000 refugees from Iraq had spilled across the border and into Jordan and were living in makeshift camps with no water or blankets.

Sir Richard offered his help in the form of a 747 with its seats taken out and, within days, with the support of UNICEF, the Red Cross, the British government, and the grocery chain Sainsbury's they had flown 40,000 blankets, several tons of rice, and medical supplies to the front line in Jordan.

Branson returned home from that mission to be confronted by images of Saddam Hussein surrounded by British and other nationals who were being held hostage in Iraq, to be used as human shields. Branson wanted to help to get the hostages released, but he had no idea where to even start. Perhaps he could fly out to Jordan and speak with the king? He was, after all, an old acquaintance of Saddam's.

King Hussain agreed to send a message, and Branson

wrote a personal letter that promised a goodwill exchange of relief supplies for the hostages. The king's aide translated this into Arabic, and it was sent by royal messenger to Saddam Hussein.

Branson returned to the UK, believing that his offer would be dismissed outright by Hussein. However, two days later word was received through the king's staff that Hussein was amenable to exchanging the women, children and sick. But with one proviso – that the request was made in person by the prime minister or a former prime minister, having flown into Baghdad.

Branson phoned former Conservative prime minister Ted Heath, who agreed to make the trip. He left the next day for Baghdad. On 23 October 1990 a Virgin Atlantic 747 with a volunteer crew also set off from Gatwick for Baghdad, not knowing what awaited it. The crew could become hostages themselves.

For Branson this was an enormous gamble. Not only could he and his staff become pawns in a high-stakes political game, but his fledgling airline was taking a huge risk; this was one of the only four 747s they had, and if it were lost the lack of insurance on this trip would spell disaster for the business. With a 'good luck' from the Jordanian air traffic controller, this lone 747 aircraft entered entirely empty Iraqi airspace, not knowing what lay ahead.

As they neared the airport at Baghdad the city was in total darkness, with only the tin string of runway edge lights breaking the darkness. They touched down without any problems and taxied to the apron, where they were met by dozens of armed soldiers and government officials at what seemed an otherwise deserted airport.

Branson remarked that it was weird seeing armed Iraqi troops in a Mexican stand-off with red-uniformed Virgin

Atlantic cabin crew; it's a vison he says he will never forget. After a while Ted Heath and Saddam Hussein emerged from the crowd of soldiers, approached Branson, and they all embraced.

The women, children and sick hostages were loaded on to the 747 and within the hour Branson and Heath bade farewell to Hussein and his team. The 747 launched from Baghdad and turned for home. As they were leaving Iraqi airspace, they all let out a cheer. When Branson touched down in the UK it dawned on him that he had probably just made a bit of history. Branson apparently kept the original letter, written in English, that was translated and sent to Hussein. Now, that is a piece of history worth preserving.

When the second Gulf War and the invasion of Iraq looked inevitable, Branson was uniquely placed to reach out to Hussein again, to try to prevent what seemed like a slippery slope towards all-out conflict in 2003. He attempted to broker a deal through Nelson Mandela and Kofi Annan, then the Secretary-General of the UN, who would try to convince Hussein to live in exile to save his country from the oncoming devastation. The outcome of these talks will never be known, as a few days before they were due to take place the coalition invaded Iraq.

Now, in 2003, Branson felt an affinity with the normal people of Iraq, who were suffering because of the actions of their leaders. He felt that this war was unjust and unfair, started on a premise that was tenuous at best, and he wanted to do whatever he could to assist the people in Basra.

Branson's team had worked with Air Marshal Brian Burridge at the RAF, together with the army, to accomplish the impossible – landing a 747 in the war zone. Within hours of President George W. Bush announcing a formal cessation of hostilities in Iraq, Branson launched a 747 brimming with medical supplies, and with a number of experts, towards Basra to assist in restoring water and electricity to the city.

On 2 May 2003 the striking white-liveried Boeing 747-400 with its cherry-red engine nacelles landed at Basra Airport carrying a massive 60 tons of humanitarian aid. The cargo included incubators, wheelchairs and lifesaving drugs, totalling around $3 million in donated aid. Speaking next to the aircraft in Basra, Branson encouraged more to do what he had done. 'The aid agencies obviously should do their part as well,' he told the assembled press. 'But Virgin has the big benefit of its own airline. My belief is that there needs to be literally hundreds of flights like this.'

Sadly, it wasn't to be. The situation on the ground deteriorated quickly and in October 2003 it became so dangerous in and around Basra that the Red Cross had no choice but to withdraw from the city. But that flight, the only civilian one of its kind, was to change the world for the better in a different way.

These two Virgin Atlantic 747 missions into Iraq were possible because of the vision of Sir Richard. He was willing to take substantial risks, using his 747s as a force for good, when others perhaps wouldn't have. While Virgin no longer has its 747s, these missions inspired Sir Richard to work with his good friend Peter Gabriel on an initiative the two men had by now been discussing for some four years. A correspondence with Nelson Mandela, and then Kofi Annan, led to the establishment of a group of statespersons called The Elders. This small group of experienced global leaders use their collective influence and know-how to tackle some of the world's biggest challenges through the non-profit Virgin Unite. This is a fitting legacy for those missions and a true force for good in the world.

And, as we'll see in the next chapter, the Jumbo has also been a force for good beyond it.

17. SOFIA

Kennedy Space Center, November 2022

It is just passing 1 a.m. and I'm standing on a patch of grass with around fifty other people. We're almost completely surrounded by water so, since I'm in Florida, it's probably odds on that there'll be an alligator or two skulking nearby. And who knows how many more are gliding past in the swamps and lakes which make up much of the real estate on this highly restricted bit of government land?

It's a clear but warm night, unseasonably so for late autumn, but the breeze blowing in adds a welcome chill to the air as the minutes tick by towards the event we've all come for, something the like of which I've never seen before and perhaps never will again. So, while behind me NASA's vehicle assembly building is lit up with what seems unnecessary glory, all eyes are trained to a spot two miles distant, where another floodlit vision sits: a rocket.

Still and silent, a ghostly presence against the unbroken inky blackness, the rocket sits on one of two launchpads, the ones from which the Space Shuttle was launched (another NASA icon that's been carried atop the 747, as we'll see in the next chapter). Even from this massive distance, I can feel a sense of pent-up energy emanating from it; it wants to leap, and in a matter of moments it will. This is *Artemis I*, the first of several rockets planned to make missions to the moon, marking the dawn of a new era of space exploration.

I am here to watch history being made.

If I felt privileged to witness a new chapter in the story of Air Force One a few years back, this new bucket-list item is an off-the-scale honour. Having spent the last two years filming the progress of the new Artemis space programme for a documentary series, I have a spot on this patch of grass tonight as a grateful guest of NASA, and I'm standing with a group of the most inspiring people I have ever met.

Astronauts Jessica Meir, Kristina Koch and Stan Love are all launch veterans, but this one is particularly special for at least one of the three, as the next time this rocket system launches, as *Artemis II*, Kristina will be atop it, and the first woman to travel to the moon. *Artemis III*, planned to launch in around 2026, is then going to land on it. It will not only be carrying the first astronaut of colour to set foot on the moon but will also see the first ever woman touch its surface. And though nothing's yet decided, my money is on that woman being Jessica.

I have interviewed Jessica and Kristina before, so we are all making space small talk as the famous countdown clock, just a few yards away from us, ticks the seconds down to launch. When it gets to thirty, however, I have a sudden thought. 'Will I need my hearing protection?' I ask Stan.

He shakes his head. 'At this distance? I'd say probably not.'

I'm a little stressed about that 'probably' – my hearing's already a little damaged from flying Hercs – but there is no time to fret. With the tannoys attached to the building behind us, we can hear as well as see it. We're almost there. Then it's the same iconic countdown that everyone of a certain age knows: 5 . . . 4 . . . 3 . . . 2 . . .

There are over a million people looking up in this corner of Florida at this moment. Some are on the bridge to Cape Canaveral, where NASA staff are gathered, and many thousands more are assembled some six miles away, lining the shore at Cocoa Beach. Those of us lucky enough to watch from the edge of the swamp are the closest any human can get. And I do mean any human, because this mission is uncrewed; up in the capsule sit two human-sized dummies with two and a half thousand dosimeters embedded inside them which will measure their exposure to radiation during the deep-space transit to the moon and back. One is also wearing a suit which the astronauts will wear and the other is not, so they can test that as well.

1 . . . And, finally, we hear the words 'lift off'. And when the Space Launch System fires, the light is so white and so blinding it feels like I'm staring into a newly birthed sun that immediately transforms night into day.

It is, however, silent, which makes it feel eerie. We all understand the physics of speed of light versus speed of sound, but it doesn't make the phenomenon feel any less strange. It seems time too has stopped. The rocket doesn't seem to move. Then – *whoosh!* – it's away, creating its own blaze of light, climbing steadily to its much-anticipated lunar date.

It's only then, seconds later, that the sound catches up, and, yes, I do wish I'd popped in my earplugs. Because the unmistakeable crackling sound now rushing towards us comes from the most powerful rocket ever to be launched. At 8.8 million pounds of thrust, it has 15 per cent more power than the Saturn V rockets used for the original Apollo missions. No wonder it's making its presence felt across the state, I think, as the force of it reverberates inside my chest.

I follow the rocket's trajectory as it ascends into the night sky, watching the 'solids' detach and the core continue on its journey, while a ripple of applause – doubtless echoed right across the country – confirms general agreement that the launch has been a success. There's an easing of tension, a collective happy outbreath, and while we're bound for bed, our hearts will stay with that rocket — on its way back to the moon some fifty years after we last left there.

I imagine almost everyone, both those here and the many millions more watching on television, are recalling the bold endeavours of the Apollo era. The audacity. The excitement. The sheer scale of the achievement. The very fact that we are trying again.

I'm not. Well, I am. But I am thinking about something else too. A specially modified Boeing 747SP. An aircraft better known as SOFIA.

Hearing the word 'Sofia' would make most think of the bohemian capital of Bulgaria, but a few of you, like me, would think of that very special Jumbo Jet — the aircraft that used the voice callsign of 'NASA747', the Stratospheric Observatory for Infrared Astronomy, which has, in no small part, made the whole Artemis endeavour possible.

Though the acronym sounds glamorous, SOFIA isn't much of a looker. A little on the short and stubby side, and with an almost comically outsized tail fin, it is one of a small number of Boeing 747 Special Performance (SP) aircraft that were made as derivatives of the Boeing 747-100 series. These SP aircraft were shortened and specifically designed to fly higher and farther than any other 747 could at that time. Due to the shortened fuselage, the fin needed to be made bigger to allow the rudder to have the same effect on the aircraft, with a smaller turning moment in the event of an engine failure.

Only forty-five SP aircraft have been built, but between them they have had a significant impact on our world. SOFIA was one such. And how. Though this airborne observatory started its life with less lofty ambitions, as an airliner for Pan Am, like any other. Well, not quite. On 20 May 1977, to mark the fiftieth anniversary of the beginning of her husband's historic flight from New York to Paris, it was christened *Clipper Lindbergh* by the wife of legendary aviator Charles Lindbergh.

Having operated in a passenger role for the next eighteen years, the aircraft, which then spent two inglorious years in storage, was finally purchased by NASA in 1997 and began the transformation into the marvel it is recognized as today.

A number of defence and space contractors, including L3 and Raytheon, worked with NASA at a facility in Waco, Texas, to convert the aircraft to an airborne observatory. To ensure success during the project Raytheon also bought another 747SP, so that the experimentation and design work, and the subsequent trials, were not done on the actual aircraft.

SOFIA had to be a 747, and, more specifically, an SP variant, because the aircraft needed to house a 2.7-metre-diameter infrared telescope and a huge gimbal stabilization system to support it. Additionally, and crucially, the aircraft needed to cruise at 41,000 feet, an altitude above the majority of atmospheric moisture, providing optimal conditions for using the telescope to research the far infrared.

Troy Asher is the director for flight operations at NASA's Armstrong Flight Research Center. He is also a highly skilled and experienced pilot – fulfilling career ambitions that had always been his childhood dream.

After attending the air force academy in Colorado and earning an engineering degree, Troy joined the USAF, where he eventually became a test pilot for bombers. Having left the air force, however, Troy didn't know what he wanted to do. But just as he was thinking that he didn't really want to work for a commercial airline, he had the good fortune to be called by someone at NASA. 'We've an opening,' he was told, 'and you're the right kind of person' – to become a test pilot on a then new and revolutionary new project: to put a telescope in an aeroplane.

One thing for which NASA is rightly famous is doing things people say can't be done. And they did – starting out small by putting a reflecting telescope in a Lear jet, then scaling up – putting the telescope on to a C141 air force transport aeroplane (a Starlifter) and developing a door that would open to the outside while in flight. And since, in astronomy, size really does matter, they started thinking big – about just how big a telescope they could fly, to do the science they wanted to do.

With the size of the telescope necessarily dictated by the aircraft that could house it, to adapt a 747 was a natural choice, and in 1997, with NASA now in partnership with DLR, Germany's Aerospace Center, work soon began to find the best place to house the whopping 2.7-metre-diameter reflecting telescope. And with the front of the aircraft soon discounted because of problems with the hump, they turned their attention to the back, cutting off a chunk of fuselage and adding an enormous sliding up-and-over door.

The telescope compartment was, as you'd imagine, extremely complex. To prevent thermal shock on the sensitive mirror and other scientific instruments, it needed to be cooled slowly to match the outside air temperature before being depressurized and the door allowed to open. Once exposed to the elements, the telescope would be subjected to significant extremes of wind buffeting, of course, which a sophisticated three-axis gimbal system was installed to mitigate.

It was similarly complex to keep the telescope working, and part of this was to ensure that condensation didn't form on the mirror and other instruments. A system was therefore put in place so that once every mission was completed, the entire compartment would be flooded with nitrogen.

Work on SOFIA, arguably the most heavily modified of any 747, took almost a decade to complete. And, in 2007, when it was finally rolled out, NASA invited Charles Lindbergh's grandson Erik to christen the aircraft once again, this time to mark the eightieth anniversary of his grandfather's epic flight.

SOFIA represented a tangible step on the road to new knowledge; as Captain James T. Kirk once observed, 'There is no such thing as the unknown – only things temporarily hidden, temporarily not understood.' SOFIA was the embodiment of that philosophy.

For Troy, being one of the test pilots at the centre of such an exciting and audacious programme was an unrivalled honour. The size of the task, the many engineering challenges, the 'doing that thing that couldn't be done'; to be able to do all of that and enable such groundbreaking science has been one of the highlights of his professional life. And of the aircraft itself – this 'ugly duckling' among all the SP variants – he has nothing but admiration. Of all the aircraft he's flown, the 747 is easily his favourite, and SOFIA, despite the flying challenges inherent in its modified form, he maintains is still a 'gentleman's aircraft'.

He is also proud of the scale of the ambition of SOFIA, and how it brought together so many like-minded souls in pursuit of enabling the same scientific goals. It was, he says, something he had never seen before. 'We had test pilots, we had fighter test pilots. We had heavy aircraft test pilots. We had research pilots, we had airline pilots – we called in guys from all over. We had active-duty guys who were flying for United Airlines who would come fly with NASA in what little bit of spare time they had. We had retired guys, right up on the age limit, that were just fantastic. The diversity of the aircrews and science crews on Sofia was something really remarkable.'

One of the key strengths of SOFIA was that it was able to fly anywhere, including over the open ocean, which opened up research possibilities that no ground-based telescope ever could. This was particularly useful far down above the Southern Pacific Ocean, where the dry air allowed them to see infrared light much more clearly.

As the astrophysics chief at NASA Ames Research Center, Dr Naseem Rangwala is clear about what makes SOFIA so special.

'You cannot observe far infrared wavelengths from the ground,' she explains. 'You have to be in space – or at least above most of the water vapour in the earth's atmosphere, because that absorbs the infrared light coming from space. Of course, everything you can do on SOFIA you can also do in space, but once up in space, it's hard to change instruments. Almost impossible, in fact. What makes SOFIA so special is that you can constantly change instrumentation, and improve it. Which means we can continue to do new science, put in new technologies, upgrade systems.'

So SOFIA allowed scientists to collect the kind of space data that would otherwise be really difficult to get. And that was all about utilizing the aircraft's unique ability to transport various suites of instruments to gather different types of data, utilizing technologies that could not be used on a space mission.

For Dr Rangwala, conducting science aboard SOFIA has been the highlight of her career. Having studied the far infrared since her days as a post-doc, she's well placed to understand just how incredible an opportunity SOFIA presented for us learning so much more. Key, too, was that SOFIA was all about community science. Every year, scientists and astronomers were able to submit proposals, which were then reviewed by a peer review panel. As you'd expect, it was oversubscribed, always, but this allowed them to choose the best of the best, which was partly what made it all so exciting.

And not just for Dr Rangwala's team at NASA. Once the selection was made and SOFIA's plans for the coming year were finalized, principal investigators (PIs) were usually invited to fly on SOFIA themselves, which gave them a whole new appreciation of what it could do.

Anyone in the world could apply for time aboard SOFIA. They obviously had to be suitably qualified to conduct the research they wanted to do – PhD astronomers, astrophysicists, and so on – but, other than that, if their project was selected there was really no barrier – the only stipulation, since NASA dollars cannot be sent outside the United States, was that they could fund it. And if so, the time aboard SOFIA was theirs. This was one of the key things that made SOFIA so special; it facilitated truly global science.

To ask Dr Rangwala what her highlights on SOFIA have been thus far is, she says, like asking a parent to pick a favourite from their children. But when pushed, she decided that it was, and still is, probably all about inspiring the world. That, and when they discovered water on the sunlit surface of the moon; it was the excitement and inspiration that went along with this, she reflects, probably brought her the most joy – getting young people enthused by, and interested in, science. Plus being the scientist charged with making that important lunar announcement which launched the Artemis endeavour, which will always be a big career highlight.

Another is the contribution SOFIA has made to broadening and deepening our understanding of magnetic fields in galaxies. In fact, it was research conducted aboard SOFIA that led to the first ever complete mapping of G47, a giant filamentary bone in the Milky Way. (The images they created, by the way, are jaw-droppingly beautiful.)

SOFIA is also credited with finding the universe's first type of molecule – helium and hydrogen combined to form helium hydride, the universe's first molecule, about 100,000 years after the Big Bang. Helium hydride was the first step in a chemical evolution that transformed the universe from simple molecules to the complex place it is today. Helium hydride therefore should be present in some parts of the modern universe, but it had never been found in space — until SOFIA detected it. SOFIA's detection confirms a key part of our basic understanding of the early universe.

Not being skilled in the art of astrophysics, the science behind this incredible scientific achievement does tend to hover a little – no, a lot – above my head. However, as Dr Rangwala explains, the implications of this pioneering space science project are immense, as they shed new light on old questions, and pose new ones too; the PRIMA Far-IR probe mission was recently selected by NASA for phase A study, along with another X-ray probe mission concept. If PRIMA is successful in proceeding to the next step, it will be NASA's next Far-IR observatory after SOFIA. PRIMA is going to study fields, and will benefit from SOFIA's measurements of polarized light.

The SOFIA project itself, originally forecast to run until 2034, came to an end in September 2022, over a decade earlier than planned. The reasons are twofold, and one, as you'd probably anticipate, is financial. The cost to launch SOFIA missions (around $80 million a year) can no longer be justified as part of the broader mix of current space exploration aims and projects. The other is that science, as always, moves apace. According to Dr Rangwala, the type of astrophysics scientists desire to do now, in the far infrared specialization, requires the kind of sensitivity that can only be achieved by sending instruments far into space.

In terms of the moon, then, it's now over to the Artemis project. In terms of everything else, including further study of those magnetic fields, well, I imagine it'll be a case of watch and wait. But SOFIA's contribution to that cannot be underestimated.

Though the SOFIA project, and the aircraft, are both now retired, the internal wall between the Crew rest/VIP guest area and the rest of the fuselage remains on display at NASA's Ames Center, having been saved for posterity. On it are scrawled the names of all the VIPs that have been aboard SOFIA, including Bill Nye the Science Guy, and even Star Trek's Lieutenant Uhura. But it also includes the names of almost everyone who ever flew on or worked on the aircraft, and serves as a reminder that delivering projects that change the world involve a great number of dedicated and differently talented people. It's an opinion that's shared by both pilot and scientist; both Troy Asher and Dr Rangwala are of the same mind that one of the best things about SOFIA was that it required such close cooperation between the engineers, technicians and pilots and the scientists conducting the research. This gave all concerned a new perspective on the others' work and disciplines, and being able to troubleshoot and problem-solve together fostered what both agree was a remarkable *esprit de corps*.

Dr Rangwala is, however, clear about what she sees as the project's most important and hopefully enduring legacy.

During SOFIA's final deployment to New Zealand, she was based at the International Antarctic Centre (IAC), near Christchurch. It was right across from the airfield where SOFIA was parked, so you could see it from the nearby Antarctic Attraction Museum.

By coincidence, they had a camp taking place there at that time – a group of New Zealand high-school students who were supposed to be heading out on an expedition. Heavy snowfall, however, meant the roads were all blocked, so the director of the centre's museum went across to the IAC and asked Dr Rangwala if she'd mind helping him out by giving a talk to the kids about SOFIA.

'It was very last-minute,' she recalls, but she was up for it. SOFIA was, after all, not just a job but a passion, and she'd spoken about the project, and the aircraft, many, many times before. 'So I went and gave this talk, with the aircraft right there, on the airfield, where they could see it. And after I'd finished talking, they were all coming up to me. Even holding on to me, in some cases – saying 'Please take me with you! I want to be doing what you're doing. I want to play on SOFIA. I want to study the universe!', and you cannot put a price to that, right? When a mission like SOFIA allows people like me and others to have that opportunity to change the world – to change, to inspire our next generation, I think, I just cannot let that story go. I always think back to it,' she finishes. '*That's* what SOFIA has done.'

Some eighteen months after watching the launch of *Artemis 1*, I find myself on a layover in Phoenix, Arizona, and realize I have enough time to visit the Pima Air and Space Museum, which is only a few hours' drive away. I love an aviation-based museum, as you've by now probably grasped, so the opportunity to visit this one feels too good to pass up.

Just outside Tucson, the museum is adjacent to the military graveyard of Davis Monthan AFB, and the final resting place of many military aircraft of note, plus some civilian ones too. And with the surrounding land flat, it is not unsurprising that, from some distance away, I can already see the tail of the bird that I have come here to see: that special 747SP, SOFIA.

I get through the formalities of parking and buying a ticket in the museum's welcome centre and then proceed outside on to the dry, sandy surface that makes up most of this desert. This ground beneath my feet is what makes storing aircraft here an easy proposition. There is no need for purpose-built aprons, for example; as hard as concrete, the desert floor can support enormous weights, even those of the very largest aircraft. The environmental conditions here are perfect too. The lack of moisture in the air means the chances of an aircraft rusting away are significantly reduced, something that is immediately evident as I head out to the 747s.

There are relics here from the Cold War, some sixty years old now, and they still look as if they could start up and fly away. SOFIA, in contrast, hasn't been here very long. Retired only in September 2022, it has only recently gone on display. I walk up to it, remembering why I love museums like this one. Ones that let you get up close and lay your reverential hands on these iconic aircraft, allowing you to see, and really feel, the engineering skill and passion that has gone into making these flying machines.

There are not many museums that allow this and, as I walk under the wing of SOFIA, my first time up close to an SP variant, I am still slightly in awe of the sheer size of it. There's also the inevitable pang of a precious memory. Of the days when, albeit on my regular 747-400, I'd do my walk-arounds before taking off.

Those days are over for me now, but I am hoping that this very special 747 will live on in people's memories for many years to come, and that its stories of space and planetary exploration will, as is Dr Naseem Rangwala's fervent hope, inspire a whole new generation of scientists.

18. Those Bits I Just Couldn't Leave Out

In any major airline, seniority is the key to everything a pilot might desire. From the work you get to do, to the leave you want to take, everything is largely determined by your seniority, and not necessarily related to your role or your status. When I joined my current airline back in 2008, I was their 3,052nd pilot in current employment, giving me a seniority number of 3,052.

You can see, then, I hope, how things work. As people leave the business and new staff are recruited, you move a little further up in the pecking order. As I have had an entire career elsewhere before coming to the airline, aspiring to be number one on the list is unrealistic for me. I will probably reach about 1,000 before I retire.

But there are also a couple of other reasons. Firstly, you may recall that in late 2008 a little global financial turmoil led to a huge downturn in the aviation industry and, just a few short weeks after yours truly joined the airline, recruiting stopped. And did not start again for three very long years, so for a good while there was hardly any movement in my number whatsoever. There are obviously much worse places to be than at the bottom of the 747 first officer list, but that number is exceptionally important. It determines your chances when bidding for your work, or, as it's known colloquially, your 'line'. All of which is allocated in seniority order of preference.

Every month the company produced thousands of rosters for two months hence, and published these in what was called the 'bid pack'. In 2008, these mini printed ledgers were pored over by all the pilots, who would pick several lines based on their preferences, days off, destinations, et cetera. They would then send the company a written note of their preferred lines of work, in the order they would ideally like to do them. This was a laborious process for both the pilots and the company, but if you were number one on the list, you obviously only needed to put in one bid, secure in the knowledge that your wishes would come to pass.

Pilots further down the list, of course, needed to be more realistic, and for me, down at 3,052, it was almost a dream sheet (or, rather, an 'in your dreams' sheet), containing hundreds of lines. At the very bottom of the 747 first officer list, I rarely got what I dreamed of and had my work allocated ... largely over weekends. But everyone has to start there, so it was fair enough, I guess, and when the airline began recruiting again I did at least move up a little. When the process of bidding is complete then you are allocated a line of work, which you will fly. This is the origin of the term 'flying the line', or 'line pilot', that many will have heard pilots talk about.

My bidding for exotic destinations was definitely a dream: I quickly realized that my work 'second home' was not, unfortunately, going to be Mauritius but New York, as my lines were largely going to involve travelling to JFK Airport.

Approaching JFK Airport, Christmas 2008

Just before Christmas 2008 I was settling into my new job as a Jumbo Jet pilot, and though I'd by now flown into JFK several times, I had yet to attempt the infamous Canarsie.

JFK airport is home to one of two approaches that are

known around the world as being particularly challenging – the other being Hong Kong's Kai Tak approach, which I've already mentioned. The Canarsie is named after the neighbourhood in Brooklyn that faces the airport and is also home to the Canarsie VOR beacon. To fly it involves a blend of an instrument approach, and then a visual manoeuvring segment, to align with the runway and land.

Seeing 747s turning so low to the ground is highly unusual, so, if the ground is your vantage point, it's always going to look pretty spectacular. From the inside of the flight deck, it is often a challenge as well; we're not generally accustomed to making turns on final approach, and it can take all of a pilot's skill to make the stars align just so, especially if the winds are across the runway.

The approach briefing on a long-haul aircraft is a weird animal, and it often takes place over several hours, almost by osmosis, as both pilots look at the weather and discuss the likely runways and approaches. Today was no different, but the runway was unlikely to change, as the easterly wind was now blowing a small gale, so it would be runway 13L and the Canarsie. I knew I was going to have to lean heavily on Al, and his experience, as he talked me through how to set up the flight management computer, and how he was going to manage the approach for my landing.

Unlike the approach in Hong Kong, there were no precision beams guiding us towards a visual decision point, there was one ground-based aid, a beacon, a VOR, that gives direction to and from the beacon only, to give lateral steering. The vertical element is managed solely by the pilots – in our case by dialling up a vertical rate of descent. As the cloud base was low today, we would be crossing that beacon 1,000 feet above the Island Channel waterway and, shortly afterwards, reaching the visual decision point. It would be here where I would turn the aircraft right through an enormous 94 degrees, to line it up with the runway, while also still descending towards it at a steady rate.

It all sounds pretty easy when you say it in the flight deck, and I couldn't understand why this approach had garnered such a reputation for being challenging – just like many other naïve young pilots before me.

Just before the descent, Al and I brushed up on any changes we hadn't previously discussed and, as I would be landing the Jumbo today, I handed him control for the approach. Around twenty-five minutes later we were south of JFK, at 2,000 feet out, over the grey waters of the Atlantic, cruising along in cold clouds. Clouds that were prime for producing icing. The engine icing protection had come on automatically, but if we were to be in this much longer, we might consider turning on the wing system as well.

At this point the Kennedy controller said, 'Speedbird 117, you're cleared for VOR runway 13L, proceed direct ASALT and at Canarsie contact the Tower nineteen-one.' I read that all back while Al entered the direct ASALT into the flight management computer. Game on. This was an initiation into a very exclusive club; landing a 747 off a Canarsie Approach was one of those rites of passage every self-respecting Jumbo pilot *must* achieve.

We banked to the right and rolled the wings level, going direct to the waypoint ASALT, which was the point where we would start the approach. Al pressed the VS (Vertical Speed) mode button, to arm the mode, which would allow him to dial in an appropriate rate of descent once we were ready.

Al then asked me to confirm the altitude crossing Canarsie and, on my answer of 1,000, dialled it into the autopilot height window.

'Descending,' Al announced as we crossed ASALT, dialling in a 700 feet per minute rate of descent into the autopilot – a little more than perhaps was needed, but when you are running out of track miles, it's easier to back off on the rate than to increase it.

As we approached Canarsie we popped out of the bottom of the cloud. Al dialled 800 feet into the autopilot and eased off on the rate of descent, to make that altitude, at DMYHL, the visual decision point. I looked out and saw the flashing lights on the ground that are there to guide you into the runway. 'Visual,' I announced. 'I have control.' Al answers with, 'You have control.'

While Al took over the radios and got a clearance for us to land on runway 13L, I was now in full concentration mode. It was a blustery day and there was no room to over- or under-cook this turn and then hope to make a correction – you just don't have time.

I was listening intently to Al's hints and tips as I took out the autopilot and started to ease 250 tons of aluminium, fuel and, of course, people around that notorious final turn.

'FIVE HUNDRED,' the automated voice of the radar altimeter called out, followed by Al, who, reassuringly, said, 'Stable.' I made yet another small correction, my eyes constantly flicking between the speed, outside, attitude, rate of descent. We were now passing 300 feet above the ground – time to start rolling the wings level. Bear in mind that our wingspan was 212 feet, so things were all now looking a teeny bit adjacent.

Two hundred feet, and we were in the groove; a small flare and a boot of rudder to straighten the drift off and, without fanfare, but a little bit of coaching from Al, I made my first touchdown at JFK, in a 747, off the famous Canarsie Approach.

As a youngster I had seen pictures of 747s coming around that final turn, and it always looked bonkers from the ground. Little did I ever dream that one day I would see it from the inside, driving, and find out that it was just as bonkers looking from in there too.

New York's JFK Airport is synonymous with Boeing 747 firsts, and not just my own. The first commercial flight took off from there in early 1970, just a year before I was born. But in August 1970, it delivered another first – one that nobody was expecting, including Pan Am Captain Augustus Watkins, who was preparing his crew to fly *Clipper Victor* (a 747 you might recall from earlier chapters) for a short flight to San Juan, Puerto Rico.

Watkins was particularly looking forward to a layover in Puerto Rico; his wife was travelling too, and it was her very first time accompanying him on the 747. It was late in the evening when the crew started to board passengers. The hot, sticky day was thankfully beginning to cool, but, despite this, many were flustered and irritable during boarding, largely due to the lateness of the hour and the knock-on effects of the crushing summer heat that had baked the city all day.

Stewardess Esther de la Fuente was welcoming passengers to their seats when she noticed a passenger with a beard who looked particularly nervous. This was nothing that unusual, of course. The 747 was a new aircraft, after all, and its size often made people nervous, especially those – and there were lots of them – for whom flying was also a new experience.

Thinking little of it, Esther continued down the cabin, settling everyone as best she could, ready for take-off, and at 01:07, the 747 lifted off from JFK and began its journey south to its destination. Some minutes later, Esther was in the galley preparing drinks when she was approached by the nervous man she'd noticed earlier.

'Take me to the pilot,' he demanded. 'I want to go to Cuba.'

Ester thought he was joking. 'No,' she quipped. 'Let's go to Rio – it's a lot more fun there at this time of year!'

At this point the man opened the bag he was holding and produced a gun and a bottle. 'This contains explosives,' he said, referring to the latter, adding, perhaps unnecessarily, 'I'm not kidding!'

Esther duly took the hijacker to the flight deck, where Captain Watkins, who would go on to describe the man as a pint-sized Che Guevara, decided that the easiest way to ensure the safety of the 12 crew and 359 passengers, including his wife, was to take him to Cuba and get him off his jet.

Despite the captain's decisive action, the crew and passengers were still obviously terrified: a hijacking of a 747 had never been done before, and what fate would await them in Havana? Still, the ensuing four hours, which were tense for all on board, were punctuated by reassuring updates from the captain, whose calm demeanour took the edge off everyone's terror.

At a little after 5.30 a.m. the 747 landed at Havana Airport, to be met by a huge 'welcoming' committee. The mood was on a knife edge, and everyone was sombre and quiet, still not knowing what fate awaited them.

What the captain didn't know, however, was that as soon as his decision to take the highjacked 747 to Cuba was made known to Cuban officials, the premier himself, Fidel Castro, was woken up and informed and, keen to take a look at this new aircraft that was making headlines across the globe, he got up, dressed and made his way to the airport.

Aboard the aircraft, meanwhile, with a set of steps having now been wheeled up, it was time to open the door and see what would happen next. Watkins went first, coming out of the door and having to jump down three feet or so, the steps obviously having been designed for smaller aircraft.

He then descended the steps and, to his astonishment, found himself face to face with a smiling Fidel Castro, communist sworn enemy of all America.

The hijacker apparently forgotten, Castro was hugely interested in the aircraft and questioned Watkins as to whether it would be possible for them to take off from the small runway in Havana. Assuring him that it could, Watkins took him on a walking tour of the outside of the Jumbo, and with Castro keen to hear all about it as they walked, told him a little more about its passenger and freight capacity.

Was Castro an avgeek at heart? In any event, he was charming enough that Watkins offered to take him for a tour of the interior as well. This, though, he politely declined, perhaps wisely. 'I wouldn't want to scare your passengers,' he said. Then, somewhat surreally, the two men bid one another farewell and, some fifty-two minutes after they had landed in Havana, the 747 took off again, leaving the hijacker, safely delivered to his chosen dictator-led destination, and whatever it was he'd been so keen to do there.

With a degree of fuel expended, they decided a quick hop to Miami would be prudent, where they were greeted by another 'welcoming' committee, this time in the form of a gaggle of FBI agents who wanted to debrief the crew and the passengers about their ordeal. For most, it's been reported, this was even more stressful than the hijack itself.

For most crews, that would have been a good day's work, and they'd be sipping mojitos on Coconut Beach within an hour. But it wasn't enough for Watkins and his crew. Once the debrief was over, they reboarded the aircraft and took off once more for Puerto Rico, landing a little under seven hours late.

But what a great story they had to tell on their layover.

The 747 has had many specialist roles in the military and civilian operations. Some became reality, and others not, and one that was realized was the YAL-01 project, in which a 747 was equipped with a laser in the nose; a bonkers idea to mount a massive laser weapon on a 747 to knock incoming nuclear missiles out of the skies.

This unique aircraft combines elements of two aircraft on the 747 family tree, the -200 and the -400. The Boeing YAL-01 was conceived in the late 1990s as a mount for a megawatt-class chemical oxygen iodine laser, in the hope that it might intercept ballistic missiles while in their boost phase.

In 2001, the United States Air Force acquired an ex-Air India -200 aircraft and brought it, without wings, to a laboratory building at Edwards Air Force Base so testing and development of the concept could begin. This work resulted in a laser being fitted to a new 747-400F in 2002 which looked like something out of a Star Wars movie.

The first firing of the laser took place in 2004. The project had a troubled test phase, but it included several successful laser firings. In 2010, the aircraft successfully engaged a test missile in the boost phase off the coast of California. Despite these successes, many senior officers within the Pentagon remained unconvinced of the operational viability of this platform – unsurprisingly – and in 2011, after sixteen years of research and over $5 billion of investment, the project was cancelled. The aircraft made its final flight on 12 February 2012 and was parked at Davis Monthan air force base. It was dismantled in 2014.

While the YAL-01 was actually built, the USAF also had a couple of other ideas for the 747 platform that were just as bold – but which, thankfully, they didn't spend billions of dollars trialling. The first was the 747 bomber – yes, an actual Jumbo bomber. This concept was considered around the time of the development of the B-1, and it was envisaged that the 747 could easily have been a launch platform for ballistic missiles. While you and I may have scoffed at the ridiculousness of this idea, a few decades later Virgin Orbit essentially did just that – as you've already read.

Now on to the last fantasy concept, and I have certainly saved the best for last: the Boeing 747 AAC, or airborne aircraft carrier. This idea was something similar to the Cloudbase concept from the *Captain Scarlett* children's puppet shows of the 1980s. A 747 would act as an airborne base for ten micro-fighter aircraft that could be launched and recovered, rearmed and repaired, and all from the mothership, which would stand off, outside contested territory. Although I laugh at this concept, the 'loyal wingman' project, which uses AI-powered UCAVs (uncrewed combat air vehicles), is something that is very much being explored now, so perhaps Boeing's idea was just before its time.

While some of these military-use ideas were never going to make it to production, one that did was the 747 air-to-air refuelling tanker. When the USAF was looking for a replacement for its ageing airborne tanker fleet, Boeing offered and demonstrated a 747 tanker (which would have been named the KC-25) for that competition. It sadly lost out to the KC-10A Extender tanker, a derivative of the DC-10 airliner, for the contract, due to being too big for the requirements, so we never saw these in USAF service. However, the remnants of that project are still visible on the first Jumbo (RA 001) at the Museum of Flight in

Seattle, where it is equipped with the boom operators' station. There were, however, a couple of orders for this variant, and from a rather unusual customer, the Shah of Iran. The Shah ordered two 747 tankers to allow him to refuel his fleet of F-4 Phantom fighters. It is still believed that these aircraft are serviceable and have in the recent past made an appearance as part of flypasts for significant national events in that country.

A Jumbo unicorn, no less.

While all these roles are unusual, they would have seen the 747 flown in a largely conventional way, something that could have easily been envisaged by those Incredibles back in the late 1960s. The next is something very different.

When you think of the world's biggest fire truck you may have images of a very large red vehicle with lots of flashing lights and, of course, a stepladder system of some sort. When I think of the largest fire truck, the only steps I am thinking of are the twelve that lead to the upper deck of the Boeing 747-400 Global Supertanker. The world's largest fire-fighting appliance.

The Global Supertanker started life as a standard passenger Boeing 747-400 and was being converted by the airline company Evergreen to a supertanker to replace its ageing 747-100 tanker. This had also been used in a fire-fighting role, when, unexpectedly to some, in December 2013 the company went into liquidation.

Seeing potential in the airframe and with lots of work already done, in August 2015 a new entity, called Global Supertanker Services, emerged and bought all the physical assets of the previous Evergreen operation. This new entity removed the tanks and dispersant system from the -100 and fitted it to the -400 and, after certification in September 2016, the Boeing 747-400 tail number 944 (N744ST) was first used in anger to fight a real fire in Chile, and then in Israel later that year. It then made its first appearance on home soil in the USA to fight the devastating California wildfires in 2017.

The aircraft, which was based in Colorado Springs, was able to be anywhere in the USA within three hours and globally within about twenty. When in firefighting mode the aircraft would configure for a landing (without gear), using those immense triple-slotted flaps to produce most lift at the slowest of speeds. It would then descend to an altitude of 400–800 feet over the target area, which, if you're on the ground, makes it look very big indeed.

The aircraft, with its smart dispersal system, could produce concentrated retardant under high pressure to target specific areas of fire or lower pressure, like heavy rain, to cover an area as long as 3 miles and 150 feet wide. No other aircraft had this capability.

If you have ever seen this 747 manoeuvring in the tight canyons of California, fighting fires, you will know it is a marvel to behold. Even in the wildest dreams of Joe Sutter, this role could never have been foreseen as a viable one, but here we are.

This was by far the largest 'fire truck' any chief could ever bring to fight a fire. It has saved countless lives and millions of acres of land from the ravages of wildfires. It was retired from service in 2021, when its operating company got into financial challenges. It is still flying, though, but hauling freight, rather than fire retardant.

Some of the most iconic images of the Boeing 747, however, are not those of the Global Supertanker winding its way through the valleys of California. They are, for me, those that show another icon, the Space Shuttle, atop the two 747s, specially adapted for the job: the Shuttle Carrier Aircraft (SCA).

These highly modified aircraft, owned and operated by NASA, were a function of practicality and, not unusually for that government entity, politics played a big part in their procurement. Because the Space Shuttle returned to earth as a glider that landed conventionally on an airstrip, NASA knew that it would have to have some methodology for transporting the Orbiter back to Kennedy Space Center, from one of its many landing sites across the globe. It also needed to be one that didn't involve it going by road, which would have been totally impractical for so many reasons.

They also needed to identify a launch platform from which they could take the Orbiter to altitude and allow it to detach and glide back to terra firma as part of the aerodynamic development of the spacecraft. The USAF offered a couple of specially modified C-5 Galaxy aircraft that would easily be capable of delivering everything that NASA desired. There was one catch, however. The USAF would crew and retain ownership of the aircraft.

Anyone who has worked with NASA, and I have worked with them a lot over many years, will realize that having another part of the government control something so fundamental to a space system such as this was never going to happen. So, in due course, after one C-5 was already converted to the role, NASA determined that the high wing design of the C-5 would interfere with the vortex testing and launching of the spacecraft during testing.

The C-5 idea was duly scrapped, and NASA identified that the pre-loved 747-100 series aircraft would meet the bill perfectly. The first to be procured was from American Airlines, and the other, in the wake of the Challenger accident, was procured some fourteen years later, an SR version from JAL.

This meant NASA could own and control the testing and movement of the Shuttle outright, which sat well with its leadership and project managers.

While the aircraft themselves were outwardly 747-100s, they had undergone significant modifications. Bar the first-class seats in the nose, the interiors were stripped, and the fuselages strengthened to take the additional weight of the Shuttle. Getting the orbiter on top of the 747 required a special gantry that lifted the spacecraft, allowing the 747 to taxi underneath; it was then lowered on to the back of the Jumbo for its next flight. The attachment points on the roof of the 747 mimicked those of the Shuttle main fuel tank attachment – heavy engineering attachments, but a good and easy solution to get the obiter atop the Jumbo. There are several pictures of these appendages online, bearing the rather flippant instructions to 'attach orbiter here' along with the note, just in case there was any doubt, 'black side down'.

Having another aircraft on the back of the 747 did somewhat alter the stability and there was a need to add extra vertical stabilizers to the tail and carry ballast to keep the aircraft balanced when the orbiter wasn't on top of it. Some may be surprised to hear that the aircraft were both fitted with infrared-missile countermeasures, something that may seem odd for a NASA aircraft. But I am sure this was done to protect the orbiter, which must have been an attractive target.

As part of the wider refit, the aircraft also received uprated gear, avionics and engines for their new role, but it was a rather unusual modification that caught my eye. The aircraft has an internal escape slide. This isn't the type of slide that comes out of the doors of the aircraft to evacuate in an emergency. Although the SCA did still have those, this is a tunnel, a chute, that runs from the flight deck to the underside of the aircraft. Should a catastrophic event happen while flying, the crew could blow out the bottom end of the slide, don their parachutes and slip to safety through their escape tunnel. What a great idea.

Or so everyone thought – until the flying test of the aircraft started with the Shuttle atop and it was discovered that the likely outcome would be the crew placed in proximity of, or ingested by, their own 747 powerplants. As this is something all crew tend to wish to avoid, the escape tunnel was removed.

Troy Asher, the Director for Flight Operations at NASA's Armstrong Flight Research Center at Edwards AFB, who we met in the previous chapter, talked with me about flying this aircraft. Troy described it as being like every other 747 he had flown, but the extra weight and drag of the eighty-ton orbiter meant you needed to think a little ahead of the jet.

Let me summarize: it is like putting an enormous roof box on your car and filling it with lead. The handling won't be the best and the fuel economy will be out of the window. That's the SCA in a nutshell.

When recovering the Shuttle from Edwards AFB to Florida, the SCA would have to make a couple of stop-offs along the way as the range with the Shuttle in tow was around 1,200 miles. Space geeks among you will know that the Shuttle Enterprise was only used for the approach and landing testing from the 747 and never actually went into space. These tests verified the Shuttle's flight characteristics and were crucial to the safe recovery of those who rode this system into orbit.

In total there were three taxi tests, eight captive flight tests and five free flight tests of the spacecraft. While I have only touched on this system briefly, if you want to know more about it, and the complexity and bravery of those on board the 747 and the orbiter during these dangerous test evolutions, they are covered in some detail in *Into the Dark*, authored by my friend Rowland White.

With the retirement of the Shuttle, the last role for these aircraft was to deliver the orbiters to their new retirement homes. The Shuttle Carrier Aircraft can themselves now both be seen at museums, and I have personally been on the one at the Johnson Space Center in Houston. It is an amazing sight.

Most, if not all, of the stories that I share within this book are about the positive way the 747 has impacted our world, our lives, or the way travel was opened to the masses. This next variant is the one that could undo all of that. This is the 'Doomsday Plane' or, as it is officially known, the E-4B Nightwatch aircraft, or the National Airborne Operations Center (NAOC) for the United States of America.

Since 1974 one of this fleet of four aircraft has been on standby to launch, to ensure the continuity of military command in a national emergency or the destruction of ground-based command-and-control centres. This is where the National Command Authority would issue the orders to launch a nuclear holocaust, if the traditional methods had already been compromised.

These four Boeing 747-200 aircraft started their life being destined for an airline which, for some unexplained reason, subsequently decided not to take delivery of them. The enterprising salespeople at Boeing then offered them to the USAF to replace their ageing EC-135J aircraft, which were based on the 707 platform, performing the same macabre mission but doing so from the air and not on ground standby, such were the tensions during the early Cold War years.

Externally, these aircraft bear a striking resemblance to the VC-25A (Air Force One) aircraft and, if you weren't a hardened aviation enthusiast, it's only the paint job that would differentiate them. The E4 is also boarded using steps to the lower cargo area, but in its case up through the right-hand-side freight hold door rather than the purpose-built extending steps and door on the left of the VC-25.

Once inside, the aircraft are very similar in that they have three usable decks and at the centre of the aircraft is a sizable conference room with state-of-the-art communications. The upper deck is accessed by the spiral feature staircase that you would routinely see on the 'classic' 747s of this era. This leads to a crew rest area with a lounge for eating and drinking. Forward of this is the flight deck, which, like the presidential aircraft, has four crew positions – captain, copilot, flight engineer, and the extra, mission-specific, navigation station. The flight deck has been upgraded over the years but still contains the elements of one designed in the 1960s, and is somewhat dated.

The main deck is dominated by the conference room and the command area, the latter filled with several banks of desks, around which mission managers and communications specialists sit. These are the people who would authenticate, and relay the order to launch nuclear weapons, assuring mutual destruction even in the event of ground command and control being obliterated. Can you imagine that being *your* job? (Me? I'm in the mutually assured destruction game . . .)

There is also a small suite named the National Command Authority area, which is an executive suite with a small lounge and sleeping area. This is potentially for the President, the Secretary of Defense or the Chairman of the Joint Chiefs of Staff. The remainder of the deck is dedicated to seating, sleeping and eating areas for the mission crew, who may be airborne for a very long time, as, like the current Air Force One, this aircraft can be refuelled while airborne.

The lower lobe of the aircraft, where your baggage would normally be, houses some of the more unique pieces of military equipment, the most notable of which is a trailing wire antenna (TWA). This TWA is a 5-mile-long wire antenna that is unfurled from the aircraft and towed behind it. This is an essential piece of the communications equipment, as it allows direct communication via the VLF (Very Low Frequency) network used to communicate with submerged ballistic missile submarines, to deliver those orders that will unleash Armageddon. As you would expect of an aircraft that is designed to provide a survivable platform from which to conduct nuclear war during an attack, the entire aircraft is shielded from the electromagnetic effects (EMP) of a nuclear detonation, but this antenna is particularly susceptible and has additional screening.

Having as a primary mission that everyone hopes they will never have to deploy the aircraft, they have also been used for other tasks in support of national disasters such as Hurricane Katrina. The aircraft is also used to transport the Secretary of Defense when they travel overseas.

But what is it like to be crew on these aircraft? I've been lucky enough to speak to both Lieutenant Colonel Brian Moone, a navigator, and Lieutenant Colonel Nicholas Haiar, a pilot, both of whom, as you'd expect, had illustrious aviation careers before joining 'The Nightwatch'. And as these aircraft are essentially there to function as a mobile Pentagon, neither is in any doubt about the importance of what they do. Or, indeed, how high the stakes are. They must also be in a state of perpetual readiness, which means keeping everyone pin-sharp through constant testing of that capability.

Alert launches, Brian explains, are initiated via speakers throughout the bases they occupy, in addition to the use of secondary pagers. His initial reaction, he says, is always 'one of pure adrenaline because you don't know if it's real or an exercise. The time between initial notification to launch is minutes, due to the fact that the aircraft is always powered up and ready for immediate launch. Because of this short time frame, you have to be focused, to ensure this happens not only quickly but safely.'

Similarly, as a pilot, Nicholas has to be strapped in and ready to fly at a moment's notice, and feels the same degree of urgency. 'I treat every practice alert launch as if it was real,' he explains. 'I run or drive to get to the aircraft, then run up two flights of stairs to get to my seat, where the maintainer is sitting and starting my engines. Around this time I find out if it's real or an exercise, then I take a breath, complete the checklist, then either go or shutdown, depending on what we are directed to do.'

Of the aircraft themselves, both men tell me they do have their quirks. For Brian, one such is something few would imagine and even fewer will ever have seen; above the spiral staircase that leads up to the upper rest area and flight deck there is still in place a chandelier that wouldn't look out of place in a 1970s hotel.

For Nicholas, the same sense of forgetting you're in an aircraft endures. 'My first time looking out of the cockpit window at the tanker aircraft,' he tells me, 'I felt I was looking out of a microwave window and had to tell my eyes to focus on the tanker and not the wire mesh. Sometimes it's hard to remember you're flying,' he adds, 'when we have so many capabilities that you wouldn't expect an aircraft to have, that it makes it feel like you're in a normal office building on the ground.'

Both have also had memorable on-board moments. For Nicholas, a lasting memory is that of having a storm pop up on the radar and of having to rush out to the aircraft with no time to change into his uniform as the storm was within minutes of their location. 'So I was able to fly in gym shorts and a T-shirt,' he recalls. 'Not our usual look . . .'

And it would possibly raise some eyebrows on the ground, I imagine, because he also tells me that they are regularly confused with Air Force One when they arrive, which he says is usually pretty entertaining.'

Brian has a particularly fond memory of flying former Secretary of Defense James Mattis. 'He always made sure to come up and thank the entire crew for our service,' Brian recalls. 'Additionally, he would wait till everyone else had eaten before he took his own meal. A true example of service before self.'

Both men's confidence in their aircraft is absolute. 'The 747-200,' Brian tells me, 'is, though antiquated, best suited to operate in a nuclear environment. While I'm sure this would normally create challenges for other aircraft, this has not been an issue for the E-4B, due to its no-fail mission.'

As a pilot, Nicholas does admit that the age of the aircraft can present some challenges, due to the lack of spare parts. 'But we work through those potential problems,' he tells me. 'And are still able to effectively continue the mission.' Indeed, both tell me that, due to all the upgrades the aircraft have, to remain compliant with FAA directives, it does not feel old at all.

Not unlike the VC-25A, the doomsday aircraft are, however, fast approaching their limit of viability – as a platform as they have been in operational service for fifty years. The problem faced by the US is that there is no single aircraft in the current inventory that can replace this aircraft's mission, so a search for a replacement, called the Survivable Air Operations Center, has commenced, with an entry-into-service date of mid-2030s.

Surprisingly, Boeing was removed from the competition early in the process and the eventual contract has been awarded to US aerospace firm Sierra Nevada Corporation (SNC). SNC subsequently signed a deal with Korean Air to buy five of their Boeing 747-8i passenger aircraft that they are decommissioning, to be replaced with newer twin-engine airliners. Although nobody at SNC has confirmed that these will be the replacement Nightwatch aircraft, it seems likely that, if it ain't broke, don't try to fix it.

So we will likely see these new 'Nightwatchers' within five years, and they will be around for a long time to come. Because the only thing that can replace a Jumbo in these niche roles is a Jumbo. When researching this piece, the team at Offutt air force base in Nebraska offered another little snippet I'd never come across before: the origin of the 'Nightwatch' moniker for these aircraft. Turns out it hails from a Rembrandt painting commonly known by the same name which depicts a group of civic guardsmen whose duties were to serve as defenders of their city gathering to maintain order. A fitting description of the mission that is to protect the peace by assuring mutual destruction, but, perhaps sadly, the nickname of the 'Doomsday Plane' is the one that strikes fear into many.

But that's obviously the point, and I think Brian Moone sums it up well: 'Most of the crew who operate on board the E-4B are selectively hired from a pool of applicants. Due to the importance of this no-fail mission, we hire the best of the best. Additionally, because the aircraft is on alert 24 hours a day, 365 days a year, our service members sacrifice a lot to make this mission happen. Their selfless dedication is what drives the E-4B and is a major factor in what makes us a huge deterrent to our enemies abroad.' So I guess it will likely endure.

For those that are interested, my current seniority number after seventeen years of service is a smidge below 2,000, just under the halfway mark of the over 4,400 pilots in our airline. Like many colleagues, I have had the seniority for command on short haul for many years but, at the moment, lifestyle is more important to me than a fourth stripe. I have chosen to remain on long haul, with excellent relative seniority in the right seat, and almost total control over my own destiny – a situation that changing seats and returning to the bottom of a new pile would lose.

Had the passenger 747 still been a regular sight at airports across the world, I might have felt differently. As it is, like the Jumbo, I am approaching the twilight of my second flying career. So will I take a long-haul command when I'm eligible for it in a few years? Who knows? 'A few years' is a long way away and, as you will now realize, relative seniority is king.

19. Hopes and Dreamlifters

Seattle, November 2018

I am in Seattle today with my friend and Emmy Award-winning director Ben. We've visits to a few Boeing sites planned as we expand our understanding of the 747 and, in particular, the 747-8i, the last passenger airliner in the 747 series.

This is not just an enthusiast's jolly. We are writing the show *The New Air Force One: Flying Fortress* for National Geographic, and today we will be doing lots of active listening as we meet key staff from Boeing. I am absolutely buzzing at the prospect, but little do I know that we will also get an opportunity to visit the Marvel Universe and meet one of the Fantastic Four.

I am of course not referring to Ben Grimm, the Thing, or any of the other characters from the comic books but the four Boeing 747 Large Cargo Freighters, or as they are more colloquially known, the Dreamlifters. These four aircraft are drastically modified Boeing 747-400 aircraft that have been specifically designed and built for one special mission: bringing the components of the next generation of Boeing 787 aircraft to the assembly lines in Charleston.

This is going to be a real treat as one of the aircraft is due to be on the ground during our visit, but first we get an insight into, and are brought up to date with, the 747 that is inspired by the design of the 787, the 747 -8. Ben and I meet with Steve Kopecki, superintendent of 747 engineering, and

Bruce Dickinson (no not that one), head of 747 programmes at Boeing.

We are sitting in a conference room overlooking the 747 production line. It is a boyhood dream of mine to see something like this, and I am trying desperately not to be like an overexcited schoolboy. We meet Steve and Bruce, and they explain to us that not long after the launch of the 747-400 series Boeing started to explore the next iteration of this game-changing aircraft.

If you have got a winning formula, it doesn't make sense to change it too much, rather to double down on what makes it so successful. In 1996, at the Farnborough Airshow, Boeing did just that and announced that they would be launching the 747-500X and -600X, stretched versions of the 747-400. They also mentioned the possibility of a 747-700X being a stretched and wider-bodied 747. All these variants did little to improve on efficiency through new design; the focus was to increase capacity and potential revenue by adding more seats. These improvements were just not enough to attract enough orders to go into production, so Boeing went back to the drawing board.

In 2000, Boeing launched the 747X and the 747X Stretch derivates, which used elements of the previous offered designs but were a little more modest, changing the wing-root design and extending the aircraft to an enormous 263 feet (80.2 metres). Again, the airlines weren't tempted to make any orders – they had fleets of 747-400s which were delivering what they needed in spades and these iterations just didn't give the improvements that justified the cost of a new airframe – the -400 was a winner; they needed a world champion to drag them away from that aircraft. So Boeing decided to take a new tack and incorporate some of the advancements offered in a new -400 variant, the -400ER or extended range.

This variant was ordered by Qantas and was known at Boeing as the '910k', as this was the maximum take-off weight (910,000 pounds) that it achieved with structural modifications and new landing gear. But the big gain was in the extended range of the aircraft, offering either one or two extra fuel tanks that were in the forward hold area, adding an extra 12,330 litres of fuel – just a little under 10 tons. Qantas opted for the single-tank variant that allowed them about 500 extra miles of range and opened routes such as Melbourne to Los Angeles direct, even when flying west to achieve this.

Despite several knockbacks, Boeing continued to explore new iterations of the 747 and pivoted to offer those elements that the customers were asking for, such as more fuel efficiency and reduced noise. Throughout the early 2000s, the 747 design team worked on a project called internally the 747-400QLR, which kept the winning formulae but added innovative engine nacelle design and a change of wing design. This design was never fully developed but merged into development of a clean-sheet design of the 747 Advanced, an aircraft that would draw on the significant technology improvements that were incorporated into the 787 Dreamliner.

In 2005, Boeing announced the launch of this new aircraft, initially called the Boeing 747-Advanced, or 747-8. Dropping the convention of having series numbers in 100s, this variant had just -8, following the new company branding standards established with the 787 programme. This model held the hopes and dreams of those who loved the aircraft. This was the airframe that would secure the continued production of the 747, and Boeing estimated a market of at least 300 aircraft, with an even split of freighters and passenger variants.

This variant emerged just at the perfect time. The market needed a replacement for the 747-400 stalwart as these aircraft were approaching two decades old, and the replacement couldn't just be another -400 as the market needed it to be more efficient and, more importantly, quieter. Boeing's fear was that the A380 was perfectly positioned to be that aircraft, and they needed something that could compete.

I think to call the new variant a 747 does the design team a disservice. They changed the aircraft so much that the only thing it retained from its older relative was the iconic humped fuselage shape. The team at Boeing had decided not to compete directly with the A380 but to design an aircraft that was in a class of its own. The main enablers for this, since Joe and his team envisioned the original, were thirty-plus years of aerodynamic and engine design developments.

The engines on those first aircraft were the first generation of high-bypass jets and were hugely unreliable. The -400 was blessed with late second-generation engines which improved reliability markedly over two decades, as tweaks were made. That very Jumbo variant, owned by General Electric, provided a platform for engine testing, which proved the reliability and robustness of the most modern engines, allowing us to confidently fly over long stretches, without suitable diversions, with only two engines rather than four. This ability has enabled the proliferation of extended two-engine operations, or ETOPS, something I will return to in a moment or two.

This leap in engine technology led to the launch of the GEnX (General Electric next Generation) engine for the 787, which is truly a fifth-generation engine. When incorporated with the newly designed 'sawtooth' composite nacelles, not only would these improve efficiency but, importantly, reduce noise by 30 per cent compared to the -400.

The second major change was enabled by developments in computational fluid dynamics. No longer were the teams using slide rules, like the Incredibles, but advanced computer modelling, allowing changes to be made to the wings and flight surfaces. Gone was the 'Sutter twist', and the original wing was replaced by a new wing with a raked wing tip that resembled the biomimicry seen in the 787 'gull' wings. The signature triple-slotted flaps were replaced by double-slotted inboard ones and single outboard.

The other changes were almost endless: new gear, increased take-off and landing weights, a redesigned flight deck, fly-by-wire spoilers and outboard ailerons, a double-hinged lower rudder, and, crucially, the body was stretched by 220 inches, making this the world-record holder for the longest passenger airliner in current service at 250 feet, over twice the distance of the first powered flight by the Wright Brothers. The best of the technologies designed for the new kid on the block, the 787, were being used to enhance the Queen of the Skies, the 747.

Boeing hoped that they had scored a home run with the 747-8 series, and they had another world-changing aircraft but, sadly, it was the world that was changing and, with that, the appetite for four-engine aircraft from consumers and airliners. These fears were borne out when the first customers for the new variant were Cargolux, a freight outfit wanting the freighter version. The era of the four-engine airliner was in decline, but there would still be a place for the freighter, and this saw over twice the number of freighters over passenger versions ordered. Rather than the market being for hundreds of aircraft, in the end only 155 were ever built.

The success of aircraft like the Boeing 787 Dreamliner have added significantly to that decline and was perhaps the final nail in the coffin for the Jumbo. The regulators had such confidence in the engines that they assessed the chance of a single failure being almost zero, and a twin-engine failure so small it is immeasurable. However, each aircraft has a rating that is expressed in minutes for the time they are permitted to fly onwards to a diversion in the event of a single engine failure; this is colloquially known as the ETOPS rating.

Back in 1990, Boeing were the first to bring an airliner into service with an approval for 180 minutes, which is now the standard for most operators. However, we are now faced with the time to diversion being extended and the Airbus A350XWB has a theoretical option for ETOPS-370, although nobody has yet used it. This all seems easy to understand, but then they changed the name of the rules to Extended Diversion Operations and applied them to four-engine aircraft as well, in a move to improve safety. In 2015, the Boeing 747-8i was the first four-engine aircraft to achieve an ETOPS-330 approval, the first two-engine one being the 787, allowing it to be the only aircraft able to fly non-stop over Antarctica without a diversion, another 747 first. Who knew?

At this point it would be remiss of me not to mention the economics as well as the technology that has led to the decline of four-engine airliners. The cost of operating a four-engine airliner is significantly more than a two-engine one – something that may seem obvious to most, but it is not just the direct operating costs such as fuel but those of servicing the engines, four instead of two, and a whole host of complexities that four of everything brings. Joe's mantra of having four of everything for safety and redundancy is no longer required and it just adds weight, and therefore cost, for the airlines.

As an example, the 777X will be able to carry as many passengers and as much freight in those lower holds as a 747 for almost 60 per cent of the operating costs. When this is combined with the lower ecological impact and the potential use of sustainable fuels, it is a much more attractive proposition for the airlines. 'Greener and more margin' is always going to win over nostalgia when it comes to shareholders and the planet.

So the era of two-engine dominance is here to stay, and we will see small variations on the same themes as manufacturers optimize this. In aviation we are unlikely to see ever again the scale of change we saw with the 747's introduction back in 1969.

Back in Everett, one of our hosts, Mary, suggests it is now time to go to the other side of the airfield and a visit to the LCF facility, and we walk out on the apron just as the LCF is taxiing in. I am awestruck by the size of this thing. I am used to flying the 747, but this is something on another level – it looks like a 747 and the Space Shuttle's fuel tank had sex, and this was the twisted offspring of that weird mating.

It is really a sight to behold, and it is rare to be able to catch one of these 'Fantastic Four' airframes as they are continually in motion between the five destinations they serve, all of which at the time either produced parts for or assembled the Boeing 787. Everett, Charleston, Wichita, Taranto-Grottaglie (Italy) and Chubu Centrair Airport (Nagoya, Japan) are the five main hubs, but Mary tells us the aircraft can sometimes be seen in Anchorage as well. This is due to the limited range of the Dreamlifter when compared to the original -400's – some 4,200 nautical miles, versus the 7,600 of the more traditional -400 freighter.

The Dreamlifter was conceived in parallel with the 787 aircraft development as it became apparent that with component supplier and manufacturers across the globe all supplying to the US assembly lines, a new 'just in time' solution would be needed as ships just wouldn't provide the efficiency needed and no current model of aircraft had the capacity to deliver the airframes.

As the engines wind down, we start to approach the aircraft, and my original shock at the size of the airframe has now changed into utter disbelief. It is enormous. We are not the only ones approaching the aircraft, though – some steps are being placed on the right forward door on the main deck and weirdly some steps up to the main hold door on the right.

I am going to go off on another tangent for a moment and explain why using the right-hand side doors is so unusual and why, traditionally, we always board from the left. In short, that was the favoured way of loading ships when they were the main mode of international passenger travel. The left side was called the port side as it was the favoured side for docking, and the right was called starboard. (The derivation of the word 'posh' is 'port out, starboard home' – referring to UK–US transatlantic trips, and passengers' (costly) preference for cabins facing the sun.) This convention was also adopted as the agreed norm for aircraft, with the loading and ancillary work taking place on the starboard side.

With the advent of jet bridges, which were always attached on the left, the right side was left unencumbered, allowing loading to take place concurrently with passenger boarding.

Mary explains that the aircraft were all bought second-hand from passenger operators Malaysian Airlines, Air China and China Airlines. She tells us, 'The initial design was a collaboration between Boeing, Boeing Rocketdyne and Gamesa Aeronautica,' and the inclusion of Rocketdyne totally explains the rocket styling of the freight area. Now it makes sense – it is essentially a rocket-casing design. As we walk around the aircraft Mary adds that they sent the aircraft to Taipei, where they were converted from their original state into this unique aircraft, which is designed for one specific mission.

They cut the roof off the -400 at main deck floor level, just behind doors one, and added this bulbous freight bay above that. The gear is uprated to handle a little more weight than the pax aircraft, but the wings and engines are the same, with one small exception. The winglets were removed as they caused some minor flutter issues during flight testing. There is also a much bigger tail on the LCF, with a 10-foot-taller one needed, and seeing it up close, I'm gobsmacked. It looks like a ten-storey building.

Tom Vize, the 747 fleet captain at Atlas, which operate this Boeing-owned aircraft, explains to me why: 'The larger rudder is needed in crosswinds as the authority needed to straighten the aircraft on landing is more. It's like flying a barn door.'

Walking around the outside, I can see why: it certainly presents a bit of surface area for the wind to catch. One thing is also clear. Aerodynamics wasn't the first consideration. The aircraft is covered in thousands of large rivets, giving it a very rough surface, unlike the smooth, sleek exteriors of modern airliners. The function of welding together this 'frankenplane', I suppose. I am expecting to see a nut with two big bolts sticking out of the plane's join next! This knobbly outside does mean that the LCF flies a little slower than a stock 747-400, at about Mach 0.82, versus 0.85.

As we approach the rear the hinges of the swing tail are apparent and a special vehicle that resembles a forklift is positioning itself under the tail. This vehicle is an adapted container forklift and is the only safe means of opening the tail and unlatching the twenty-one locks that hold it securely in place. The vehicle plugs into the bottom of the tail, provides the hydraulic power to unlock the locks, and while supporting the tail then swings back in a motion that splits open this massive jet. It is like a mechanical ballet watching the tail swing out in this way, revealing the 29x23-feet opening. I am curious why it needs to be so complex and am informed that, 'This was the simple solution.' This method doesn't require any aircraft systems integration for the locks, and once locked they cannot open as they are not pressurized or powered. Also, supporting it in this way negates the need for more robust hinges to support the weight and a complex swing system to power it open and closed. Simple indeed.

As we discuss the hinges, the most enormous aircraft cargo loader I have ever seen has arrived. I am told that this is the DBL-100, the largest cargo loader in the world. It is specifically designed to take an entire load from the Dreamlifter in one go, which seems incredible.

We watch as the loader aligns with the rear of the aircraft, and I am told this is done by laser guidance. There are two small lasers on the rear of the aircraft floor that align with the loader to ensure a safe transfer of the load. Sure enough, it is aligned very quickly, and the load, the mid-section of a 787, starts to emerge from the rear opening. For those technically minded, these are the 43, 44 and 46 sections of the Boeing 787. With the load off and moving away, the door is in motion again and moving towards closed. Time for us to grab a look at the inside.

We enter the aircraft at the right-hand side door via some steps. This is what would have been the first-class cabin, but it is now very different. The area is open, barring a box containing a life raft and some safety equipment. Looking down what would have been the aisle towards the rear of the aircraft is a bulkhead. This wall runs the entire full height of the aircraft just to the rear of doors one. It then becomes apparent that the flight deck and nose area are entirely isolated from the freight area.

This sanctuary is the only part of the aircraft that is pressurized and can support human life during those high-altitude transits. That makes total sense to me now that I think about it – but I just never thought about it before.

A stair takes us up to the flight deck area, which is very familiar to me, having flown the -400 for many years. There is also a toilet and small galley area for those essentials. After a few photos, we exit via the door, and it now dawns on me why there were steps going to the forward lower-hold door – this is how you gain access to the freight area. We mount the steps up to the lower-hold area and, on entering, we are told that this area can still hold seven pallets and is often used for smaller component carriage between the factories.

At the front of the hold there is a set of steps up into the main cargo area. As I reach the top, I look left and am presented with an architectural engineering masterpiece. At 65,000 cubic feet, three times the volume of a normal 747, it feels as if you could hold a concert in here; it's certainly the best dinner venue I could suggest for a 747 reunion. (Or even a book launch, perhaps!)

I just stand there, stunned, while Mary reels off some stats to Ben. I am trying to find the words to convey the size of the interior of this aircraft, but nothing I can think of is even coming close. It's the same awestruck feeling I had when I looked towards the tail. No, scrub that. Even more so. It looks like a frigging cathedral!

Walking down the aircraft towards the rear allows me to view the complexity of the 'simple solution' for the locks and the door. There was certainly some heavy engineering thought put into those twenty-one locks and the safeguards to ensure the tail stays put for the entire flight, something I am sure the pilots are entirely behind as well.

Looking up, I also realize a few other things. Firstly, the control wires for the rudder and elevators would normally go down the centre of the aircraft, but on this variant they are diverted to the hinge (left side) so they aren't damaged when the tail swings open. Additionally, there is no APU in the tail, something that I didn't spot from the outside. In any other 747 there is a small jet engine in the tail that provides power and air conditioning on the ground and air for engine starting. To prevent the need for a fuel line going to the tail, increasing the potential for a fire, they just removed it. This does mean that to start the aircraft it requires air from a ground-support trolley, but that's not an issue when you only have five main destinations.

Although all the aircraft are owned by Boeing, since 2010 they have been entirely operated by Atlas Air, which utilizes its existing fleet of experienced 747 pilots to fly this monster across its network of airports. From a licensing perspective, the aircraft is flown using the Boeing 747-400 rating and, like the -8 series, is just differences training (extra training for when two aircraft fly almost the same, but there are some vagaries between the two types) from the core 747-400 series rating. While I will never have the privilege to fly this aircraft, I am reliably informed by Tom that with the exception of landing in a crosswind, 'It flies just like any other 747.'

As I walk away from the aircraft, I feel exceptionally privileged to have had the opportunity to get inside it. It's unusual for anyone who isn't employed by Boeing or Atlas to be anywhere near it, and I am truly grateful I could visit the '747 Cathedral' to worship the iconic form in one more variant. It is rare for the aircraft to be away from its primary role, and few members of the public have ever seen it, never mind been inside it. But in 2023 Boeing and Atlas brought one of these giants to the small Wittman Regional Airport in Oshkosh, Wisconsin, for the largest airshow on the planet, the Experimental Aircraft Association's AirVenture. Almost 700,000 attendees had the privilege to see and touch this amazing aircraft, likely a once-in-a-lifetime opportunity to do so.

This is such a unique aircraft that it deserves its place in this book. It is going to change the face of aviation for many years to come, facilitating that 'just in time' ability to get 787 parts across the globe, and into the factory, to make the next generation of world-beating airliners. Still, I do find it a little weird that the components of the 787 are brought to the assembly lines in a four-holer.

It's like turkeys voting for Christmas, is it not?

20. Forever Incredible

Boeing Plant, Everett, 9 February 2022

Seattle is famously known as the rainy city and, as I drive north from the centre to the Boeing plant at Everett, it certainly delivers. The sky is grey, and the rain – which comes in lots of different flavours here – is that awful drizzle that wafts around in sheets and soaks everything. But despite the gloominess of the day, my spirits cannot be dampened. I am here to witness something special. The end of an era. The last chance to see something iconic in the world of aviation.

I am the only guest today, and I am being hosted by Steve Kopecki, the superintendent of 747 manufacturing operations for the Boeing company. We're here to witness the laying of the 'keel' of the last 747, the beginning of the build process as they place the wing spars for line number 1574, the last Jumbo that will go down the line. The date is accidentally significant as well: it is exactly fifty-three years since the first flight of the 747 from this very airfield.

Steve talks as he walks me through the factory. The last run of aircraft is on the line, with the exception of the final one, 1574; the last three, of four, all destined for Atlas Air, are there and it is truly a sight to behold. This is not my first time in this building, but it will be the last time I'm here with a line of 747s, in differing states of the manufacturing process, down the middle of this aviation basilica.

There is almost no automation here. Every rivet, every panel, is fitted by a mechanic, and though Boeing did introduce production improvements, including the drill tracks developed for the 787, to improve precision and give better ergonomics, it feels to me not unlike the process those Incredibles used some five decades earlier. The noise of these mechanics at work is oddly reassuring. Their faces may have changed, but the tooling and processes they are using would still be recognized by their late-1960s counterparts – the very first mechanics who graced that then brand-new building and began the 747 manufacturing line even as it was still being finished. I feel sure they would have felt the same pride in being first as these mechanics feel about being the last to work on this aviation giant. But as Steve points out, 'It isn't over until the last aircraft rolls out that door.' He and his teams will be working diligently until it does, and that final countdown starts today.

Before we watch the start of the process, Steve walks me through how the last aircraft is to be assembled, using its sister aircraft to demonstrate each stage. Steve describes this build process as 'an aerial ballet of sorts, with tons of aircraft sections being moved around the factory by cranes, 60 feet above the floor, and coming together with thousandths of an inch to spare'.

The process starts with the laying of the three wing spars. This is essentially the keel of the aircraft and is the core around which the wings are built. These are built on their sides so both sides of the wing surface can be worked on at the same time. Once these are ready, they are lifted from the vertical and laid down in a more recognizable fashion, on the factory floor, on specially built trestles, for their final pieces of work. These wings are then 'flown' across the factory by crane and laid at the beginning of the assembly line.

The wings then start their journey down the line, where they are mated together with the body sections in what is called the 'wing-to-body join'. The sections of the entire aircraft are brought together in what can only be described as some Harry Potteresque way, with them all flying across the factory on cranes to merge on the line and on to the wings.

The enormity of this operation is hard to explain in words. This is an entire 200 tons of 747, all coming together like some Lego kit. But this is for real and, Steve explains, has significant jeopardy for the mechanics. Once these pieces, front, mid and aft, are in place the tolerance for the join for all these enormous body parts is less than 1/5000th of an inch. For context, the width of a human hair is 5/1000th of an inch. The precision and patience required to do this accurately, and only once, and without damaging the airframe or injuring an engineer, is truly astonishing. I've flown 10,000 hours in the 747 and had no idea this is how it's put together.

Steve tells me this is the point 'where a jumble of sections and components become an aircraft', and marks the beginning of the end of the nascent aircraft's journey down the building, where, just before it enters the final testing phase, it will be lowered on to its own gear for the first time, and similarly, roll on its own wheels for the first time, to final assembly and testing, where the aircraft is adorned with its beating hearts: the four GEnX engines, which can be fitted in one shift. This is the point where the aircraft will be powered up for the first time, and all the functionality tested, before it is cleared to roll out of those enormous doors at the end of the building.

My Jumbo assembly education complete, Steve and I watch the main event, and I manage to squeeze in a picture of the main wing spar of 1574. This is the last time I, and possibly anyone outside this factory, will ever see this piece of precision-shaped metal in this form.

Boeing Plant, Everett, December 2022

A small pool of invited guests has gathered outside the Boeing plant at Everett to witness a historic yet solemn moment. The roll-out of the last 747 from this plant. For Mike Lombardi and the rest of the guests, all waiting for the doors to part, this is an emotional moment; it's the end of an era.

It's night-time, clear and cold, and once the doors begin to open the darkness of the apron is flooded with light from the brightly illuminated inside of the factory. And there it is: now exposed, this beautiful aircraft – this icon, the last of its kind, a Jumbo, looking regal and sparkling as it's pulled out by the tug.

This moment is reminiscent of those images of the first 747 when it was revealed to the world almost exactly fifty-four years previously. It is difficult to believe this is the last that will ever emerge from this factory, and I can see I'm not the only one moved. Captured by the lights, I catch the glisten of unshed tears. It's a bit like the end of high school, all the mechanics and teams now going their separate ways, unlikely to work or meet again in the same cohesive way as they have on the Jumbo. I totally understand their sadness, their feeling of loss.

The aircraft is towed down the taxiway and the moment has passed. The last Jumbo has left the building and is now handed over to the Boeing Flight Operations Team, who put it through its paces on the ground and in the air. Their job is now to test every single piece of machinery to ensure that, when Atlas Air take delivery in a few months' time, the aircraft is working entirely as advertised. They will then take it on a short hop to the Boeing painting facility in Portland, where the aircraft will be painted in what was rumoured to be a special livery for this final aircraft. It will then be brought back to the delivery centre at Everett, where it will be handed over to its new owners. But first, Boeing has a little something special planned.

To my joy, I am invited.

Seattle, 31 January 2023

It's a pre-dawn start for me, as I'm scheduled to meet media teams from Boeing and Atlas, who will be my hosts for this historic event. I know them quite well now, as I've spent a year working with them while chronicling this journey, but there will be no filming or working for me today. I am purely here to see the old girl off with one last hurrah.

As dawn breaks, I board a comically clapped-out old bus and I am reminded that almost fifty-four years to the day, those who were here to see the first flight of this groundbreaking and innovative aircraft – which many thought was simply too big to fly – would have also been clambering on transport across to the factory. Not much has changed and, judging by the noise it is making, I think the bus might have been there as well.

The view that we have on the way to the factory is somewhat different. We pass rows of twin-engine airliners, the future of aviation, the Boeing 787, and a few 777X aircraft with their distinctive folding wing tips. As we turn the corner, all thoughts of the new kids on the block vanish, as the aircraft version of an elder statesperson come into view, the Queen of the Skies, the Jumbo.

The dullness of the winter's morning does not diminish the glow of the paint on the aircraft: a stunning white, with blue engine nacelles and tail. The tail is adorned with the Atlas Air logo in yellow and the words 'ATLAS AIR' are in 15-foot-high blue-and-yellow lettering on the side of the fuselage. What a sight.

The aircraft is slightly angled towards the hangar doors, and we stop adjacent to the nose, where we are invited to debus, and are ushered quickly inside the building. Since my last visit, the 'Jumbo line' is no more and, for this event, the entire space has been filled with seats: some 10,000 guests (yes, ten *thousand*) are expected to arrive in the next hour to watch this celebration of the 747. There is a stage set up and numerous huge screens hanging from the roof.

I am not sure what I expected, but the set-up is hugely impressive – dozens of camera teams and, despite the chill outside, it has a cosy, welcoming feeling. I settle down in my allocated seat, near the front of the general seating, just behind the VIPs, which includes the few 'Incredibles' who are still living. It's only fitting that they are here for the last delivery as they were here for the first. What a circle to complete, over fifty years in the making.

The celebration starts with a disembodied voice making the announcements. I cannot quite place it, but it is definitely familiar. The show itself is a multimedia spectacular, with archive footage, customer testimonials and, of course, bits of the build of the final airframe. The show then starts building to an obvious crescendo; we are all awaiting the big reveal. The voice now says, 'I couldn't not be here for this . . .' and on walks acting legend and, of course, commercially licensed 747 pilot John Travolta.

The crowd goes wild. This is not what anyone was expecting. Travolta is a well-known Jumbo pilot himself, through his affinity with Qantas, where he learned to fly the iconic jet. He talks about his love of the aircraft, describing it as 'the most thought-out aircraft ever built', and thanks all those present who have designed, built and tested the aircraft, telling them, rightly, that 'you are awesome'. He then speaks for everyone there, I think, by adding, 'There is nothing like seeing a 747 take flight to remind you that there is also magic here.'

John Travolta is followed by a number of other speakers, all sharing the same joyful sentiments. Then the hangar doors begin to open and the space is flooded with a bright shard of light and a cool winter breeze.

There is music too, but, frankly, I cannot hear anything but the clapping and whooping from the crowd as the Queen of the Skies makes her regal entrance. The flags showing the brands of every airline that has ever bought the aircraft are fluttering in the wind as the entire aircraft is framed by the now-open doors. It's another hugely moving moment that has been choreographed to perfection, and yes, I shed a little tear too.

There is also something more. Back in 2011, to celebrate Joe Sutter's ninetieth birthday, Boeing's 40-87 building in Everett, the main engineering building for Boeing Commercial Airplanes division, was renamed the Joe Sutter Building. Today, they've another surprise, something that's been a closely guarded secret until today. On the right-hand side of the aircraft, just below the flight-deck windows, is a huge decal depicting an image of Joe Sutter and the legend 'Forever Incredible'. A fitting tribute to the man whose vision, tenacity, and some may even say stubbornness, delivered the world one of those rare things that comes along every so often – something that makes such a positive impact on our lives and the world. Joe Sutter died in 2016. How proud would he have been? But at least members of his family were there to see it, including his grandson Jon, who now works for Boeing and in the same Boeing location where his grandfather designed the Queen of the Skies.

I wander outside to have some photos with the aircraft and bump into Captain Thomas Vize, the 747 fleet captain with Atlas. We talk about the decal and what Tom and his team have planned for the big departure tomorrow, when he has the privilege of taking delivery of the last 747 and flying it away from the factory. He explains that he has had the privilege of flying every variant of the 747, apart from the SP, but his logbook does also include the Dreamlifter, which few others have. He has even flown the -300 – a rare bird indeed.

Thomas is without a doubt the most experienced 747 pilot I have ever met, and I can see why Atlas have chosen him to drive the final one away from assembly. He also tells me they 'have a little surprise lined up for tomorrow, something our flight-planning team have been working on for months'.

'A flypast?' I suggest, but he shakes his head. It is *definitely not* that. Flypasts are famously banned by Boeing, and the airport, after a previous delivery, of a 747, went viral. It was a Cargolux delivery of a 747-8F from Paine Field in October 2014, and shortly after departure, at about 20 feet off the ground, the aircraft did a highly dangerous wing-waggle manoeuvre. Though the wings just about managed not to hit the ground, heads certainly rolled, not least that of one of Cargolux's vice-presidents, a senior training pilot who subsequently found himself redeployed elsewhere.

As Tom will have his CEO and the head of comms on board for the departure, it would be career-limiting to do anything out of the ordinary. That said, there is a sparkle in his eye as he bids me farewell and is ushered away to meet some VIPs.

I stand and marvel at the aircraft, taking it all in and giving it a little tap of reassurance to wish it good fortune for tomorrow. With that, I reboard the bus and am transported back to 1969. Or the car park. You decide which.

Boeing Future of Flight Building, Everett, 1 February 2023

Your body being in another time zone does sometimes have its advantages. After a long day at the factory, I am tucked up in bed by 8 p.m., meaning that I'm up and about before the vast majority of Seattle has even stirred the next morning or, in some cases, given the racket outside, gone to bed. The roads are quiet, though, by the time I wind my way northwards towards Everett, and Boeing's Future of Flight building.

As I drive through Seattle, despite the overcast and dreary morning, I manage to keep a keen eye out for any billboards asking me to turn out the lights, but don't see any. I am the first of the guests to arrive and the security guard takes pity on me and invites me in out of the cold. For those who have not been to this building, it is on the north-west corner of Paine Field at Everett, adjacent to the northerly end of the runway. The building houses a number of interactive education pieces about aviation and space, while also having as a centrepiece a tail from a 747.

It is only when you see this on the ground that you realize the enormity of the tail and the entire aircraft. There is also another key part of the building, one I am banned from entering. Not by Boeing, but by Sharon, my wife. It is the largest ever Boeing store and is a jamboree of all things aviation, from models to decommissioned aircraft parts. I apparently must not fuel my addiction for such things by entering this den of temptation.

The real reason I am here is to use the deck at the back of the building that overlooks the plant and affords an unrestricted view of the runway. I set up my camera then go and have a coffee.

Over the next hour or so the deck fills with some familiar faces from yesterday, and I am standing chatting with my friend and global aviation media afficionado Sam Chui when we are disturbed by the air traffic control transmissions coming out of the speakers around the deck: 'Paine Tower, Giant 747 Heavy, request push and start.' The controller replies in the affirmative and, in the distance, at the Boeing delivery centre, we can see the blue tail of the 747 beginning to move backwards away from the building. This is it, our opportunity to view and record yet another piece of aviation history.

I wonder how Tom is feeling at this moment. There are quite a few eyes on him now as this is being streamed live and captured by dozens of media outlets. 'Giant 747 Heavy, Taxi,' comes the next call from the aircraft, with instructions following on from the tower. We are lucky. They were going to depart from the northerly end of the runway, right in front of us, and I feel like a little kid, so excited to see this jet roar into the skies.

Then we all see something out of the ordinary. The airport fire trucks are rolling, lights and sirens on. What's happening? The trucks wheel on to the grass and position themselves either side of the exit from the parking area, then start spewing gallons of water. Then it becomes apparent – there is no emergency. The fire teams are delivering their own unique tribute to the 747, in a way only they can, with a huge water archway through which Tom and team now taxi.

As they approach the end of the runway, the tower transmits, 'Giant 747 Heavy, Paine Tower, call ready for departure,' and, after what seemed like an eternity for those watching, but is in reality three or four minutes, Tom and team reply, 'Giant 747 Heavy, ready for departure.' And as the aircraft turns on to the runway I can't help but think back to those grainy film images from the first flight, as RA 001 did just the same, over five decades earlier.

'Giant 747 Heavy, Paine Tower, runway 16 Right, clear for take-off.' With that, Tom stands up the engines and we hear the noise increase and pause, then, with a press of the TOGA switch, the engines accelerate to take-off thrust and this giant starts its roll down the runway, with the background of a dark sky. Tom rotates the aircraft and flies into the history books. It's a fitting end to the 747 story at Everett.

But is it?

I'm just packing away my camera and saying my goodbyes to Sam when I notice the unmistakeable outline of a 747 appearing from the south. Are Tom and the team coming back for that flypast after all? It looks like it's configured for a landing, with gear down and landing flaps, so is there a problem that necessitates them coming straight back? I scramble to get my phone out of my pocket. This needs recording, whatever it is.

At the approach end of the runway the aircraft seems to pitch up and the gear is retracting. Is this a go-around? Because that's what it looks like. The aircraft very slowly gains height and speed as it flies down the runway and, as it flies past the main factory building, it tips its wings in a final wave before climbing away to the north.

I have recently caught up with Tom and asked what the final go-around/flypast was all about. He reminds me that flypasts are banned at Paine Field, but it appears that instrument approaches to carry out a go-around weren't. So, after the first departure, they requested and were approved for an instrument approach to go-around on the opposite runway. They made a normal approach, and he was, perhaps, a little less prompt with the application of go-around power on the missed approach. That's all. So though this may have *looked* like a flypast, it wasn't. It was just a slower than normal go-around. Honest.

Back on the ground, that final little wing tip to the factory, a salute from the Queen of the Skies as she departed for the last time, hits me in the feels. As I pack up my stuff, making sure they aren't coming back again, little do I realize that Tom and Team Atlas have one final hurrah for the aircraft to deliver, and this time it's huge, and one they can't get wrong.

Tom and his team are now en route to Cincinnati, but they don't seem to be climbing in the way you would expect – they're level at about 12,000 feet and routing towards the Moses Lake area of Washington State, to the east of Seattle. I wonder if this is the surprise that Tom alluded to, the one his 'flight-planning team have been working on for months'. Very quickly it becomes apparent that this *is* the big surprise – in fact, an enormous one.

In a special salute dreamed up by Michael Steen and his team at Atlas, the last 747 is drawing a huge piece of sky art. Over the next two hours and thirty-five minutes, Tom and team draw the number 747, adorned by a crown – obviously befitting a queen – 94.5 miles long and 59.5 miles high. I cannot tell you how difficult it must have been to work out the waypoints and fly it so accurately, and to get something that is so sharp when viewed. And boy has it been viewed. Some 20 million people have viewed it on the various flight tracking apps.

When I catch up with Tom later, he tells me that this was

the most nerve-wracking part of the entire day; they had flown it in the simulator and it had seemed to work, but nobody really knew until they did it for real. Like me, the entire Atlas Team was watching this unfold over the skies of Washington in the hope that they had nailed it. They did. Tom then flew the aircraft to Cincinnati, where the tower made an unusual request: could they see the type of go-around that the 747 had performed at Paine Field? So Tom obliged, then returned to land the aircraft, and, once parked, have a very well-earned celebratory glass of champagne.

My own flying journey with the Jumbo ended on 20 October 2019, when I landed Boeing 747-400 G-CIVS back at Heathrow from Los Angeles. I had decided that after over a decade of flying this beautiful aircraft the time had come for a change. The planned out-of-service date for the fleet was looming in 2024, and I wanted to go and take the opportunity to fly a brand-new aircraft, the one that, where I work, would replace the 747: the Airbus A350-1000. Little did I know that in just the few months after I left, the Jumbo fleet had been mothballed and, within weeks after that, it was retired for ever. Such was the immediate decision-making needed within the industry to cut costs during the global pandemic.

While the pandemic accelerated the retirement of these icons, the days of the four-engine airliner were already numbered, with those 'light twins' waiting in the wings to topple the reign of the Queen. Notwithstanding the challenges of the time, the airline still managed to give them a send-off fitting of their service.

I consider it to be an honour to have been able to fly the 747. I am part of a small group of pilots who all feel a weird affinity, a kind of love even, towards this one-of-a-kind aircraft. And I am not alone in being a weirdo. Many pilots I have spoken to feel the same way about these 400 tons of aluminium – so much so that we are even a family. One that meets annually to discuss (and discuss, and discuss . . .) the best of our Jumbo-sized adventures.

I am not an emotional person, but I felt genuinely sad to leave the 747 fleet. The day I stepped off the aircraft after flying it for the last time I touched the registration plate on the door – a small act to thank her for getting me safely across the globe.

Not unlike the show I had the privilege of making for Smithsonian, this book is a final love letter to the Boeing 747, the Queen of the Skies. This aircraft is truly like no other our planet has ever seen, as I hope I've been able to convince you. During some 118 million flight hours (had to cram that last fact in) it has carried us, delivered to us, saved people from persecution, extinguished fires, flown presidents, blown up ballistic missiles, carried and launched spacecraft, and, of course, facilitated some of the most sophisticated and groundbreaking space science.

Although I have reached the end of the last chapter in this book, it is by no means the last chapter for the Boeing 747. Those of us who love the Jumbo will, for many decades to come, be able to stop and marvel, as it takes to the skies as a cargo carrier, or for a few of us, as the new 'Air Force One'.

John Travolta got it right. There *is* magic here.

The Jumbo will be Forever Incredible.

Epilogue

As part of the process of making *The Last 747* documentary, we got the chance to interview Willie Walsh. Now director general of IATA, the International Air Transport Association, he's also the former CEO of British Airways. As a pilot himself, his take on the 747 was a familiar one. 'It is the only aircraft,' he told me, 'that makes me stop and watch it depart, even now.'

It probably goes without saying – I've said it often enough in these pages – that there isn't a 747 pilot out there, past or present, who doesn't feel the same deep respect for the Jumbo. As such, then, is this a book for all the aviation professionals? The flight crews? The cabin crews? The aeronautical engineers?

Yes, of course. But it's a story for many others too, because, arguably more than any other aircraft, past or present, the 747 transcends that. All kinds of people have fallen under the Queen of the Sky's spell.

It's late September, around dusk, and I'm with my co-writer, Lynne, standing in a field in a remote part of rural Cheshire. In the distance, up on a crag, sits the picturesque ruin of Beeston Castle and, closer to home, the landscape is definitely screaming 'rural idyll'. Though we're not here for country pursuits.

We're here at the invitation of a guy called Dan Chang whose passion for the 747 (and 'passion' is not a word I use lightly) is what he's excited to show us today. And not just us; in and around the teepee under which we're standing I see a lot of familiar faces. Many are pilots, of course, some of whom I've flown with, plus former cabin crew and engineers and a smattering of virtual pilots, like Mikey, who isn't a pilot at all. He's an air traffic controller at Heathrow Airport but can probably (more likely definitely) fly the Jumbo sim better than I can.

But there are also others who are here because they share Dan's specific passion, to own a piece of the epic 747 story. Like my mate Darren Lewington, who runs Aerotiques, in Gloucestershire, and makes beautiful creations out of 747 parts. I have one at home, in fact – a piece of art made from three cabin windows and a turbine blade from a 747 I actually flew, and which even my long-suffering wife, Dr Bateman, finds acceptable.

Darren tells me he's also recently turned a 747 main wheel into a one-of-a-kind coffee table, and even used an entire 747 first-class galley to make a sewing-room storage unit for a former cabin-crew client.

Darren and his business partner, also called Darren, assumed when they started the aircraft upcycling business in 2016 that it would be pilots and aviation enthusiasts who would be their principal clients. But with the Covid-19 pandemic hastening the retirement of the Jumbo, the pair were soon inundated with requests for mementos and memorabilia, sometimes with a surprising level of detail. Darren is in no doubt that what drives demand is the 747's iconic status, and is genuinely happy that these airframes will live on beyond their flying days.

Darren's not alone in making art out of aircraft scrap either. Another close friend, Dave Hall, does the same thing in Los Angeles, creating everything from ultra-high-end furniture for Hollywood clients to plane tags from the skins of retired Atlas Air 747s. And a few ambitious souls have gone even further. There is apparently a house in the Santa Monica mountains which has 747-100 wings as its signature roof, and a building being constructed in Seattle – where else? – with a 747 fuselage as its centrepiece. Heck, there's even an Airbnb in Stockholm that is an *entire* 747.

Dan Chang is cut from slightly different cloth, however. He doesn't just want to preserve, or refashion, or incorporate. He has done something so extreme that if I ever even contemplated it, I think I'd need to find a good divorce lawyer.

Dan's an aviation enthusiast, no question. He is witty and urbane, and has the kind of verve and energy that you can sense the very moment you meet him. And while we met him a few hours back, now the light's started fading he's standing before his assembled guests, about to unveil what he's been up to.

Dan speaks emotionally about a personal journey that, inspired by his deep love of the 747, started back in 2020. He and a few friends, having seen the demise of various Jumbo fleets due to the pandemic, had the mad (his words) idea to try and save one.

Now, having flown a few Jumbos in my day, I know they are pretty large. So saving a whole 747 would certainly be a challenge – unless, of course, you have your own airfield. Dan and co. didn't have an airfield but they did have a large piece of farmland, and a bucketload of ambition, so, undeterred by the various raised eyebrows they encountered, they began forming a plan.

Dan is standing adjacent to the teepee, in front of a large building that, were I a farmer, I'd definitely have the correct name for. As it is, I can only offer 'very, very large barn'. And as the roller door on the front begins moving gracefully upwards, I'm looking at the entire upper deck of a 747-400.

And I mean entire. This is no shell that they've salvaged. As well as a loving recreation of every aspect of the passenger space, it also includes the entire – working – flight deck.

I say 'working'. It doesn't fly anywhere, obviously. But it's a simulator, and a great one, with amazing visuals. Prior to the official opening I've even been able to impress my long-suffering co-writer (yes, there *is* a theme here) by executing a Canarsie and landing smoothly on runway 13L at New York's famed JFK airport.

This is not just an enthusiast's folly, of course. As well as simulator sessions for would-be pilots, they do cream teas, and parties, and candle-lit dinners – a piece of theatre for those who either would like to, or already have, turned left and gone up those fabled spiral stairs.

For me, though, the hit is a different one. As I step aboard, I am immediately transported back to those days when this – *exactly* this – was the walk to my office. And with the sights, and the smells, and the *familiarity* of it all, I almost have to pause and take a moment, I feel so lucky.

Dan and his team have devoted thousands of hours of their time and hundreds of thousands of pounds to make this project a reality, but many, I imagine, simply don't get it. Why would they do all that work? Invest all that money? After all, the 747 is just an aircraft.

But it isn't.

It is the aircraft that changed the world.

– Scottie Bateman, November 2024

Afterword

by Michael Lombardi, former Senior Historian, Boeing

It was a cold and dark December night when the last 747 rolled out of the Boeing factory. It seemed appropriate, as the environment not only added to the sense of finality but also to the sense of magic as the ghostly white giant emerged from its birthplace into the darkness. Even though I've seen hundreds of 747s in the factory or out on the flight line, taxiing, taking off or flying overhead, the aeroplane's size, beauty and majesty still filled me with awe – she truly is the Queen of the Skies. But that awe soon turned to something else as I glanced back at the cavernous assembly building that had just a moment before been filled with a 747 and now was filled with a vast emptiness. It hit me then, and it hit me hard, that this was indeed the end of the line: the last 747.

For my entire career at Boeing, there has always been a 747 in the Boeing Everett plant. Looking back at the empty assembly building was a lot like moving from a long-time home and remembering that the empty rooms were once filled with family and memories.

That empty space where the brilliant and talented men and women of Boeing assembled 747s for more than fifty years echoed with their imagination, courage, hard work, dedication and, above all . . . passion. It's where that first team made real something that the world said couldn't be done. They earned the name 'The Incredibles' for their pioneering spirit and the amazing accomplishment that continues to inspire the latest generation of Boeing employees.

But that December night was not the end of the story, merely the end of a chapter. The 747 – the Queen of the Skies – is still flying overhead and still doing what she has always done: providing for the greater good of all.

It's the end of a chapter in a story that began more than a century ago when Bill Boeing launched his aeroplane company with the goal of building something better, to advance the technology of flight and to make the aeroplane into something that would serve all of humanity and bring people together. Today his vision is realized every day as millions of people fly. Air travel is an accepted way of life – but that hasn't always been the case. From the early days of commercial aviation, flying was limited to business travellers and those with the means to purchase the very expensive tickets. Destinations were also limited, requiring a number of connections to fly between major cities.

On 28 September 1968, that all changed as an incredible invention was revealed to the world when the 747 rolled out of the Everett plant. Boeing called her 'Super Jet', the press dubbed the new plane 'Jumbo Jet', but to all who have loved the plane through the years she is the 'Queen of the Skies'.

Bill Boeing not only wanted to build something better but also something safer. He demanded perfection: 'I would rather close up shop than send out substandard work!' Since that time quality and safety have remained foundational.

But simply fulfilling Bill Boeing's vision was not enough for the 'Father of the 747', Joe Sutter. He knew he had to go even further. While leading the 747 design team, Sutter doubled down on safety. In fact, he quadrupled down on safety, pioneering quadruple redundancy for many of the 747's systems. His new aeroplane would be more than twice the size and carry double the passengers of the largest commercial jet, therefore his most important work was to prevent any chance of an accident. He enforced a safety and quality culture by the sheer strength of his character and the respect he had earned as a leader, every programme and every day started and ended with safety – it was a strong step towards perfection.

The 747 design team did their job; they created an aeroplane as close to perfect as possible, and history has proven their perfection as the accidents detailed in this book were not the result of a design flaw. In fact, very few accidents were related to the design, and in many instances the 747 overcame human errors and natural occurrences because of the genius of the designers and their leaders.

To say that the 747 was born from great leadership would not be an exaggeration. The 747 came about from the bold and brilliant direction of Boeing CEO William Allen. It was his decision to take the great financial risk to 'bet the company' on a plane that many said would not fly both literally and financially. It was also his friendship with Juan Trippe, the legendary leader of Pan American Airways, that formed the catalyst for the launch of the 747.

The partnership of Boeing and Pan Am ushered in the Jet Age on 15 August 1958, when Pan Am took delivery of the United States' first commercial jet airliner, a Boeing 707-120, and began plans for 26 October 1958, when Pan Am and the 707 would make history by inaugurating the first 707 service and the first daily transatlantic jet service from New York to Paris. As a result, air travel began to grow, and by the early 1960s the gates at major airports were reaching capacity. That's when Juan Trippe began the search for a bigger aeroplane. Trippe and Allen made an 'if you buy it, we will build it'/'If you build it, we'll buy it' agreement for an aeroplane that would be twice the size of the 707. And with that, the 747 programme was launched with a formal agreement in April 1966.

When it entered service, the 747 quickly became the icon of commercial aviation. It was the first aeroplane with two aisles. Most who fly have no idea what aeroplane they are on, but the 747's size and its distinctive hump make the plane easily recognizable. That distinctive shape is a result of the art that is inherent in great engineering; its design is often recognized as an outstanding work of architecture. The 747 has also become a part of popular culture, starring in numerous movies, TV shows and in the lyrics of many songs.

It did not take long for the 747 to have a giant impact on air travel. It was the must-have flagship for the world's airlines, and it attracted passengers with its huge, luxurious cabin, its unique first-class experience and, of course, its famous upper-deck lounge. But it was the Super Jet's size, world-spanning range, capacity and economy that had the greatest impact. For the first time in history anyone could fly anywhere on the planet – the Super Jet shrank the world and made real humanity's ancient dream of flight.

After shrinking the world, the 747 does not fly into the sunset to be forgotten . . . the Queen of the Skies will fly on for years to come, and the most recognizable and famous version of the 747, the VC-25 'Air Force One', will serve for decades as a proud symbol of the United States.

But even after the last 747 touches down for the last time, the venerable Queen of the Skies will live on as a legend in aviation much like the DC-3, the B-17 flying Fortress, the Spitfire and the P-51 Mustang.

The 747 will live on as inspiration for anyone who dares to dream big, to take risks and to create something magnificent . . . something that will change the world and contribute to the greater good of all humanity.

The 747 is a reminder of the power of the human spirit, a testament to what we can accomplish with our hearts, minds and our hands. Even though we may lose hope in a world that seems filled with strife, we can turn our eyes skyward to see the great contrails of the Queen of the Skies crossing the heavens and know that we can still overcome great adversity and accomplish incredible things.

Acknowledgements

I have really enjoyed collaborating on this book with my co-author Lynne and I would like to start by thanking her for her patience with my awful admin, timekeeping and grammar. Without Lynne I could not have crafted this book to make it such an engaging and cohesive read. Thank you.

Several airlines and corporate entities have participated in the drafting of the text to ensure accuracy of the stories. However, I should stress that views and opinions expressed here are solely my own, in a personal capacity, and are in no way endorsed or represent the views of my employer, or any of those individuals or entities mentioned herein. Notwithstanding this, there are some people who have gone above and beyond to assist, some of whom I would like to single out for thanks here.

Boeing have supported this project throughout and I would particularly like to thank Mike Lombardi, their recently retired corporate historian. Mike was a fount of knowledge on all things Boeing and shares my passion for the company and this amazing aircraft. I would like to thank him for his unwavering support and for writing the afterword. As well as Mike, Paul Lewis, at Boeing HQ, has been of huge support in helping remove what sometimes seemed insurmountable barriers. Also, Steve Kopecki, the last Superintendent of 747 Manufacturing Operations, who has an encyclopaedic knowledge of all things technical on the 747 – information us pilots just don't have. Last thanks at Boeing goes to Ray Conner, the former CEO of Boeing Commercial Airplanes, for writing the foreword.

The last 747 was delivered to Atlas Air and I would like to acknowledge their CEO, Michael Steen, for sharing some of his precious time with us and allowing us the opportunity to speak with his staff (Captains Thomas Vize – Chief Pilot 747 – and Rick Ruiz) about this aircraft and their amazing 747 operation, all facilitated by their Chief Communications Officer, Debbie Coffey, to whom we are eternally grateful.

We would also like to thank the following: Tom at the Pan Am Museum for allowing us to use their archive and podcasts as reference material, Charlotte Sjoberg (Virgin Group) for her wise counsel and for acting as a conduit to Sir Richard Branson and Dan Hart (former CEO at Virgin Orbit). Sir Richard himself, for his tips and first-hand insight for chapters 15 and 16, along with our deepest sympathies on the passing of his beloved wife, Joan. Nicola Pearson, Anthony Coombes and Simonetta Sohal (British Airways), who supported the project through the edit process.

Although an individual, Sam Chui is an institution in his own right, and I would like to thank him for his engaging chat whilst we waited for the departure of the last 747, and for allowing us to use elements of one of his articles. Also Ben Goldsmith: though his harrowing 747 story sadly could not be included, we appreciated his time with us enormously.

Without the amazing team at the Department of Defense and the United States Air Force, we would not have been able to bring you the amazing insight of the operations of the VC-25 and E-4B aircraft. The operation of these aircraft is rightly cloaked in secrecy, and I would like to extend my thanks to the teams at JBA Andrews and Offutt Air Force Base for their service and for allowing me to have a little peek under the hood of these amazing machines. Whilst there were too many people involved to name them all, I would like to single out Develyn Watson (Deputy Director, Entertainment

Liaison Office, USAF) without whose support none of this privileged insight would have been possible.

Whilst I am thanking government agencies, I would also like to extend my sincerest thanks to the comms team at NASA, in particular Erica Heim, who facilitated the access to Troy Asher (Director of Flight Operations, NASA Armstrong Flight Center), who shared his love of flying SOFIA, and the Shuttle Carrier Aircraft, plus his test career on the B-2, but that's another book entirely. I want to also thank Dr Naseem Rangwala who absolutely blew my mind with the science that was achieved with this unique 747, that will impact our planet and everyday lives for decades to come. Thanks to both for sharing your adventures aboard SOFIA with Lynne and me.

The loss of the Pan Am 747 over Lockerbie shocked the world, as the images of the aftermath were beamed onto our televisions and newspapers, bringing tragedy into our lives like none before. I am extremely thankful to Dave Bywater (Lead Consultant Paramedic) at the Scottish Ambulance Service for introducing me to retired Paramedics Paul Malner and Sam McNeish and reacquainting me with an old friend, retired senior officer Mike Cassidy. All shared their very personal and harrowing accounts of that evening. I know how that night still impacts their lives and I feel hugely privileged to be able to share their perspective with you. Thank you, gents.

There are a couple of individuals who I feel I would like to single out for special thanks, as their contribution to the book means so much to me, albeit for different reasons. Firstly, Captain Iain Moody, with whom I have shared the flight deck on many an occasion, talking pilot nonsense as we traverse the globe. Iain's dad had sadly passed before we could get his personal recollection of the fateful flight over Indonesia detailed in *Jumbo*. Iain, however, stepped up, providing us with his recollections of his dad's many stories about that night. I understand how difficult this was, and I am hugely grateful that he agreed to do this so soon after his dads passing. Hopefully this is a fitting and lasting tribute to the remarkable acts of airmanship that his dad and crew achieved that night.

The second individual that I want to single out for thanks for their contribution to the book is Dr Sheila Nutt. Sheila is an inspiration for so many, and Lynne and I now include ourselves in that gang. Sheila's aviation career was so different to my own. I have male privilege in a profession dominated by males, and I have never had to endure discrimination in my workplace. Sheila was, and is, a trailblazer, being one of the first black flight attendants in Pan Am and on the 747. She was an early and unexpected ambassador for inclusivity at a time when that was far from popular in much of the world, including travel to places where apartheid was the norm. Sheila will hate me for saying this, but she was hugely brave and played a pivotal part in changing the culture of many within the industry and among passengers alike. I thank her for doing all that she did then and now continues to do at Harvard University. I would love to say that aviation was still blazing a trail with inclusion, and in being a safe place to work, but it embarrasses me to say that we still only have a small percentage of female pilots and those who do work in the flight deck are often subject to unacceptable behaviours. Taking a lead from Sheila, I will be a champion to help set standards and root out these behaviours. As males we must do better.

Whilst writing this book we have relied on the expert knowledge of Mike Lombardi and his intimate knowledge of Boeing and the early days of the 747, including recollections from his friend Joe Sutter. We also referred to Joe's own biography *747* for some of those minor details that we couldn't glean from elsewhere. Although no longer in print, if you can find one, this is a great autobiography, one I can wholeheartedly recommend for any aviation geek. During my research for the book, I also used various sources to help me highlight the ways the Jumbo changed the world, including accident reports, and transcripts of ATC and military communications, all of which are open source and far too numerous to list individually. Should I have inadvertently not credited a source then this is my omission, and not deliberate, and I apologize.

My last thanks go to a group of people who are keeping the legend of the 747 alive, with pieces of art and experiences that will outlive even the lifetime of the last 747 to leave the factory. Dave Hall and his team at Moto Art, who have made enormous pieces of 747 furniture, as well as their staple product of PlaneTags, made from the skins of retried 747s. Dave has been gracious with his time and allowed me into his aviation mancave to talk Jumbos. Darren Lewington at Aerotiques has made a few bespoke pieces of 747 art for my home, for which I am hugely grateful, and although my wife may not share that enthusiasm, she too has bought some 747 items. Darren has been a friend for many years and continues to honour the 747 legacy.

The last person to thank for their support whilst researching the book is Dan Chang, owner of the 744 Experience. Dan hosted Lynne and I at the launch of this unique venture, and we had the opportunity to fly the 747 at Heathrow, an experience that took me back to my first flight and one Lynne will treasure for ever. Thanks to you all.

Finally, I want to thank my friends and fellow aviators, Mark and Lyndsay, for sanity checking the final drafts, and my wife Sharon for putting up with my never-ending mad aviation schemes and ideas.

Index

Specific aircraft are listed under their manufacturer's name

accidents
  1928 KLM Fokker F.III 107
  Air India bomb 212
  first crash, pilot error 56–58
  hull losses 205
  Japan Air flight 182–8
  Korean Air Boeing 007 flight navigation errors 164–77
  Lockerbie 207–11, 214–15, 217, 218–20
  Los Rodeos Airport, Tenerife 93–105
  National Airlines flight 102 227–31
  Operation Babylift 250–1
  Qantas Flight 01 201–3, 205
  UPS Flight 06 192–9
  volcanic ash 113, 122–6
ACMI (Aircraft, Crew, Maintenance and Insurance) operation 88
advertising 82
aerodynamics
  Dreamlifters Large Cargo Freighters (LCFs) 311
  Dutch Roll 185
  wings 52–5
Afghanistan 11–13, 223–5, 227
Air Force One
  carpet 142–3
  communications 146–7, 151
  costs 133, 149, 152
  departure process 148
  food and cooking 143–4
  layout 140–2, 144–6, 151
  livery 152–3
  pilot training 90
  Presidential Airlift Group (PAG) 133, 136–8
  previous aircraft 129–30
  Ravens security 140
  refurbishment 150–1
  specifications 138–9
Air India bomb 212
air pressure, cabin 117–18, 183, 184–5, 192
air-to-air refuelling tanker 290
air traffic instructions 107
Airbus 89, 306, 308, 329
aircraft carriers, airborne 290
Airline Deregulation Act 82
airport security 212, 213, 214–17, 220
al-Qaeda 216
Allen, Bill 47, 50
Allen, William 337
Altman, Beau 108–10
Anchorage 124, 164–5
Annan, Kofi 264
Antarctica 278, 308

Apollo space program 51, 77, 78, 162, 269
approach 33, 35, 283–5
Armstrong Flight Research Center 271
art from aircraft scrap 332–3
Artemis space program 267–70, 275, 277
Asher, Troy 271–2, 273, 277, 295
assembly-lines 17
astronomy 270–6
Atlas Air Worldwide 88–90, 311, 314–15, 317, 320, 321, 322
Aviation Corporation of the Americas 65
aviation graveyards 132
aviation safety
    crash investigations 107, 175–7
    dangerous cargo 191–2, 194–5, 198–9
    Emergency Vision Assurance System (EVAS) 199–200
    evacuation requirements 42
    human error prevention 178–9
    Human Factors Training 188
    safety cards and briefings 109–11
    Staten Island collision 1960 19
Aviation Safety Art International 109

baggage screening 215–16
Bagram Airport 228–9
ballistic missiles
    guidance systems 162
    Soviet tests 166–7
Bangkok Airport 201–3

Barrett-Lee, Lynne 217, 331
Bateman, Scott
    Air Force One flight 147–50
    Air Force One handover 130–1, 133–6
    Airbus flights 91, 113
    childhood 233
    documentary films 17, 129, 132–6, 238, 303, 326, 331
    first flies 747 Jumbo 5, 6–8, 15–16
    first solo flight 9
    flight simulator training 221–2
    humanitarian aid flights 249–50
    last 747 flight 329–30
    military background 6, 10–12, 224
    New York JFK landing 282–6
    rosters 282
    seniority 281, 302
    training period on 747 Jumbo 29–37
Bell, Matthew 192, 193–8
Beta Israel 255–7
BigJet TV 201, 203
black boxes 19, 175–6, 229
BOAC 41
Boeing
    707 26, 41, 79, 337
    727-200 41
    737 8, 79
    747 see Jumbo Jet
    777X 308
    787 Dreamliner 305, 306, 307–8

2707 Supersonic Transport (SST) 18–19, 40, 51, 75–9
B-47 Stratojet 78
C-5 38, 39–40
C-17 Globemaster 242–3
Dreamlifters Large Cargo Freighters (LCFs) 303, 309–15
Flying Fortress 78
Future of Flight building 325
'Model 733' 20–21, 23
Saturn V rocket 41, 51
Boeing, William E. 78, 336
bombers 290
bombs
  airport security 213, 214–17
  Dawson's Field Hijackings 213
  Lockerbie 207–11, 214–15, 217, 218–20
Borger, John 45, 48
Boston Logan Airport 31–32, 34–5
Boullioun, Tex 44
Bragg, Robert 'Bob' 97, 99, 100, 102, 105, 107, 113
Branson, Richard 233–4, 235, 236, 237, 248, 261–4
British Aircraft Corporation 20
British Airways 190, 248, 331
British Pathé News 67–8
Brokaw, Jamie-Lee 227–8
Brown, Row 43
Bruns, Larry 109
Burridge, Brian 263
Bush, Barbara 142
Bush, George H. W. 130
Bush, George W. 146, 264

cabin air pressure 117–18, 183, 184–5, 192
Camp Bastion, Afghanistan 223–5, 227
cargo *see* freight
Cargolux 307, 324
Carousel system 162, 165
Cassidy, Mike 209, 210, 219
Castro, Fidel 287–8
Chang, Dan 331–2, 333–4
Chowdry, Michael 88
Chui, Sam 91, 326
Chung Byung-in 164
Civil Aviation Authority (CAA) 243
Civil Rights Act 72
climate change 200, 248
Clinton, Bill 145
Cokely, Ralph 61–63
Colonial Airways 65
communications
  crew training 188–9
  emergency services 219
  trailing wire antenna (TWA) 298
  waypoints 34, 156–7
computer modelling 306–7
Concorde 19, 21, 22, 60, 76, 77, 78
Congo 86–7
Cornwall Spaceport 242–3
Covid-19 pandemic 90–92, 329
Cranebank training centre 35
crew
  recruitment 69
  training 71, 93–7, 109, 110, 188–9

Crew Resource Management 106, 110
Cuba 287

Dawson's Field Hijackings 213
de Beaulieu, Françoise Colbert 95
De Havilland Comet 4 18
de la Fuente, Esther 286
Defence Research Agency 215
Dickinson, Bruce 304
Digital Dan 238–9
DLR 272
DME (Distance Measuring Equipment) 161
'Doomsday Plane' 296–302
doors, boarding side 310
Douglas Aircraft Corporation 108
Dreamlifters Large Cargo Freighters (LCFs) 303, 309–15
Dubai International Airport 192
Dyer, Jerry 201, 203

E-4B Nightwatch aircraft 296–302
ejector seats 70
El Al 258–9
elephant transport 89
emergency services 218–19
Emergency Vision Assurance System (EVAS) 199–200
engines
 delivery schedule delays 66–7
 ETOPS ratings 308
 failure due to volcanic ash 116–21, 122–4

GEnX (General Electric next Generation) 305
high-bypass turbofans 38, 39, 306
low-bypass turbofans 39
Newton rocket 240
Rolls-Royce 190
turbojet 38–9
Ethiopian Jews 255–7
European Aviation Air Charter 126
evacuation
 aviation safety requirements 42, 108
 crew training 71, 90–1
Everett, Washington State 17, 55–6, 309, 325
Evergreen 291
Experimental Aircraft Association 315
Extended Diversion Operations 308
Eyjafjallajökull ash cloud 113, 125–6

factory
 building 50–1
 location 49–51
 size 50
Falasha 255–6
Falkland Islands 234
Farnborough Airshow 304
Federal Aviation Administration (FAA) 20, 59–60, 62, 217
FedEx 87
fire fighting, Global Supertanker 291–2

fire trucks 105–6
fires *see* accidents
first responders 219
Flanagan family 208
flight attendants 69–73
flight briefings 7, 9
flight preparations 8–10, 14
flight recorders 19, 175–6, 229
flight simulators 221–2, 334
flower transportation 89
food on board 71
Ford, Gerald 249, 254
Formula 1 89–90
Frankfurt Airport 217–18
freight
   capacity 81
   Combi 200M 86–7
   dangerous cargo 191–2, 194–5, 198–9
   DBL-100 cargo loader 312
   design requirements 42, 43
   Dreamlifters Large Cargo Freighters (LCFs) 303, 309–15
   freight on passenger craft 80, 85
   NOTOC (notification to captain) 191
   operators 87–8, 307
   outsize loads 224–32
   profits 85–6
   turnaround time 87
Fried, Jack 202, 203
fuel requirements 7
Fukuda, Hiroshi 183
Future of Flight building 325

Gabriel, Peter 264
Gamesa Aeronautica 310
Gates, Bill 75, 79
General Dynamics F-111 21
General Electric 24, 38, 75, 306
GEnX (General Electric next Generation) engine 305
glide ratio 117–18
Global Supertanker 291–2
go-arounds 203–5, 327–8, 329
GPS (Global Positioning System) 157, 159–60, 163, 178
Greaves, Roger 114, 115–16, 118, 119, 120
Grubbs, Victor 94, 95–6, 97, 100, 103–5, 111

Haiar, Nicholas 298–300
Halaby, Najeeb 20, 21, 22
Hall, Dave 332
Haneda Airport, Tokyo 182, 187
Hart, Dan 238, 241, 243–4, 246, 247, 248
Hartov, Steven 228–9
Hasler, Brad 224, 225, 227–8
Havana Airport 287
Heath, Ted 262, 263
Heathrow
   Cranebank training centre 35
   security 217
   Storm Eunice 201
   Terminal 5 6
Heinemann, Milt 45–6, 47
helium hydride 275
Hercules 10, 14
hijacking 95, 213, 287–8
Hong Kong 7, 157

Hood Canal, Washington State 24
Howard, Larry 176
Howland, Ruth 25
hull losses 213
Human Factors Training 188
humanitarian aid 89–90, 249–55, 257–63, 264–5
Hurricane Katrina 298
Hussain of Jordan 261–2
Hussein, Saddam 261, 262, 263

IATA (International Air Transport Association) 331
Iceland 113, 126
ILS (Instrument Landing System) 34, 35, 157–8
Imperial Airways 107, 202
IMUs (inertial measurement units) 162
INS 162, 163, 165–6
International Civil Aviation Organization (ICAO) 175, 176–7
Iran Air 87
Iranian Air Defence Forces 178, 291
Iraq 260–4
IRU (Inertial Reference Unit) 157, 159–60

Jakarta 121
jamming, GPS 163–4
Japan Air flight 123 183–8, 189
Japan Airlines (JAL) 41, 81, 112, 182
Japan, Tohoku earthquake and tsunami 249

JFK Airport 66, 282–6
Johnson, Daniel 108–10, 130
Johnson, Lyndon 20
Johnson Space Center 296
Joint Base Andrews 136–8
Jumbo Jet *see also* Air Force One; freight; manufacturing
  8 series 305–7
  200 series variants 86–7, 189–90
  300 series variants 190
  400 series variants 190–1, 223, 304–5
  certification 59–60, 62
  costs 308
  design built in redundancy 43–4, 91, 336–7
  design changes since launch 181–2
  design requirements 40–1
  engines 38, 39–40, 66–7
  ETOPS ratings 308
  first one completed 55–6
  freight 80
  fuel requirements 7, 223
  Global Supertanker 291–2
  hydraulic system changes 189
  initial design 41–42
  last ones constructed 17, 90, 317–21, 322–5, 326–7, 335
  maiden flights 56, 58, 67–8
  maintenance procedures 184, 188
  military concept programs 289–91
  National Airborne Operations Center (NAOC) 296–302

nose opening 43, 87, 89
operating costs 82
passenger numbers 80–81, 257–8
range 81, 305
Shuttle Carrier Aircraft (SCA) 293–6
size 8–9, 14, 81, 142
SOFIA (Stratospheric Observatory for Infrared Astronomy) 270–1, 273–8, 279–80
speed 30, 190
switch from double-decker design 42–4, 47–8
weight 54, 55
wing design 37, 43, 51–55, 306–7

Kabul 11–13
Kai Tak Airport, Hong Kong 157–8
Kamenski, Valeri 167, 171–2
Kangaroo Route 201–2
Kelly, Dorothy 95–6, 101–2, 103–4, 111–12
Kennedy, Jackie 152
Kennedy, John F. 20, 22, 23, 130
Kennedy Space Center 267
Kim Eui-dong 164
Kirsanov, Pytor 176
KLM 87, 95–101, 105–6, 189
Koch, Kristina 268
Kopecki, Steve 303–4, 317, 318, 319
Korean Air 301

Korean Air Boeing 007 flight navigation errors 164–77
Kornukov, Anatoly 169–72, 173
Kuwait 261

L3 271
Laker Airways 233–4
Laker, Freddie 233
Lamp, Doug 192, 193–6
landing *see also* approach
    Boston Logan Airport 31–32, 33, 34–6
    design requirements 55
    go-arounds 203–5, 327–8, 329
    JFK Airport 285–6
    Los Angeles (LAX) 156
    maiden flights 59
    navigation 157–9
    weather conditions 201, 202–3, 204
laser weapons 289–90
Lepley, Kelly 87
Lewington, Darren 332
Lindbergh, Charles 'Slim' 68–70, 271
Lindbergy, Erik 273
lithium batteries 194–5, 198–9
Lockerbie 207–11, 214–15, 217, 218–20
Lockheed
    C-5 44
    Jetstar 18
    L-1011 Tristar 62
    SST developments 23, 75
Loewy, Raymond 152
Lombardi, Mike 81, 86, 320, 335–9

Long Island Airways 65
Los Angeles (LAX) 31–3
Los Rodeos Airport, Tenerife 93–105
Love, Stan 268

Macauley, Robert 252
maintenance procedures 184, 188
Malner, Paul 207, 208, 219
Mandela, Nelson 264
manufacturing
 assembly-lines 17, 303, 304
 factory 49
 parts transportation 303, 309, 315
 tooling and processes 317–19
Marine One 148
Maylasian Boeing 777 shot down 178
McDonnell Douglas 106
Meir, Jessica 268
Meurs, Klaas 97, 98, 106
Miazga, Suzanne 219–20
military concept programs 289–91
military showers 12–13
'Model 733' 20–21, 23
Moody, Eric 114–15, 117–20, 126–7
Moody, Iain 113
Moone, Brian 298–300, 301–2
Mount Galunggung 122, 124, 126
Murray, Jean 207, 208
Museum of Flight 17–18, 290–1

NASA 51, 267–8, 271–5, 276, 293–6
National Airborne Operations Center (NAOC) 296–302
National Airlines 224, 225, 226
National Airlines flight 102 229–32
National Supersonic Transport programme 23
navigation
 GPS (Global Positioning System) 157, 159–60, 163, 178
 historical development 160–3
 INS 162, 163, 165–6
 IRU (Inertial Reference Unit) 157, 159–60, 162
 Korean Air Boeing 007 flight navigation errors 164–77
 landing 157–9
 waypoints 34, 156–7
NDB (non-directional beacon) 161
net zero 248
New Zealand 278
Newquay Airport 242–3
North American Aviation
 B-70 Valkyrie 23
 SST developments 23–5
Northwest Airlines 190
NOTOC (notification to captain) 191
nuclear weapons launch, National Airborne Operations Center (NAOC) 296–302
Nutt, Ambrose 80
Nutt, Sheila 69–70, 72–3

Obama, Barack 133
Offutt air force base 301
Operation Babylift 250–5
Operation Solomon 257–9
oxygen masks 118, 119, 185, 194, 196

Paine Field International Airport 15, 49, 50, 324, 325–7
Pan Am flight 103, Lockerbie 207–16, 218–20
Pan American Airlines 26
   747 contract signed 41, 43
   advertising 82
   after Lockerbie 220
   aircraft names 66
   crew recruitment 69
   foundation 65–6
   Jumbo Jet design requirements 40–41
   maiden flight 67
   New York JFK – Heathrow route 67–8, 73
   passenger experience 71–72
   shown single deck design 45–8
Paris Airshow 60
passengers
   capacity 80–1
   numbers 80
   Pan Am experience 71–72, 82
   record numbers 258
Pathé News 67–8
pilots
   approach and landing 33
   flight simulator training 221–2
   the 'heavy' 155–6
   rosters 281–2
   seniority 281, 302
   training 93–7, 107
Pima Air and Space Museum 278–9
plane-spotting 200–1
Pope 122
Pratt and Whitney 24, 38, 43, 66
Presidential Airlift Group (PAG) 133, 136–8
PRIMA Far-IR probe 276
Project Horizon 20, 21–22

Qantas 81, 191, 322
Qantas Airlines 81, 305
Qantas Flight 01 201–3, 205
Quesada, Elwood Richard 20

Rangwala, Naseem 274–5, 276, 277–8, 280
Raytheon 271
Reagan, Nancy 144
Reagan, Ronald 130, 148, 178
Redmond, Tony 210
Redoubt volcano 124
Renton Airfield 60–1
RMI (Radio Magnetic Indicator) 161
rocket launches, Virgin Orbit 238–42, 243–8
Rocketdyne 310
Rolls-Royce 190
Rouzie, Dick 26
Ruiz, Rick 87–8
runway numbering 32–3

Sabena 86–7, 190
safety cards and briefings 107–11

Samper, Mal 44
Sasaki, Yutaka 182–3, 184–7
Saturn V rocket 341, 51, 269
Schreuder, Willem 97, 103
Sea Tac Airport 79
Seattle 303, 317
Second World War 78, 208
security restrictions at airports 212, 213, 214–17, 220
Selassie, Haile 256
'servant leadership' 72
shipping 31–33
Shuttle Carrier Aircraft (SCA) 293–6
shuttle operations 29
Sierra Nevada Corporation (SNC) 301
sky art 328–9
Skytrain 233
Slingsby Firefly 9
Smithsonian 15, 330
Snohomish County Airport 49, 50
SOFIA (Stratospheric Observatory for Infrared Astronomy) 270–1, 273–8, 279–80
solar flares 244
Southern California Logistics Airfield 132
Soviet Union
 Korean Air Boeing 007 flight navigation errors 166–77
 supersonic aircraft development 21, 76
 Tupolev 144 76, 77
space program 51, 77, 78, 162, 267–70, 275, 277

Space Shuttle 293–6
spoofing, GPS 163–4
SST (2707 Supersonic Transport) 18–19, 40, 51, 75–9
St Elmo's Fire 115–16, 120–1, 123
standard operating procedures. SOPs 30
Staten Island collision 19–20
Steen, Michael 89, 328
Steiner, Jack 53
stewardesses *see* flight attendants
storm watching 200–1
Sud Aviation 20
Sun Dong-hui 164
Sundhnúkur volcano 126
supersonic aircraft 18–19, 20–24, 40, 75–8
Survivable Air Operations Center 301
Sutter, Joe
 assigned design project 25–7
 background 24–5
 begins design 38, 40, 41–43
 C-5 engines 39–40
 design changes after launch 68
 design legacy 336–7
 engineering building name 323–4
 factory location 49–50
 first crash, pilot error 60–2
 maiden flight 58–9
 recognition of design quality 68–9
 switch from double-decker design 42–4, 47–8
 turning solution 57–8

wing design 37, 43, 51–53
Sutter, Nancy 24, 25
Swift, Taylor 89
Swissair 190

Takahama, Masami 182–3, 184–7
take-off 15, 59, 135–6
taxiing 14, 57–8, 98
telescopes 270–8, 279–80
Tenerife 93–4
terrorism *see also* bombs
   hijacking 95, 213, 287–8
The Elders 264–5
ticket prices 82
TOGA button 15, 202, 327
toilets 134, 135
Topping, Al 252–3
Townley-Freeman, Barry 114, 117, 118, 120, 122
trailing wire antenna (TWA) 298
Travolta, John 322–3, 330
Trippe, Ed 22–3
Trippe, Juan
   background 65
   character 44, 65
   design requirements 40–41, 337–8
   plans to buy Concorde 22–3
   'servant leadership' 72
   shown single deck design 45–8
   Vietnam War refugees 252
Trump, Donald 133, 152–3
Tupolev 144 74, 75–6
turbulence, climate change 200
TWA 41
two crew operation 29

UNICEF 249, 260, 261
Unit Load Devices (ULDs) 225–6
United States Air Force 289–90
UPS 87
UPS Flight 06 192–9
Upset Prevention and Recovery Training (UPRT) 222
USAF Academy 23

Van Zanten, Jacob 97–8, 99–100, 106
Vietnam War refugees 250–5
Virgin Atlantic 233–4, 235–8, 248, 262–3, 264
Virgin Orbit 238–41, 243–8
Virgin Unite 265
Vize, Tom 311, 314, 324, 326, 328–9
volcanic ash 113, 122–6
Volcanic Ash Advisory Centres (VAACs) 124–5
VOR (VHF Omnidirectional Range) beacon 157, 161

Waddell, Jack 56–7, 58, 59
Waddell's Wagon 57
Wallick, Jess 58
Wallis, Barnes 208
Walnut Creek, California 49, 50
Walsh, Willie 179, 331
Warns, George 94, 96
Watkins, Augustus 286, 287–9
waypoints 34, 156–7
weather conditions 200–1, 202–3, 204

whale transport 87
White, Jimmy 209
Whittle, Frank 38
Williams, Paul 200
wing design 37, 43, 51–55, 306–7

Wright Aircraft Laboratory 70
Wright, Orville 142
Wygle, Brien 58, 59

YAL-01 project 289–90
Yeltsin, Boris 177

Picture Credits

Insets

- p1. Care of author
- p2. Wikimedia Commons
- p3. Top, Wikimedia Commons; bottom, care of author
- p4. Top left & right, source unknown; middle & bottom, Wikimedia Commons
- p5. Top & middle, source unknown; bottom, Wikimedia Commons
- p6. Top, Wikimedia Commons; bottom, public domain
- p7. Care of author
- p8. Getty
- p9. Virgin Image via author
- p10. NASA via author
- p11. NASA via author
- p12. Top two, care of author; bottom, USAF via author
- p13. Wikimedia Commons
- p14. Care of author
- p15. Care of author
- p16. Wikimedia Commons

Every effort has been made to trace copyright holders and to obtain their permission for the use of copyright material. The publisher apologizes for any errors or omissions and would be grateful to be notified of any corrections that should be incorporated in future editions of this book.